An Introduction to Forensic Linguistics

'Seldom do introductions to any field offer such a wealth of information or provide such a useful array of exercise activities for students in the way that this book does. Coulthard and Johnson not only provide their readers with extensive examples of the actual evidence used in the many law cases described here but they also show how the linguist's "toolkit" was used to address the litigated issues. In doing this, they give valuable insights about how forensic linguists think, do their analyses and, in some cases, even testify at trial.'

Roger W. Shuy, *Distinguished Research Professor of Linguistics, Emeritus,*
Georgetown University

'This is a wonderful textbook for students, providing stimulating examples, lucid accounts of relevant linguistic theory and excellent further reading and activities. The foreign language of law is also expertly documented, explained and explored. Language as evidence is cast centre stage; coupled with expert linguistic analysis, the written and spoken clues uncovered by researchers are foregrounded in unfolding legal dramas. Coulthard and Johnson have produced a clear and compelling work that contains its own forensic linguistic puzzle.'

Annabelle Mooney, *Roehampton University, UK*

From the accusation of plagiarism surrounding *The Da Vinci Code*, to the infamous hoaxer in the Yorkshire Ripper case, the use of linguistic evidence in court and the number of linguists called to act as expert witnesses in court trials has increased rapidly in the past fifteen years. *An Introduction to Forensic Linguistics* provides a timely and accessible introduction to this rapidly expanding subject.

Using knowledge and experience gained in legal settings – Coulthard in his work as an expert witness and Johnson in her work as a West Midlands police officer – the two authors combine an array of perspectives into a distinctly unified textbook, focusing throughout on evidence from real and often high profile cases including serial killer Harold Shipman, the Bridgewater Four and the Birmingham Six.

Divided into two parts, The Language of the Legal Process and Language as Evidence, the book covers the key topics of the field. The first part looks at legal language, the structures of legal genres and the collection and testing of evidence from the initial police interview through to examination and cross-examination in the courtroom. The second part focuses on the role of the forensic linguist, the forensic phonetician and the document examiner, as well as examining in detail the linguistic investigation of authorship and plagiarism.

With research tasks and suggestions for further reading provided at the end of each chapter, *An Introduction to Forensic Linguistics* is the essential textbook for courses in forensic linguistics and the language of the law.

Malcolm Coulthard is Professor of Forensic Linguistics at Aston University, UK and **Alison Johnson** is Lecturer in English Language at the University of Leeds, UK.

An Introduction to Forensic Linguistics
Language in Evidence

Malcolm Coulthard and Alison Johnson

Routledge
Taylor & Francis Group

LONDON AND NEW YORK

First published 2007
by Routledge
2 Park Square, Milton Park, Abingdon, Oxon OX14 4RN

Simultaneously published in the USA and Canada
by Routledge
270 Madison Ave, New York, NY 10016

Routledge is an imprint of the Taylor & Francis Group, an informa business

© 2007 Malcolm Coulthard and Alison Johnson

Typeset in Goudy by
HWA Text and Data Management, Tunbridge Wells
Printed and bound in Great Britain by
Antony Rowe Ltd, Chippenham, Wiltshire

British Library Cataloguing in Publication Data
A catalogue record for this book is available from the British Library

Library of Congress Cataloging-in-Publication Data
Coulthard, Malcolm.
An introduction to forensic linguistics : language in evidence /
Malcolm Coulthard and Alison Johnson.
    p. cm.
  1. Forensic linguistics. I. Johnson, Alison, 1959– II. Title.
K2287.5.C68 2007
363.25—dc22   2007040179

ISBN 10: 0–415–32024–0 (hbk)
ISBN 10: 0–415–32023–2 (pbk)
ISBN 10: 0–203–96971–5 (ebk)

ISBN 13: 978–0–415–32024–5 (hbk)
ISBN 13: 978–0–415–32023–8 (pbk)
ISBN 13: 978–0–203–96971–7 (ebk)

This book is dedicated to our families

Carmen Rosa and David

Simon and Zel, Richard,
Flavio and Bela, Catherine,
Robert and Regina, Rebekah and Chris,
Adam and Jayne, Robert,
Sylvia and Wob, Michael and Geraldine

Josh, Sam, Luc, Zander, Sienna, Max, Joe and Rory

Contents

Acknowledgements

We are deeply indebted to Krzysztof Kredens, who read and commented in detail on an early draft of Part II and to David Woolls for his superb work in harmonising the varied referencing styles of the authors with that of the publisher. We also thank Peter French who not only produced the spectrogram in Figure 7.1 especially for the book, but has also been a constant source of information and encouragement for the past 20 years.

Most of the material in this book has been presented over the past 15 years to literally thousands of students on undergraduate and postgraduate courses at the Universities of Aston, Birmingham, Cardiff and Leeds and has benefited immensely from their perceptive observations. We learned a great deal from innumerable colleagues who have discussed texts and responded to ideas following papers at conferences and university research seminars. Particular thanks for insights, stimulation and critical comments must go to our friends in the 1990s Birmingham Forensic Linguistics Research Group: Jenny Ball, Sue Blackwell, Janet Cotterill, Tim Grant, Chris Heffer, Charles Owen, Frances Rock, Jess Shapiro, Anne Smith and Michael Toolan. And last, but by no means least, Roger Shuy, Larry Solan, Diana Eades, John Gibbons, Ron Butters and Peter Tiersma whose friendship, perceptive writings and generous personal communications have influenced the whole book.

Acknowledgement is due to Troika Talent for their permission to reproduce the excerpts from *Little Britain* in Chapter 1 of the book.

Introduction

Shipman jailed for 15 murders
Family GP Harold Shipman has been jailed for life for murdering 15 patients, as he goes down in history as the UK's biggest convicted serial killer. He was also found guilty of forging the will of Kathleen Grundy, one of his patients.

(BBC News 31 January 2000)

Court rejects Da Vinci copy claim
The *Da Vinci Code* author Dan Brown did not breach the copyright of an earlier book, London's High Court has ruled.

(BBC News 7 April 2006)

Google pays the price of common usage
There is a risk that the word 'Google' could become so commonly used that it becomes synonymous with the word 'search'. If this happens, we could lose protection for this trademark, which could result in other people using the word 'Google' to refer to their own products, thus diminishing our brand.

(Max de Lotbinière quoting Google in: *The Guardian Weekly*
Learning English 21 July 2006)

Man remanded in Ripper hoax probe
A 49-year-old man has been remanded in custody charged with being the infamous Yorkshire Ripper hoaxer known as Wearside Jack. The clerk at Leeds Magistrates' Court read the charge to Mr Humble, which said he was accused of sending the letters and audiotape between 1 March 1978 and 30 June 1979 [27 years earlier]. She said: 'You sent a series of communications, namely three letters and an audio tape, to West Yorkshire Police and the press claiming to be the perpetrator of a series of murders that at that time were the subject of a police investigation.'

(BBC News 20 October 2005)

Introduction – falsification, plagiarism, trademarks and hoax

Linguistic aspects of legal stories often make headline news around the world, indicating the high profile given to such material by newsmakers. Four such headlines and reports taken from the British news media form the epigraph for this introduction. The first refers to the case of Harold Shipman, a doctor who was convicted in January 2000 of the murder of 15 of his patients. The judge, the Honourable Mr Justice Forbes, observed that 'there has never been another case in this country which has required the investigation of as many possible murders committed by a single individual as needed to be investigated in this case' (The Shipman Inquiry 2001).

The second story relates to the alleged copying of material by Dan Brown, the author of *The Da Vinci Code*, from an earlier work of non-fiction, *The Holy Blood and the Holy Grail*. This claim for damages, brought by the authors of the earlier work, delayed the launch of the film of the same name and thereby raised the profile of copying, plagiarism and copyright violation in the minds of the general public.

The third story – about trademark protection for the Google name – is concerned with the interesting question of how far companies can claim to 'own' words and have the right to decide who can use them and in what circumstances – and it gives an insight into what happens when they try Canute-like to stop their word(s) slipping into common usage with a generic meaning, as when, 60 years ago, people used to talk about 'hoovering the carpet' (with their Goblin vacuum cleaner).

The final story is about the uniqueness of voices and whether a tape recording of a speaker committing a crime a quarter of a century earlier can be successfully matched with the contemporary vocal output of a recently arrested suspect, in spite of the passage of time and its effect on the voice.

Of particular interest in the Shipman case was his forgery of the Last Will and Testament of one of his patients, Mrs Kathleen Grundy, which led to his arrest after the suspicions of her daughter, Mrs Angela Woodruff, were aroused. Unfortunately for Dr Shipman, the daughter was a lawyer and she had previously drawn up her mother's will and always dealt with her legal affairs, so when a new will was discovered, made only days before her mother's death, she investigated it. In particular, the phraseology, the choice of individual words and the signature differed from her mother's usual style, and there were errors in the typescript, although Mrs Woodruff described her mother as usually 'meticulous'. The handwriting too was larger than normal (Shipman Trial, Day 4).

A Forensic Document Examiner was employed to make comparisons of the alleged forged signature with documents such as her driving licence, which contained her authentic signature. His evidence during examination in court was the following:

Q. And what was the result of your comparison?

A. The questioned signatures on items BB 1 and BB 2 are superficially similar in their appearance to the specimen signatures of K. Grundy. However, neither of the questioned signatures is fluently written and there are differences, significant differences in the fine detail shown by the two questioned signatures as opposed to the fine detail shown by the specimens.

Q. Can you point specifically please to such differences?

A.   Looking at the two uppermost signatures, the two questioned signatures, both of them have a letter D in the word Grundy written with an open loop here and the tail, the top part here is very tall. It is taller than the K and it is taller than the G, the initial letters. By contrast [in] the specimen signatures, the tail of the D is closed, sorry the loop of the D is closed and the upright is actually much smaller than the K and the G.

(Shipman Trial, Day 6)

In this way significant textual evidence was introduced to the court and presented to members of the jury to consider. This, along with other evidence, including Mrs Woodruff's testimony in relation to the forged will – that it contained inaccurate information about her mother's ownership of a single house, when she actually owned two – meant that the evidence against Shipman was compelling. This story highlights some of the ways that forensic linguistics and the work of linguists enters the popular press, through cases that involve authorship and handwriting analysis. We return to handwriting analysis in Chapter 7, while in Chapter 4 we consider the collection of verbal evidence by the police, by examining in detail one of the interviews with Dr Shipman.

The second headline, referring to a High Court case in 2006 in the UK concerning the alleged copying or plagiarizing of material for Dan Brown's novel, *The Da Vinci Code*, involved Baigent and Leigh's claim of 'non-textual infringement of copyright', meaning that the central theme from their book, *The Holy Blood and the Holy Grail* (HBHG), had been copied by Brown. They sued the publisher, The Random House Group Limited, and a long legal battle ensued. The headline in the epigraph (*Court rejects Da Vinci copy claim*) reports the ruling in favour of the defendant, Random House, that they (and Brown) did not infringe copyright in the novel. The judge's conclusion was that 'there is no copyright infringement either by textual copying or non textual copying of a substantial part of HBHG by means of copying the Central Themes' (*Baigent v. Random House*, 7 April 2006). The ruling made way for the delayed distribution and screening of the film, *The Da Vinci Code*. Plagiarism and copyright are treated in more detail in Chapter 9.

The third headline throws the spotlight on a further area of interest: trademarks and their protection. Major companies vigorously defend their trademarks and, as the headline and report reveal, any slippage can result in the trademark falling into common usage and therefore becoming open to use by another company. McDonald's, for example, have defended their trademarks – usually successfully though occasionally unsuccessfully – including the golden 'M' arch, the prefix 'Mc' and individual product names such as 'Big Mac'. In *McDonald's Corp.* v. *Arche Technologies* (17 USPQ 2d 1557 (N.D. Cal. 1990)) the computer firm, Arche Technologies, successfully defended their use of coloured arches in their logo. The court ruled that use of the golden arch did weaken the McDonald's trademark, but allowed the use of other coloured arches. However, in *McDonald's Corp.* v. *McBagels, Inc.*, (649 F. Supp. 1268, 1278 (S.D.N.Y. 1986)) McDonald's were successful in their defence of the Mc trademark and McBagels were prevented from using it as a name. Threatened litigation was also brought by McDonald's against McMunchies in 1996 (Muir 24 September 1996) and other companies and individuals who have tried to use the Mc prefix.

Trademark law means that companies must defend their trademarks to protect them, since the novel coining that goes into producing trademarks is usurped if these words slip into common usage, as they are liable to do. If they do, anyone can use them and benefit from the marketing and publicity of the well-known company. Chapter 6 discusses linguistic evidence in trademark disputes.

The fourth headline draws us into the world of forensic phonetics and speaker identification. Baldwin and French (1990), French (1998,1994), Hollien (1990b), Kniffka (1990) and Künzel (1987, 1994) all report forensic phonetic practice and research. In work on speaker identification forensic phoneticians analyse the voice, often working with the police who have voice recordings, which may be of poor quality, in order to try to identify the individual implicated in a particular investigation. The most significant case in England is without doubt that of 'The Yorkshire Ripper', a serial killer who, between 1975 and 1979, murdered ten women in the Leeds and Bradford area of Yorkshire. In June 1979 Stanley Ellis, a phonetician, dialectologist and lecturer at the University of Leeds, was called in by police after a tape recording, purporting to be from 'The Ripper', was sent to them. At the same time Jack Windsor Lewis, another linguist, was employed to analyse three letters sent to the police apparently from the same person (see Windsor Lewis 1994).

The West Yorkshire police asked Ellis to try to identify the accent of the speaker and pinpoint his regional origin. Ellis reported to the police: 'in my opinion the man's voice represented someone who had been brought up in the Southwick or Castletown areas [of Sunderland], but that I had reservations concerning the possibility of his no longer living there' (Ellis 1994: 202). There followed a long investigation during which Ellis and Windsor Lewis became concerned that the letters and tape recording could be a hoax and that therefore eliminating from the murder investigation all suspects who did not have a north-eastern accent was a mistake.

In January 1981, Peter Sutcliffe, a lorry driver from Bradford, was arrested and accused of the Ripper murders and in April 1981 he pleaded guilty to manslaughter on the grounds of diminished responsibility. But Sutcliffe did not have a Sunderland accent, so, as Ellis noted, 'the identity of a man who sent [the] tape and letters ... has never been discovered' (1994: 206). The final twist in the tale came in October 2005, 26 years after the tapes had been sent, when a Sunderland man, John Humble, was arrested and charged with sending the hoax letters and the tape to the police. A review of 'cold cases', using the latest DNA tests, had managed to identify Humble by matching his genetic profile with a sample of saliva taken from one of the hoax letter's envelopes from the original case. The BBC's online news archive carries the Humble story (BBC News 21 March 2006), complete with audio recordings from the original 1979 tape and his 2005 arrest interview, where he was asked to read out the text for comparison by voice analysts. This case highlights the way that forensic phoneticians' work is used alongside other investigative processes – see French *et al.* (2006) for a report by the phoneticians involved. Humble's address was given in court as Flodden Road, Ford Estate, in the suburb of South Hylton in Sunderland, half a kilometre away from Southwick and Castletown, which had been identified by Ellis as the two likely places of origin. The case demonstrates that forensic phonetic work, criticized at the time by the harassed police officer in charge of the investigation, can be amazingly accurate, even though the speaker was not identified at the time.

These four UK cases and their headline prominence highlight some of the concerns of forensic linguistics and phonetics. Other central concerns of forensic linguistics that will be treated in subsequent chapters are:

- the language of legal documents;
- the language of the police and law enforcement;
- interviews with children and vulnerable witnesses in the legal system;
- courtroom interaction;
- linguistic evidence and expert witness testimony in courtrooms;
- authorship attribution and plagiarism;
- forensic phonetics and speaker identification.

A brief history of forensic linguistics

Forty years ago Jan Svartvik published *The Evans Statements: A Case for Forensic Linguistics*. In it he demonstrated that disputed and incriminating parts of a series of four statements which had been made to police officers by Timothy Evans about the deaths of his wife and baby daughter, had a grammatical style measurably different from that of uncontested parts of the statements and thus a new area of forensic expertise was born. (Interestingly, almost 20 years earlier, the term *forensic English* was used by Philbrick (1949) in the title of his book on legal English, *Language and the Law: the Semantics of Forensic English*, but the phrase was never taken up.)

Initially, the growth of forensic linguistics was slow. In unexpected places there appeared isolated articles in which an author, often a distinguished linguist, analysed disputed confessions, or commented on the likely authenticity of purported verbatim records of interaction, or identified and evaluated inconsistencies in language which had been attributed to immigrants or aboriginals by the police in their written records of depositions, or assessed the linguistic similarity of rival trademarks (Eades 1994; Levi 1994a, b; Shuy 1993, 1998, 2002b).

There was, however, in those early days, no attempt to establish a discipline of, or even a methodology for, forensic linguistics – the work was usually undertaken as an intellectual challenge and almost always required the creation, rather than simply the application, of a method of analysis. By contrast, in the past 15 years there has been a rapid growth in the frequency with which courts in a series of countries have called on the expertise of linguists. In consequence, there is now a developing methodology and a growing number of linguists who act as expert witnesses, a few even on a full-time basis. In addition there are now two professional associations, the IAFL (International Association of Forensic Linguists) and the IAFPA (International Association for Forensic Phonetics and Acoustics), and a dedicated journal, *Forensic Linguistics*, was launched in 1994. The journal was renamed in 2003 as *The International Journal of Speech, Language and the Law*, in order to indicate more clearly to potential readers the wider definition of forensic linguistics with which the journal's editors, as well as the authors of this book, have always worked. Not all the researchers to whom we will refer in this book would identify themselves within a field called forensic linguistics, but their work is, nevertheless, included in bibliographies of forensic linguistics, as students and researchers seek out prior work in this fast-growing field.

The cases in which expert evidence has been commissioned from linguists range from disputes about the meaning of individual morphemes in a trademark dispute and of individual words in jury instructions, through the 'ownership' of particular words and phrases in a plagiarism case, to accusations in certain murder cases that whole texts have been fabricated. Usually, the linguist uses standard analytical tools in order to reach an opinion, though very few cases require exactly the same selection from the linguist's toolkit. Occasionally, however, cases raise new and exciting questions for descriptive linguistics, which require basic research, such as how can one measure the 'rarity' and therefore the evidential value of individual expressions, or how can one assess the reliability of verbal memory.

Early forensic linguistic research originated in a wide range of disciplines: linguistics, law, psychology, anthropology and sociology and included topics as diverse as handwriting analysis, forensic phonetics and role of the linguist as an expert in court, covering work in Australia, Europe and North America. Research since 1990 has continued to come from all these disciplines, making forensic linguistics a multi- and cross-disciplinary field, with any up-to-date bibliography now reaching considerable proportions by comparison with the early work. (See, for example, the online bibliography of the IAFL at: <http://www.iafl.bham.ac.uk/bib/biblio.php> [accessed May 2007], or the one on Peter Tiersma's website at: <http://www.languageandlaw.org> [accessed May 2007] and compare it with Levi 1994a.)

In the early years the majority of the research was published in articles, book chapters and edited collections, with the exception of O'Barr (1982), whereas it is notable that since the millennium many more book-length studies have been produced, particularly those with the word 'forensic' in the title. These continue to be in the key areas, such as legal language (Solan and Tiersma 2005; Tiersma 1999), courtroom interaction (Archer 2005; Ehrlich 2001; Heffer 2005; Matoesian 2001, 2003; Solan 1993; Stygall 1994), language and power (Conley and O'Barr 1998; Cotterill 2003) and the linguist as expert in court (Shuy 2002a, 2006; Berk-Seligson 2002). Police and law enforcement officers' use of language has also produced book-length studies, focusing particularly on interview and interrogation, and has been researched from a case study (Rock in press; Shuy 2005), psychological (Gudjonsson 2003) and conversational analytic (Heydon 2005) perspective. Forensic phonetics has been the focus of four books (Baldwin and French 1990; Hollien 1990b, 2001; Rose 2002). A new area of forensic stylistics and author identification has developed (McMenamin 1993, 2002) and in recent years language testing, particularly in relation to asylum seeking, has been the focus of much discussion and report. Eades (2005) brings together multicultural issues in forensic linguistics.

Books covering the field of forensic linguistics include this volume along with Gibbons (2003) and Olsson (2004). In addition, a large body of research is to be found in *The International Journal of Speech Language and the Law*, and also in articles published in a range of other journals such as: *Applied Linguistics, Journal of Pragmatics, Research on Language and Social Interaction, Discourse Studies, Text* and the *Yale Law Review*. In subsequent chapters reference is made as appropriate to articles in these journals and full details can be found in the references at the end of the book.

On forensic discourse analysis

In the 30 years since *An Introduction to Discourse Analysis* was published (Coulthard 1977) descriptive linguistics has been transformed. The creation of massive corpora and the rapid development of the worldwide web have contributed to major changes in the way that language itself is viewed and have increased the availability of real language for analysis. The domain of education has been relatively open to researchers during the period, because of the constant interaction of research and practice by practitioner-researchers. However, by contrast, reasearch in forensic linguistics has mainly developed through interaction with researchers from outside the legal domains – an approach which has inbuilt advantages and disadvantages. There are advantages to crossing boundaries and we do this in different ways, through using knowledge and experience gained in legal settings – Coulthard in his work as an expert linguist with the police, lawyers in and out of court, complainants and defendants, and Johnson in her work as a West Midlands police officer and as expert linguist. This array of perspectives has, we hope, been combined into a distinctly unified text, with a singular focus on text and its description and its applied and theoretical potential.

In 2003 Michael Stubbs, in The Third Sinclair Open Lecture (Stubbs 2004), asked the question: what happened to discourse analysis? The term 'discourse analysis' is now found preceded by a wide range of modifying adjectives: *anthropological, child, cognitive, critical, educational, ethnographic, feminist, legal, medical, multimodal, political, psychotherapeutic* and, of course, *forensic discourse analysis.* The answer, then, to Stubbs' question is clearly that discourse analysis has proliferated and branched off into a number of specific sub-domains, one of those being forensic discourse analysis. It is, like many of its sisters, concerned with specific institutional functions and uses of language. Indeed, the adjective *institutional* is one of those that can be found modifying the term 'discourse analysis', as is the adjective *social*. One of the primary concerns of forensic linguistics is with institutional discourse and its intersection with lay and social meanings.

The term 'institutional discourse' very simply means discourse that takes place within a professional or work-based setting. 'Talk at work' (Drew and Heritage

1992) is motivated by the needs or goals of the institution to which it belongs, whether that be legal, educational, medical, religious or political. Each of those institutional discourses can be identified by a particular selection and use of grammar, vocabulary and structure. In Chapter 2 we look at what legal language is like and in Chapter 3 we look at the structures of a range of legal genres. But institutional discourse is also defined functionally in terms of discourse roles and goals and in chapters 4 and 5 these are the focus of our examination of evidence collection from initial encounters with emergency services, through police interviews to courtroom interaction.

In Part 2 we look at cases where institutional practices have been disputed and where discourse analysis is employed through the reports and evidence of experts to uncover what might have happened. Chapter 6 discusses a number of cases that use discourse and pragmatic analyses of notes and interview records. Institutional discourse in a forensic context, therefore, is engaged in legal activities related to the collection and interpretation of evidence. Some of these activities are later disputed usually by a lay participant. In the first volume of *Forensic Linguistics: The International Journal of Speech Language and the Law*, Shuy (1994) reports how he acted as an expert in a civil lawsuit against a car dealership in which a deaf man brought charges of false imprisonment and fraud. Because he was deaf, the interaction, which involved inquiring about purchasing a car, had been carried out through handwritten notes, which both the dealer and the customer produced. Each of the 101 separate pieces of paper consisted of an exchange as in 22:

22. *Salesperson.*   Which one do you like? Lower Price. Demo.
     Bien.   Demonstration model.

(Shuy 1994: 134)

Shuy's task 'as an expert linguist' was to produce a report that analysed the exchanges 'for clues to temporality and to either verify or correct the sequence they [the plaintiff and his attorneys] proposed' (Shuy 1994: 134). To do this Shuy looked at topic and response, speech acts and the sequence of service encounters, to uncover what the judge called 'an anatomy of a car sale' (Shuy 1994: 148). Linguistic evidence using discourse analysis supported the plaintiff's case, the jury found in his favour and he was awarded $6 million in damages.

Organisation of the book

The book is divided into two parts: 'The language of the legal process' and 'Language as evidence', resulting from a combined approach, both in terms of having two authors and in those authors' roles as teachers, researchers and experts. Johnson was lead author for the first part and Coulthard for the second. However, one of the first five chapters is a joint production with both authors contributing significant input. As an authorship attribution exercise (once you have read chapters 8 and 9) you are invited to attempt to identify which chapter it is. The answer, together with a discussion of issues surrounding computer assisted attribution, can be found via a link on Johnson's personal webpage (http://www. leeds.ac.uk/english/staff/pages/staffindex.php?file=john).

Descriptive linguistics and forensic linguistics work hand-in-hand and corpora and real data, though they are often limited in size and availability, are central to our endeavour. All of the texts used in this book are real and the majority have been the focus of teaching or research, or are taken from cases where linguistic expertise has been called upon. The book represents the authors' belief in the centrality of the text as the basis of teaching and research. Increasingly, forensic texts are publicly available, though not always in their original form. The Harold Shipman trial, referred to in this chapter and also later in the book, is available electronically from the Shipman Inquiry website (The Shipman Inquiry 2001), though unfortunately not as an audio recording, but only in official transcript form. For ease of reference it is referred to simply as 'Shipman Trial, Day X' throughout the book. Other texts are available in audio form, though often substantially edited, while newspaper and television news is often accessible through the huge archives available on the Internet.

Forensic texts are often sensitive in nature. The words are those of our fellow citizens who have found themselves involved in civil and criminal cases, or are used in the course of professional life. Law courts are, as any visitor will know, solemn and yet emotional places, both in the ways that they deal with the law, and as a forum for the physical expression of some of the most unusual and disturbing aspects of human life. This context has been constantly in our mind. We do not claim to understand the motives and intentions of its users, but simply seek to understand language itself and how it is used in a variety of legal settings.

Part I, chapters 1 to 5 of the book, offers a thorough grounding in forensic approaches to language analysis and is intended for use by students and lecturers for courses on language and the law, to explore key ideas of legal language, legal genres and context, and questioning and narrative in interviews and the courtroom. The text extracts promote critical analytical discussion and the chapters are aimed at developing an understanding of current research, field-specific vocabulary, skills and knowledge and stimulating new thinking. Part II, chapters 6 to 10, discusses forensic linguistic and phonetic casework, research and practice. Students and researchers are equipped in this section to carry out research tasks in relation to authorship attribution, speaker identification and trademark law. The book could, equally well, be used by advanced students and researchers as a stand-alone introduction to forensic linguistics and by lecturers planning courses.

Reading and research tasks and how they function

Each chapter ends with Suggested Readings. These vary in number, but are intended as a fairly comprehensive starting point for students at all levels. Since it is impossible to guess what any given reader knows already, we suggest that you concentrate on those texts that are new to you. For some readers this will be all, and for others perhaps only one, of the readings. It is intended that each chapter be used as an introduction to one area of forensic linguistic study and that follow-up reading and selection from the references will develop a wider understanding of some of the underpinning linguistic concepts.

Most chapters have developed from seminars with undergraduate and postgraduate students, for whom this kind of additional reading is required, particularly in university courses where students are able to choose a specialist option module such as forensic linguistics with perhaps only one introductory course in linguistics or English language behind them. The readings for Chapter 1, selected from Jaworski and Coupland (2006), are specifically chosen with that audience in mind. In our experience, students often have insufficient expertise in discourse analysis to tackle this applied discipline and the readings therefore aim to fill potential gaps. Readers will quickly establish whether the readings cover new ground or not. In any case, many of the readings bear revisiting, so even if you have encountered the article before, do not make an instant decision to ignore it.

We have tried to ensure that some of the readings are available electronically to give wider access to material. We have also referred to a number of websites where data, cases or news articles can be accessed. The intention here is to facilitate access where students have limited resources in libraries, but, since URLs are not stable, we have attempted to limit ourselves to websites with permanent URLs and large archives.

Each chapter also contains a set of Research Tasks related to issues raised in the chapter. Sometimes they suggest research that replicates a published study, sometimes a more detailed analysis of a text referred to in the chapter, while yet others propose investigations that could be the basis of undergraduate or postgraduate projects or theses. The set of tasks sometimes works as a series (as in Chapter 10), but more often provides a set of options. Individual tasks can be used by students for independent research or set by teachers as tasks to be reported on in class. Equally, they could be set or adapted as assignment or project questions. Research tasks are included to engage readers in two central ways: in a reflective response to the ideas raised in the chapters and in a practical response through applying the ideas and descriptive methodologies outlined in the chapter.

Part I

The language of the legal process

1 Approaching a forensic text

Little Britain, Series 1, Episode 4: Magistrates' Court
LAWYER: Vicky Pollard, you have been charged with shoplifting. On the 11th April, it is alleged you went into the Erskine branch of Superdrug. Once there you attempted to steal an eyeliner pencil and a can of Red Bull by concealing them in your leggings. Now in the face of the overwhelming evidence we've heard today against you, do you stand by your plea of – 'Not guilty'?
VICKY: No but yeah but no because what happened was right this thing happened what I don't know nothing about shut up I wasn't meant to be anywhere even near there. Then Meredith came over and started stirring it all up started calling me all these things about this thing I didn't even know about.
THE LAWYER IS STUMPED

(Lucas and Walliams 2004: 104)

The Hutton Inquiry: Examination of Prime Minister, Tony Blair
MR ANTHONY CHARLES LYNTON BLAIR (called)
Examined by MR DINGEMANS (MR D).
LORD HUTTON: Good morning ladies and gentlemen. Good morning Prime Minister.
TONY BLAIR: Good morning my Lord.
MR D: I do not think we need an introduction. May I start with the dossiers? We have heard that a dossier was being produced in February 2002 which related to four countries, one of which was Iraq. Could you explain the background to that?
TB: After September 11th there was a renewed sense of urgency on the question of rogue states and weapons of mass destruction and the link with terrorism, and there was some thought given to trying to bring all that together, identifying the countries that were a particular source of concern to us, one of which was Iraq.

(The Hutton Inquiry 2003c)

Introduction

We can make some instant observations on the two extracts in the epigraph. The fictional exchange from the popular British television and radio series, *Little Britain*, is markedly different from the real courtroom examination of a witness. Vicky Pollard behaves very differently from the British Prime Minister, Tony Blair, in her responses to the lawyer's opening turn. This deviation in the fictional text creates dramatic tension and surprise for the audience, but also draws into sharp focus the norms of interaction for this genre: politeness, expected cooperation between the interlocutors in relation to known facts, and control by the legal professional over the organisation, distribution and length of speaking turns and the selection of topic. In this chapter we examine the fictional text from *Little Britain* alongside two extracts from a real courtroom, in relation to these and other issues, concentrating on discourse and text analytic theory that can inform our understanding and interpretation.

Little Britain is a situation comedy, which is described by the BBC as 'all that is mad, bad, quirky and generally bonkers about the people and places of Britain' (BBC 10 January 2007). Characters are ludicrously exaggerated stereotypes, who exhibit extremes of behaviour and talk that draw on norms of talk-in-interaction for comic effect. 'The Hutton Inquiry' (The Hutton Inquiry 2003a) was a public inquiry by a judge into the circumstances of the death of Dr David Kelly, a UK weapons expert with experience in Iraq, who was found dead in July 2003, apparently having committed suicide, after he had been revealed as 'the source of a *Today* radio programme report claiming the government had "sexed up" its dossier on Iraq's weapons of mass destruction' (BBC News 16 March 2004). A public inquiry is different from a trial in England in that it does not always take place in a courtroom, though this one did, and there is no jury. The judge listens to witnesses who are questioned by lawyers in order to present their evidence and at the conclusion he or she writes a report containing findings. There is no prosecution, so no prosecuting or defence lawyers. Instead there is a single lawyer for the Inquiry, Mr Dingemans, and then there are lawyers for each of the relevant parties involved. In The Hutton Inquiry the parties included the BBC, the British Government and Dr Kelly's family; witnesses are called on behalf of these differing parties.

Our aim here is to demonstrate how a contrastive analysis of fictional and real interaction between lawyers and witnesses can be instructive in casting light on their linguistic behaviour in one specific legal context: the courtroom.

Approaching a forensic text – discourse and text analytic tools for forensic contexts

When, as linguists, we analyse a text, we draw on many diverse interpretative tools, methods and theories. In approaching a text in a forensic context the analyst needs to consider how it is similar and what distinguishes it from other texts in other contexts and which theories and methods are most appropriate to analyse it. Often it is an eclectic selection of tools and a developmental approach to methodology that is necessary. Nevertheless, there are well-researched, grounded linguistic theories that are generally considered useful. Since the texts we shall be examining here are spoken, although we are actually dealing with written transcripts of recordings of spoken interaction, *text* will be used to refer to both the written and the spoken. We will consider some of the key features of spoken discourse, including cooperation between participants, politeness and the rules for turn-taking: turn design, allocation, distribution and function. Though not always designed as questions with interrogative syntax, the lawyers' turns in witness examinations in court function to *elicit* information or confirmation. Although each speaker gets the same number of turns, turn length is distinctive, with the witness often responding only minimally with *yes*, *no* or *hmm* to quite long sequences of lawyer-led request-for-confirmation moves. Power, control and status are unequally distributed too, producing an asymmetrical relationship between lawyers and witnesses that is oriented to and understood by participants in the courtroom.

When asked a general question about the essential differences between speech and writing, people sometimes observe that writing is highly structured and that speech is unstructured. This is untrue. Speech is just as rule-governed as writing, but the rules and organisation are different. In conversation we talk of openings and closings, whereas in writing we talk of introductions and conclusions. We would not expect an essay or a book to conclude with *I'm afraid I've got to go now* or *Ok see you tomorrow then*, nor would we normally close a telephone conversation with *The End* or *In conclusion*. If we did, we would be marking or foregrounding the manner of production, and the interlocutor or audience would draw inferences from this rule-breaking. Norms and conventions are, therefore, a background against which any text producer's deviations invoke interpretative activity in receivers. Texts and text types (or 'activity types' (Levinson 1979)) have norms and conventional ways of speaking or writing. Over the course of a text these conventions contribute to creating the distinctive and recognisable features of a genre, which users recognize and by which they abide.

Institutional interaction is typically asymmetrical, since power and control are located in the institutional participant, rather than being equally distributed. This results in the institutional speaker directing and controlling the discourse rather than the lay speaker and institutional transactive goals being pursued at the expense of social or phatic ones (see Malinowski 1923 in Jaworski and Coupland (2006)). Different rules of politeness therefore operate, with institutional speakers having negative rather than positive face needs (see Goffman 1967 in Jaworski and Coupland (2006)) – they have a right to be unimpeded rather than needing to be liked – meaning that interruptions and uncooperative responses are more constrained in this setting and therefore marked when they occur. Speech acts are sometimes indirect (Tony Blair's response in the epigraph could be interpreted as an indirect way of saying 'I'm not going to tell you') and the illocutionary force is often different from that implied by the locutionary form. For example, locutions in the form of questions often perform a variety of illocutionary acts, from eliciting information ('Can you tell me your name and occupation?') to requests for confirmation ('You started work at 7 a.m. Is that correct?'), and then sometimes questions are intended as commands requiring compliance and therefore expect no response at all ('Are you going to keep interrupting me?').

Institutional talk is characterized by Drew and Heritage (1992: 22) as having:

- an orientation to core goals, tasks or identity conventionally associated with the institution – 'goal orientations';
- constraints on 'allowable contributions';
- specific 'inferential frameworks' in the context (Levinson 1979: 72 refers to these as 'inferential schemata').

This means that the institutional members of legal conversations – police officers in interviews or barristers in court – are in control of the legal goals and agendas in talk and are aware of the constraints on the meaning of particular words or phrases, such as *intend* or *admit*, whereas lay members do not understand the talk in the same way and could be described as being at the mercy of these goals. These aspects of the interaction contribute to the asymmetrical relationships that exist in institutional discourse settings, with the institutional member having the upper hand and the lay member often occupying the less powerful position.

The asymmetrical relationship does not always mean that the institutional member is always powerful in a negatively constraining way. For example, in a courtroom the lawyer, when questioning a witness called for his own side or party, uses his powerful position and linguistic skills to support the witness's testimony, designing his turns to help her present her case in the best way. However, when cross-examining a witness, lawyers use very different tactics. Dominance, facilitation and restriction in institutional discourse have, therefore, to be viewed in terms of who is speaking, when and for what purpose. As Drew and Heritage (1992: 21) point out, 'the character of institutional interaction varies widely across different institutional tasks and settings'. As the tasks change, so does the status and identity of the institutional speaker and his relationship to the other. Drew and Heritage (1992: 20) say that the question that is posed for empirical research is how we identify the ways in which activity in institutional settings is 'done differently'. Text and talk in forensic settings are done differently from social talk. A legal conversation takes place in both a physical and an interactive context, one which constrains social evaluation – we do not expect institutional speakers in legal contexts to evaluate stories with interjections like 'Oh my God' or 'You don't say' – and instead produces no reaction or a legal evaluation – 'Did you intend to injure him?'. Lay speakers collaborate in this institutional work by making their stories factual.

In institutional interactions such as courtroom examinations or police interviews there is also the interesting complication of the issue of 'shared knowledge' (Labov and Fanshel 1977). Many of the questions posed are not real information-seeking questions, since the questioner already knows the answer and the questioned person generally knows that they know the answer. This is not an unknown type of interaction, since it is present in much teacher–pupil and parent–child interaction, but it presents particular challenges for the interlocutors in institutional settings. The lawyer in the *Little Britain* extract in the epigraph reasonably expects the events mentioned in his question to be shared knowledge. The response from Vicky, though not the one expected, is not unusual in courtroom and interview data since, as questions become challenging, witnesses start to resist them, but it is particularly marked here as it is at the very beginning of the interaction. Witnesses may resist what they see as unnecessary questions or questions that challenge their view of events, but expect to be asked some questions that in other settings would appear unnecessary. Labov and Fanshel (1977: 73) refer to a second level of shared knowledge, information that is 'known to everyone present' or could reasonably be considered to be shared. For example, it could be assumed that adults would agree that for a shopper to conceal items in their garments, rather than put them into a shopping basket, is the action of a thief, not a shopper; see Chapter 4, for a discussion of real examples.

The texts

In order to examine some of these issues we can move on to examine the three texts referred to briefly earlier. Extract 1.1 below is from *Little Britain*, while extracts 1.2 and 1.3 are both transcripts of witness examinations from 'The Hutton Inquiry' (2003c). The Hutton Inquiry (2003a) considered, amongst other things, the UK Government's behaviour in relation to Mr Kelly and whether the Ministry of Defence took proper steps to protect its employee from the media interest in him. The two Hutton witnesses are very different. The first is one of the ambulance technicians called to the scene when Dr Kelly's body was found and he describes how he and his colleague examined the body for signs of life. The lawyer's questioning of the ambulance man is straightforward and is selected here as representing a prototypical example of a witness examination. The ambulance technician, although a professional within his own work situation, is a lay member in the courtroom setting. The second witness is the Prime Minister, who was himself a courtroom lawyer. Tony Blair is an unusual and exceptional witness and was selected for analysis and commentary here because the lawyer treats him rather like an expert witness, in that he is allowed, indeed expected, to produce extended responses, and, because of his professional status, he is also more able to respond without the long narrative eliciting moves typical of the examination of lay witnesses. Heffer (2005: 101) notes that 'expert witnesses gave by far the highest proportion of extended turns [over 100 words] (6.6)' in his trial corpus, compared with 0.6 for lay witnesses.

Since *Little Britain* was written as a script to be performed and the Hutton texts are transcripts made from live unscripted court recordings, all three texts are representations of what was actually said. Even so, there are limitations on the comparability and equivalence of the texts, because, as one of the writers of the script, Matt Lucas, says, 'what ended up in the show isn't always what was scripted' (BBC 20 January 2007). Also, as Heffer (2005: 58) observes about transcripts made from courtroom recordings, 'there will always be a considerable degree of subjectivity in the transcriber's interpretation, such that ambiguity in the text may well be reporter-induced' and also 'the possibility must exist that the transcript data set is skewed by the motives leading to the production of transcripts'. In addition, the real witnesses are witnesses in a public enquiry, rather than appearing as the accused in a criminal court. With those limitations in mind, we can still profitably compare the texts to see how the fictional example deviates from the norms exemplified in the real examples.

Extract 1.1 is from a satirical comic creation that draws on audience expectations of what is right and acceptable in the setting of the courtroom. When we compare it with actual courtroom interaction we can ask how the *Little Britain* text subverts the conventions of genre, register, transitions in turn-taking, turn length, interruption, politeness, question and answer pairs, cooperation and topic control that are expected in the courtroom.

Extract 1.1

Vicky Pollard: 'Magistrates' Court', *Little Britain*, Series 1, Episode 4. (Interruptions are indicated by ellipses … where the turn is cut off.)

1	Lawyer	Vicky Pollard, you have been charged with shoplifting. On the
2		11th of April, it is alleged you went into the Erskine branch of
3		Superdrug. Once there you attempted to steal an eyeliner pencil
4		and a can of Red Bull by concealing them in your leggings.
5		Now in the face of the overwhelming evidence we've heard
6		today against you, do you stand by your plea of – 'Not guilty'?
7	Vicky	No but yeah but no because what happened was right this thing
8		happened that I don't know nothing about shut up I wasn't meant
9		to be anywhere even near there. Then Meredith came over and
10		started stirring it all up started calling me all these things about
11		this thing I didn't even know about.
		THE LAWYER IS STUMPED
12	Lawyer	Right, but you admit you were in Superdrug at the time?
13	Vicky	No but yeah but no because there's this whole other thing what I
14		didn't even know about and Meredith said it weren't a thing but it
15		was but don't listen to her because she's a complete slag.
16	Lawyer	Sorry, Meredith? Who is Meredith?
17	Vicky	She's the one who done that thing about the thing but if she gives
18		you sweets don't eat 'em because she's dirty.
19	Lawyer	Thing? What thing?
20	Vicky	Yeah I know and anyway and there was this whole other thing
21		what I didn't even know about or somefink or nuffin' because
22		nobody told Wayne Duggin that Jermyn fingered Carly round the
23		back of the ice rink.
24	Lawyer	Right.
25	Vicky	But I was supposed to be doing Home Ec. But I wasn't right I
26		was on the phone to Jules. But anyway don't listen to her because
27		she had a baby and didn't tell anyone.
28	Lawyer	Vicky, were you at Superdrug at the time?
29	Vicky	No but yeah but no but yeah but no but yeah but no because I
30		wasn't even with Amber.

31	Lawyer	Amber? Who's Amber?
32	Vicky	Yeah exactly. I wasn't even with her and anyway I didn't even
33		know who she is so you'd better ask her.
34	Lawyer	Vicky, I don't think you realise the gravity of the situation you …
35	Vicky	No but there's something right what I didn't …
36	Lawyer	If you're found guilty …
37	Vicky	No you definitely can't say that right because …
38	Lawyer	You'll have a criminal record.
39	Vicky	No but I'm allergic to cat hair so I don't have to go into lessons.
40	Lawyer	This is a court of law, you have … are you going to keep interrupting me?
41	Vicky	No no no no no no I'm not, I'm going to let you speak.
42	Lawyer	Oh. Now we've heard from the social workers …
43	Vicky	Oh my God! Right. There was this whole other thing I completely
44		forgot to tell you about …
45	Lawyer	Oh I give up.
46	Vicky	You know Craig? Well he felt up Amy on the corkscrew at Alton
47		Towers and her mum totally had an eppy. But then Dean went on
48		the Mary Rose and was sick on Louise Farren's head.

(Lucas and Walliams 2004: 104–6)

Extract 1.2, from The Hutton Inquiry transcripts, is the examination of an ambulance technician. (The date of the Inquiry appearance and page and line numbers from the transcripts are preserved in the extracts below. The extract begins on page 77, line 23. Q marks the lawyer turns and A the witness. When, occasionally, Lord Hutton speaks, his turns are marked LH.)

Extract 1.2

Page 77 (2 September 2003)

23		MR DAVID IAN BARTLETT (called)
24		Examined by MR KNOX (counsel to the Inquiry)
25	Q.	Mr Bartlett, what is your full name?

Page 78

1	A.	David Ian Bartlett.
2	Q.	And what is your occupation?
3	A.	Ambulance technician.
4	Q.	And who are you employed by?
5	A.	Oxford Ambulance.
6	Q.	And you are based at?
7	A.	Abingdon.
8	Q.	Abingdon ambulance station?
9	A.	Yes.
10	Q.	Were you on duty on the early morning of 18th July?
11	A.	Yes.
12	Q.	And what time did you get in?

13 A.   0700 hours.
14 Q.   What is the number of the ambulance you were working in
15   that day; can you remember?
16 A.   I cannot remember to be honest without going back to the
17   computer readouts. We use so many different ones.
18 Q.   If I say number 934, does that sound right?
19 A.   Could be, yes.
20 Q.   Do you remember what happened about 20 to 10?
21 A.   Yes, we had a call to attend the Longworth area and on
22   the way there – excuse me, I have a bad cold –
23 LH.   Yes, do you have a glass of water there? That
24   might help.
25 A.   Yes. We got an update saying it was a male query kilo 1

Page 79

1   which as my colleague explained is a person presumed
2   dead.
3   Q.   You say you got an update, was that?
4   A.   On the computer readout in the ambulance.
5   Q.   That meant what?
6   A.   They had come across a body or a body had been reported
7   and had not been certified but presumed dead.
8   Q.   Can you remember when you arrived at the place you were
9   going to?
10 A.   The time?
11 Q.   Yes, the time.
12 A.   9.55.
13 Q.   That was at Harrowdown Hill, is that right?
14 A.   Yes.
15 Q.   Off Tucks Lane?
16 A.   Yes.
17 Q.   What happened when you arrived?
18 A.   We parked at the end of the lane where there were some
19   cars already parked, a lot of police officers there. We
20   asked one police officer who directed us to the police
21   that were in the combat uniforms and they asked us to
22   bring some equipment and follow them down into the
23   woods.
24 Q.   And you did that?
25 A.   Yes. We took a defib monitor with us and our own

Page 80

1   personal kit.
2   Q.   You walked down into the woods, is that right?
3   A.   Yes.
4   Q.   What did you eventually come across?
5   A.   We got to the end of the lane, there were some more

6   police officers there. I think it was two or three,
7   I cannot remember, I think it was two, took us up into
8   the woods which was like right angles to the track. As
9   we walked up they were in front of us putting the marker
10   posts in and told us to stay between the two posts.
11 Q. So you stayed between the two posts and carried on
12   presumably?
13 A. Yes.
14 Q. What did you then come across?
15 A. They led us up to where the body was laid, feet facing
16   us, laid on its back, left arm out to one side
17   (indicates) and the right arm across the chest.
18 Q. What about the hands? Did you notice anything about the
19   position of the hands?
20 A. It was slightly wrist up, more wrist up than down.
21 Q. What about the right arm?
22 A. That was across the chest, palm down.
23 Q. Did you notice any injuries?
24 A. Just some dried blood across the wrist.
25 Q. Which wrist would that be?
Page 81
1   A. The left wrist.

Extract 1.3

The Hutton Inquiry – Examination of the Prime Minister, Tony Blair (28 August 2003).

Page 0
3   MR ANTHONY CHARLES LYNTON BLAIR (called)
4   Examined by MR DINGEMANS (counsel to the Inquiry)
5   LH. Good morning ladies and gentlemen. Good
6   morning Prime Minister.
7   A. Good morning my Lord.
8   Q. I do not think we need an introduction. May
9   I start with the dossiers? We have heard that a dossier
10   was being produced in February 2002 which related to
11   four countries, one of which was Iraq. Could you
12   explain the background to that?
13 A. After September 11th there was a renewed sense of
14   urgency on the question of rogue states and weapons of
15   mass destruction and the link with terrorism, and there
16   was some thought given to trying to bring all that
17   together, identifying the countries that were
18   a particular source of concern to us, one of which was

19   Iraq.
20 Q.   We have heard that the dossier was then pursued against
21   Iraq alone in about February/March time. Why was the
22   decision made to concentrate on Iraq alone?
23 A.   Again, as I say in my witness statement, I think given
24   history Iraq was a special case. It was in breach of
25   United Nations resolutions. It had a history of using
Page 1
1   weapons of mass destruction against its own people. So
2   there was a sense that Iraq as it were fitted a special
3   category.
4   Q.   We know that the dossier got at least in its earlier
5   stages to a final state in early March time but was not
6   published.
7   A.   Hmm.
8   Q.   What was the reason for that?
9   A.   We had a draft, but this thing was already beginning to
10   build as a very major story. Frankly we were months
11   away from deciding our strategy on this issue. I took
12   the view in the end, and discussed it with the
13   Foreign Secretary, and we both agreed that it would
14   inflame the situation too much in order to publish it at
15   this stage.
16 Q.   We have also heard that on 3rd September you do announce
17   that dossier is going to be published.
18 A.   Yes.
19 Q.   What changed?
20 A.   What changed was really two things which came together.
21   First of all, there was a tremendous amount of
22   information and evidence coming across my desk as to the
23   weapons of mass destruction and the programmes
24   associated with it that Saddam had. There was also
25   a renewed sense of urgency, again, in the way that this
Page 2
1   was being publicly debated. I recall throughout the
2   August break last year literally every day there were
3   stories appearing saying we were about to go and invade
4   Iraq. Military action had been decided upon.
5   President Bush and I had a telephone call towards
6   the end of that break and we decided: look, we really
7   had to confront this issue, devise our strategy and get
8   on with it and I took the view, in the end, and said
9   this at the press conference I gave in my constituency
10   on 3rd September, that we really had to disclose what we
11   knew or as much as we could of what we knew. That was

```
12        because there was an enormous clamour. Here we were
13        saying: this is a big problem, we have to deal with it.
14        Why did we say it was a big problem? Because of the
15        intelligence. And people were naturally saying: produce
16        that intelligence then.
17   Q.   What was the aim of the dossier?
18   A.   The aim of the dossier was to disclose the reason for
19        our concern and the reason why we believed this issue
20        had to be confronted.
21   Q.   We have heard evidence that after your announcement on
22        3rd September, there was a meeting in Downing Street
23        chaired by Alastair Campbell on 5th September, where the
24        presentational sides of the dossier were discussed, and
25        after that meeting an e-mail was exchanged. Can I take
Page 3
1         you to that? That is CAB/11/17.
2    A.   That is going to come up here, is it?
3    Q.   I hope so. What you can see is about 13.50 – we
4         understand the meeting was about noon – Mr Powell
5         e-mailed Mr Campbell:
6         'What did you decide on dossiers?'
7         'Re dossier, substantial rewrite, with JS
8         [John Scarlett] and Julian Miller in charge, which JS
9         will take to US next Friday, and be in shape Monday
10        thereafter. Structure as per TB's discussion.
11        Agreement that there has to be real intelligence
12        material in their presentation as such.'
13        Had you at this stage discussed the structure of the
14        dossier with Mr Campbell?
15   A.   I think I had discussed it in outline at least, that it
16        was important that it dealt with Iraq and the question
17        of weapons of mass destruction. We would obviously have
18        to deal with the main elements of that because that
19        after all was our case.
20   Q.   And had you been aware of the proposed role that
21        Mr Campbell was going to take in assisting with the
22        presentation?
23   A.   Well, I was in no doubt that he would assist with the
24        presentation. I cannot recall exactly when but
25        certainly around that time. However, I also knew that
Page 4
1         it had to be a document that was owned by the Joint
2         Intelligence Committee and the Chairman, John Scarlett.
3         That was obviously important because we could not
4         produce this as evidence that came from anything other
```

```
 5          than an objective source.
 6  Q.      We have heard that there was a draft of the dossier
 7          produced on 10th September, and we have seen that.
 8          I will not take you to that, if that is all right. What
 9          was the first draft of the dossier that you actually
10          saw?
11  A.      As I say in my statement I believe I saw the
12          10th September draft and I commented on drafts of the
13          16th and 19th and I made certain comments on that. But
14          obviously in the end, of course, it all had to be
15          produced and done through the process of the JIC.
16  Q.      We have also seen some JIC assessments, redacted JIC
17          assessments of 5th and 9th September which deal with the
18          45 minute issue. When did you see those?
19  A.      I have seen the JIC assessment on 9th September but
20          other than that, I do not think I made a comment on the
21          45 minutes in respect of the dossier.
22  Q.      But you may have seen it as it went through in the draft
23          of the 10th September?
24  A.      Yes, I suppose that – if it was in the 10th September
25          draft I would have seen it.
```

Text analysis

There are many contrastive points that can be made here. Readers are invited to follow-up our analysis with their own analyses of these texts. Questions to guide your investigation are posed in the research activity at the end of this chapter.

Schemas

What is immediately obvious to readers in Britain is that Vicky Pollard represents a social stereotype of a working-class, delinquent, unintelligent chav and in keeping with that character she is disrespectful of institutional authority. Since this is a cultural stereotype it is less likely to be accessible to readers outside Britain, but what will be noticeable is the surprising lack of respect shown for the lawyer. Snell's (2006: 59) analysis of the *Little Britain* extract takes us to 'schema theory', which is linked to concepts of 'frames' and 'scripts' (see Schank and Abelson 1977; Schank and Nash-Webber 1975; and also Tannen and Wallat 1987). Snell argues that schemata (mental representations of events or 'scripts') 'are activated by linguistic items in the text [... and] once activated ...generate expectations [...which] may be subverted, resulting in incongruity, and this incongruity may give rise to humour'. She suggests that schemata can be 'activated' (Snell 2006: 64) by characters' catchphrases, such as Vicky Pollard's *no but yeah but no*, and that schema theory can be used to explain why audiences 'both in Britain and outside may not appreciate its humour'. Schema theory can also 'account for the different reactions that distinct sections of the audience may have [... and] because people have different kinds of background knowledge and beliefs, it is possible for different people to construct quite different interpretations of the same text' (Snell 2006: 64). This also explains how audiences share humour if they 'have very similar schemata' (Snell 2006: 63).

This is a powerful set of concepts for analysing the interpretative processes that are activated when audiences respond to speakers and to drama in particular. It also takes us one step further in our consideration of how real courtroom interactions are encountered by an audience in a *similar* way. In open court the interaction is 'played' to a public audience and then, through journalistic reporting, transmitted to a wider public audience. Lord Hutton, in his ruling on applications to broadcast the Inquiry on television and radio, refers to 'the vital significance of the work of the journalist in reporting court proceedings and, within the bounds of impartiality and fairness, commenting on the decision of judges and justices and their behaviour in and conduct of the proceedings' and quotes Lord Denning calling the newspaper reporter 'the watchdog of justice' (The Hutton Inquiry 2003b). Participants in court are to greater and lesser degrees aware of this wider audience, but are nonetheless aware of the more immediate audience and their presentation to them. There is therefore a degree of staging and drama even in the non-dramatic text.

Quantitative observations

If we move to a quantitative analysis, we can compare the texts statistically in terms of the number of words uttered by each speaker over a comparable number of turns. This is useful in analysing the proportion of talk allotted to each speaker and the length of turns in the three extracts, which tells us something about control and topic movement. We notice that extracts 1.1 and 1.2 are similar in length, 494 and 504 words, respectively. However, extract 1.1 contains 13 turns per speaker (lawyer and witness) and extract 1.2 contains 27 per speaker, demonstrating that the Hutton Inquiry examination is more efficient, speaker turns occurring and recurring more rapidly and smoothly, in line with Sacks *et al.*'s (1974) 'simplest systematics' of turn-taking in conversation. Only once does Vicky Pollard answer a yes/no question with a firm *no* (lines 40–1) despite being asked several polar interrogative questions, whereas the ambulance technician cooperatively (see Grice 1975 in Jaworski and Coupland 2006), provides ten *yes* responses (p. 78, lines 9, 11, 19, 21, 25; p. 79, lines 14, 16, 25; p. 80, lines 3, 13).

Extracts 1.1 and 1.2 are also different in terms of the amount of talk that is produced by witness and lawyer. In extract 1.1 Vicky Pollard produces 66 per cent of the talk and the lawyer 34 per cent (Vicky 326 words, the lawyer 168), whereas in extract 1.2 the witness produces 61 per cent and the lawyer 39 per cent (witness 306 words, lawyer 198). This difference is statistically significant, particularly when viewed in combination with the distribution of turn length in relation to questions. When a short answer is required, Vicky Pollard produces a long and irrelevant one, unlike the real witness. When information is required

Vicky Pollard fails to give it or gives irrelevant information, whereas the real witness recognizes when more than a *yes* is required and makes his contribution relevant. The ambulance technician's response schema is active, whereas the writers of the *Little Britain* sketch deliberately create a character whose courtroom response schema is inactive or totally lacking.

Qualitative comments on quantitative data

The examination of Prime Minister Blair (extract 1.3) is different from both the fictional one and that of the ambulance technician's. Although it is twice the length of the other two (1,020 words, as opposed to 494 and 504 respectively), it has a very similar number of turns to extract 1.1, 28 compared with 26 in 1.1. Comparing it with extract 1.2, which we have said is efficient in terms of turn exchange, extract 1.3 has twice the number of words with half the number of turns. When we look at the real texts qualitatively, that is in relation to the turn form and content, we can see that the nature of the questions and answers is very different, as is the degree of shared knowledge.

Differences in length of turn are only partially due to the status of the speaker. The ambulance technician is an important witness, being the first non-police officer on the scene, apart from the woman who found the body. Since he is able to give important expert evidence on the signs of life found on the body and the position, clothing and appearance of the deceased, he has high status in relation to the inquiry's goals of 'investigating the circumstances surrounding the death of Dr Kelly' (The Hutton Inquiry 2004a). However, the Prime Minister's evidence is more important for pursuing the evaluative goals of the inquiry: the consideration of the issues of 'whether the Government behaved in a way which was dishonourable or underhand or duplicitous in revealing Dr Kelly's name to the media' and 'whether the Government failed to take proper steps to help and protect Dr Kelly' (The Hutton Inquiry 2004b).

This underlines a point made by Heffer (2005: 101) that the extended turns of complainants, defendants and lay witnesses are usually narrative in content, whereas those of police and expert witnesses are predominantly non-narrative. This fact illustrates the difference between the two kinds of witnesses: those who are there to tell their story as eye-witnesses who have experienced the event or as an integral part of it (its immediate precedent or aftermath) and those who are there to explain procedural, scientific, or, in the case of the Hutton Inquiry, political details surrounding the event. In extracts 1.2 and 1.3 the institutional discourse is oriented towards the goals of the legal and political communities, the parties represented in the Inquiry and the public's interest in those issues in society, whereas the primary goal of the *Little Britain* sketch is to subvert the legal and political issues in the pursuance of satirical comic goals and the audience's interest in the humorous portrayal of aspects of social life and satire as entertainment.

The cooperative principle and Gricean Maxims

Let us return to the cooperative principle (CP). Since the courtroom setting is so highly constrained and formal, adhering to the CP could be even more strongly expected. The CP presupposes that one's conversational contribution should be 'such as is required, at the stage at which it occurs, by the accepted purpose or direction of the talk exchange in which [one] is engaged' (Grice 1975: 45). This clearly has additional relevance in the courtroom context. However, Levinson (1979) also points out that there are activities that are not inherently cooperative. They might include a psychiatric interview or interrogation. Of interrogation, Levinson says: 'it is unlikely that either party assumes the other is fulfilling the maxims of quality, manner, and especially quantity (requiring that one say as much as is required by the other' (1979: 76).

Relevance, though, is something that is expected. The ambulance technician does vary the length and informativity of his turns in relation to the purpose of the question. Where it is merely expecting confirmation of a narrative detail that is already shared knowledge, but which needs to be articulated in court, the technician simply replies *yes* (e.g. extract 1.2: p. 79, lines 14 and 16), but where a simple *yes* would be interpreted in the context as insufficient, he replies with an informing move (extract 1.2: p. 80, lines 20 and 24) or a *yes* plus informing move (p. 78, line 21 and page 79, line 25). In relation to the Gricean maxim of quantity – 'make your contribution as informative as is required (for the current purposes of the exchange)', but 'do not make your contribution more informative than is required' (Grice 1975: 45–6) – the technician orients to the local conditions of the question in order to produce a turn whose length is appropriate to the cooperative constraints operating at the time.

At the same time he is orienting to the other Gricean Maxims:

relevance	He asks a clarification question on p.79, line 10 in order to be relevant to the question in line 9.
truth	He says *I cannot remember, to be honest* on p. 78, line 16 to indicate that he is orienting to the need to be truthful – 'do not say what you believe to be false' – and in relation to 'do not say that for which you lack evidence' (Grice 1975: 45–6) on p.78, line 19 he answers *could be, yes* in response to the lawyer's provision of the ambulance number he was driving as *number 934*. He is unable to simply confirm this without violating the maxim of quality by agreeing with something for which he has already stated he does not have the evidence, since it is a computer record that he does not have to hand.
manner	He is brief, clear and unambiguous. When asked to give the time and confirm the place he went to, he gives the time 9.55 and replies *yes* (p. 79, lines 14 and 16) in response to requests to confirm the place as Harrowdown Hill (p. 79, line 13), Tucks Lane (p. 79, line 15).

Vicky Pollard, on the other hand, is presented by the scriptwriters as someone who flouts and violates all of Grice's maxims and openly disregards the CP, choosing or neglecting to be relevant, truthful, informative, unambiguous, brief or orderly. Her flouting of the maxim of relevance is apparent in the irrelevant details she supplies about her associates and their activities and in her neglecting to supply details of her own activities that are relevant to the allegation of shoplifting. Her lack of truthfulness is a violation of the truth maxim, since it is apparent in her reply to the lawyer's question, about whether she is going to keep interrupting him, that she is lying. She replies *no*, but then immediately interrupts him (extract 1.1: lines 41–2). When asked an information-seeking question (*Who's Amber?*, line 31) she fails to provide the required information and when asked to confirm with a simple *yes* or *no*, she is consistently unforthcoming. Her *no but yeah but no* response is annoyingly ambiguous to the lawyer, and all of these aspects of her flouting of the principles of conversation constitute the humour of the text and contribute to the satirical position taken by the writers to entertain the audience.

Prime Minister Blair, in extract 1.3, produces responses which seem to relate to Levinson's point about settings where the maxim of quantity is flouted, in a way that is distinctive of politicians. This political uncooperativeness – supplying more information than is required – was noted by Fairclough (1989) in his analysis of a political interview with the former British Prime Minister, Margaret Thatcher. Blair is frequently invited to take long turns, where more detailed information is sought (*Could you explain...?*, p. 0, lines 11–12; *Why...?*, p. 0, line 21; *What was the reason...?*, p. 1, line 8), but he also produces lengthy turns where a shorter one would have been acceptable (p. 1, line 20 to p. 22, line 16: 209 words; page 3, line 23 to p. 4, line 5: 68 words). In other places, where a statement inviting a clarificatory response is produced, rather than taking a proper turn, he produces a minimal response, *hmm* (p. 2, lines 4–7), thereby inviting the lawyer to continue. Thus Tony Blair flouts the maxim of quantity by producing sometimes more and sometimes less than required and in doing so signals his authority, since the lawyer accepts this behaviour.

Speech acts

The *Little Britain* extract both conforms to and resists the generic conventions surrounding the witness examination genre. In its conventional start, the lawyer takes a fairly lengthy turn, which is formulaic and which informs the witness of the reason for her being there. The function of the words, though, is to do more than inform – both she and the audience know why she is there. The speech act is one of warning the witness that her actions have now taken on a new meaning; the context of the courtroom provides for the possibility that she will be convicted of theft. In Speech Act Theory (see Austin 1962; reprinted in Jaworski and Coupland 2006), which has developed from the work of Austin (1962) and Searle (1969), the locutionary act (what is said) in the lawyer's opening in extract 1.1 is a declarative, information-giving turn, but the illocutionary force (what is done by uttering those words) is to warn or advise the witness about the possible implications of her actions.

The perlocutionary effect (what is actually achieved through the uttering of the words) is more complex. There are two effects: one for the witness and one for the 'overhearing audience' (Heritage 1985). The effect for Vicky Pollard is that the warning misfires and she ignores it, producing for the audience a surprise, because she resists the more powerful speaker and fails to cooperate. This has the effect of 'stumping' the lawyer, reducing his control to zero. Despite repeated attempts to regain control, by using constraining positive polarity *yes/no* declarative questions (*but you admit you were in Superdrug at the time?*, line 12) and by addressing her by first name as a preface to a powerful informing move that requires no response (*Vicky, I don't think you realise the gravity of the situation*, line 34), he concedes that he has to *give up* (line 48). The perlocutionary effect, therefore, of the lawyer's attempt at lawyer talk, is impotence rather than control, since his interlocutor is singularly unimpeded by his attempts at constraining and controlling her talk. She says what she wants in the way that she wants to, using non-standard and informal speech that is inappropriate here, with no recognition of the lawyer's negative face needs – immunity from outside interference or pressure.

Face threatening acts

This behaviour violates the interactional norms of the courtroom. In real courtrooms, when questioning witnesses, many of the lawyer's turns are 'face threatening acts', which challenge the witness (see Brown and Levinson 1978; reprinted in Jaworski and Coupland 2006). In this way the lawyer's role in the courtroom (particularly in cross-examination) allows him to interfere with and put pressure on the witness in pursuance of the interactional goals of the Crown or State, by whom he is given his power. When we compare extract 1.1 with extract 1.3 we can see that the lawyer threatens Blair's positive face, his status as Prime Minister, by attempting to elicit evidence of dishonourable, underhand or duplicitous behaviour: some of the primary goals of the inquiry. The lawyer therefore mitigates the potentially face threatening acts by using a polite modality (*may I...?* (p. 0, lines 8–9), *could you...?* (p. 0, line 11) *can I...?* (p. 2, line 25)). Tony Blair both underlines his honesty and reaffirms his status through his use of discourse markers in the adverbs *frankly* (p. 1, line 10), *obviously* (p. 3, line 17; p. 4, line 3) and in his use of imperative (*look* p. 2, line 6) and performative verbs *I recall, I believe, as I said in my statement*, which attend to the veracity of the statements he is making and are therefore displaying cooperation with the quality maxim and underlining his response to the negative face needs of the lawyer who is asking the questions and of the judge to whom he is addressing his words. His use of the discourse marker 'look' appears to be a favoured one. Although only used once in extract 1.3, it is used five times later in the same examination. For example:

Q.   Was that the main charge to which you were responding at the time?
A.   Yes, I mean, look, this was an absolutely fundamental charge.

(p. 20, line 24 to p. 21, line 2)

This strategy constitutes authority-marking at this moment and at others where it is used.

There are two particular points in extract 1.3 where the lawyer seems to successfully undermine the status of Tony Blair's testimony and these are interesting, particularly in relation to Blair's underlining of his authority at other points. The battle between the authority of two powerful opponents is evident. In the first instance (p.3, line 20 to p. 4, line 2) the lawyer uses an *and*-prefaced question to append a more challenging positive polarity question to a previous unproblematic one, thereby inducing Blair to mark his reservation and disagreement through the use of *well*, *but* and *however* and through negation (*cannot recall*) that is qualified by the adverb *exactly*, which indicates orientation to the truth maxim.

```
20   Q.   And had you been aware of the proposed role that
21        Mr Campbell was going to take in assisting with the
22        presentation?
23   A.   Well, I was in no doubt that he would assist with the
24        presentation. I cannot recall exactly when but
25        certainly around that time. However, I also knew that
page 4
1         it had to be a document that was owned by the Joint
2         Intelligence Committee and the Chairman, John Scarlett.
```

This use of pragmatic markers underlines the concession Blair is making to the threat to his positive face. The perlocutionary effect of his defensive speech act here is that the audience realizes he reluctantly acknowledges that his blameless reputation has been successfully challenged. This is also a side-effect of saying more than is required and denying the implication in the question and it clearly demonstrates the institutional inferencing resources that are available here.

In the second example of the lawyer undermining Blair's status (p. 4, lines 16–25), the question in lines 22–3 takes an adversarial stance with respect to the previous answer, which had contradicted an earlier statement that he saw a draft of the dossier on 10 September. This makes the response in 19–21 appear untruthful and therefore open to challenge. The question in 22, then, marked by an adversarial discourse marker *but*, is a threat to both Blair's positive and negative face. His status as a truthful witness is threatened and his desire to be unimpeded is also challenged, as he is made to reconsider his statement. His response concedes the challenge as successful and he marks it as such, reluctantly, with the concessive verb and hedging *Yes, I suppose* and in the use of the condition plus concession clause pair (*if ... [then] I would have...*).

```
16   Q.   We have also seen some JIC assessments, redacted JIC
17        assessments of 5th and 9th September which deal with the
18        45 minute issue. When did you see those?
19   A.   I have seen the JIC assessment on 9th September but
20        other than that, I do not think I made a comment on the
```

21   45 minutes in respect of the dossier.
22 Q. But you may have seen it as it went through in the draft
23   of the 10th September?
24 A. Yes, I suppose that – if it was in the 10th September
25   draft I would have seen it.

These face threatening acts used by the lawyer to challenge Blair and threaten his positive face, constitute indirect speech acts which fail to disrupt the generally polite conduct of the interaction in extracts 1.2 and 1.3 and which contrasts starkly with the 'bald on-record' (Brown and Levinson 1987; reprinted in Jaworski and Coupland 2006) face threatening acts and impoliteness used by Vicky Pollard in extract 1.1: *shut up* (line 8), *No you definitely can't say that* (line 38). These are unmitigated by any politeness or hedging tokens and this level of directness is one that assumes a relationship of social intimacy and knowledge that is not operating here in a reciprocal way. Audience expectations are further confounded, as the status of the lawyer is reduced to that of a schoolmate or family member, or to use schema theory and Snell's (2006: 63) analysis, 'the script for COURTROOM gives way to TEENAGE GOSSIP'.

Turn-taking, preference and interruption

By contrasting the real and fictional texts we can see how turn-taking operates normally and where deviation from norms occurs. The notion of 'projectability' is an important one in conversational analysis. Because speakers understand that turns are constructed in terms of units that are predicted by the previous one – yes/ no question expects a *yes* or *no* answer; information-seeking question requires an informative answer – we are able to predict their possible completion at transition relevance places (TRPs), which are indicated by such things as a change in the pitch or volume of the voice, the end of a syntactic unit, nomination, silence or body language.

    Turns to talk are allocated by means of three ordered options (Sacks *et al.* 1974):

1 the current speaker selects the next
2 a listener self selects
3 speaker continuation.

This is a powerful distributional device and an important structuring feature of talk. In extract 1.1 Vicky Pollard breaks these turn-allocation rules by failing to observe TRPs and interrupting the lawyer when he is still in the middle of a syntactic unit (lines 35, 37, 41 and 43). Both witnesses in extracts 1.2 and 1.3, however, observe the rules more strictly.

    'Preference' too is an important principle (see Pomerantz 1984; reprinted in Jaworski and Coupland 2006). Conversation analysts note that talk is organized by means of structural pairs: question with answer, invitation with acceptance or rejection, into which speakers build preference for particular responses. For example, in the case of yes/no questions the preference is for an affirmative or negative response. The lawyer's declarative question to Tony Blair: *But you may have seen it as it went through in the draft of the 10th September?* additionally constrains in its preference for a *yes* answer.

Sacks *et al.* (1974: 700) noted a number of 'grossly apparent' or obvious facts about conversation which are useful to consider here:

1   Only one participant speaks at a time – overlap, when it occurs, is brief.
2   Order and distribution are not determined in advance and vary within and between conversations.
3   Size of turn varies: different sized units – word, phrase, clause; speaker continuation allows speakers to say more.
4   What is said or done is not determined in advance. There is local management (within social and institutional norms).
5   Speaker change recurs.

Against this background of conversational norms, we can see how Vicky Pollard breaks the rules for interrupting and misinterprets TRPs, failing to provide the long narrative turns and short confirmation turns that the lawyer expects of a cooperative witness. We can also say that 'conversations' in institutional settings have differing norms in relation to such things as order and distribution of turns and the degree to which the talk is prepared in advance; because the evidence-giving in court will have been preceded by interviews, statement-making and conversations with lawyers, much of the talk is not fresh and new, but revisited, already said. The turn length of witness answers therefore varies (in the real witness responses) according to the constraints of the question and what is being done at the time. What is said and done is to a greater extent determined by a planned agenda that can be identified in the interaction and in the local management of activity. In question and answer sequences the number of turns per participant is equal, but the proportion of talk time occupied by the participants differs according to their role, status and the degree to which their responses are managed by the lawyer.

Some contrastive observations on the texts

Extract 1.1 can be contrasted with extracts 1.2 and 1.3 in terms of the ways in which they do or do not conform to the expectations of the 'context of situation' (Halliday and Hasan 1989). The 'tenor' of discourse selected for Vicky Pollard subverts the formal and distant relationship, which is expected between lawyer and witness, and converts it into something disconcertingly familiar. There also appears to be a mismatch of 'field' of discourse, with Vicky using lexis and a style that is more appropriate for a casual conversation amongst peers than one in a legal context. Tony Blair and the ambulance technician, on the other hand, situate their talk firmly in the legal field with adherence to the maxim of quality made explicit through the use of expressions such as *to be honest, frankly, I believe.*

From looking at these real courtroom examinations, we can see that lawyers, not witnesses, control the topic, topic change and ask the questions, though Tony Blair resists the lawyer in some ways that are similar to the fictional example, through adversarial responses and choosing turn length. Vicky Pollard surprises the lawyer and the audience in her marked resistance, dominating the talk by asking questions and giving commands. Vicky's dominance is apparent from the quantitative analysis of the turns in the extracts, particularly in turns that are expected to be simply confirmatory *yes* or *no* responses.

Our understanding of the ways in which we recognize the generic conventions or schemata employed in extracts 1.2 and 1.3 is highlighted by the sharp contrasts with extract 1.1, through the script writers' representation of Vicky Pollard as a witness who violates the conventions of courtroom examination. When we see the unmarked form (particularly in extract 1.2) we recognize the marked form of extract 1.1 (and to some extent 1.3) more clearly. In extracts 1.2 and 1.3 we can identify the greater and lesser degrees of control exerted by the lawyer in relation to the content of turns (noted also by Heffer 2005: 43) produced by lay and professional witnesses. Extract 1.2 illustrates the control of evidence by the lawyer and extract 1.3 the relative freedom given to and taken by Tony Blair, as a more expert witness, to organize the content of his own speech. He also derives authority from his status outside the courtroom.

Conclusion

This contrastive vignette brings into focus some of the operational norms of the activity of examining witnesses in courtrooms. We have seen how each witness orients to the goals, norms and rules of the activity, whilst at the same time negotiating meaning, inference and responding to the expectations of the lawyer. The ambulance technician's use of the informative spectrum (interpreting when *yes* or 'more than *yes*' is required) is seen as cooperation without coerced capitulation, whereas Tony Blair operates at a level of authority that retains some of his Prime Ministerial status within an otherwise status-diminishing activity framework. He is given authority by the nature of his potential contribution to the Inquiry's goals and performs his right to retain authority through his use of discourse markers such as *frankly* and *look*. In the way that he responds to the lawyer's questions with long turns taken confidently, his authority is negotiated as part of the unfolding discourse in which his performance constructs and is constructed by the authority he assumes.

Further reading

There are some key readings in relation to the theories mentioned in this chapter. All seven of these can be found in Jaworski and Coupland (2006).

The readings are (in alphabetical order): Austin (chapter 2); Brown and Levinson (chapter 22); Goffman (chapter 21); Grice (chapter 3); Malinowski (chapter 20); Pomerantz (chapter 17); Tannen and Wallat (chapter 24).

Research tasks

1 Using the texts introduced in this chapter and other witness and lawyer interactions from the same or other sources (as well as knowledge gained from the readings), explore the following questions:

 a How far do witnesses cooperate with or resist the preferences built into lawyers' questions?

 b How do witnesses negotiate their own authority and assume rights that are not given to them by the lawyers' constraints on response?

 c In what circumstances are maxims flouted or violated by witnesses?

 d Do lawyers flout or violate maxims; if so why and what is the effect?

 e What part does the non-participating overhearing audience – that is the judge, jury, public observers, etc. – play in these settings?

 f How are discourse markers such as *well, to be honest, in fact, I think, I believe* (and any others you identify) used by witnesses and lawyers? What is marked and what is the effect?

2 On the basis of your reading generate other questions to research in witness examinations. These may be in relation to length and types of turn, whether the cooperative principle holds true and many more.

2 The language of the law

Melinkoff suggests that one reason for the use of French in legal documents was the urge to have a secret language and to preserve a professional monopoly.

(Maley 1994: 12)

Sir Edward Coke's (1628) definition of murder
When a man of sound memory and of the age of discretion, unlawfully killeth within any country of the realm any reasonable creature in *rerum natura* under the King's Peace, with malice aforethought, either expressed by the party or implied by law, so as the party wounded, or hurt, *et cetera*, die of the wound or hurt, *et cetera*, within a year and a day after the same.

(Coke 1979)

Blair interviewed again by police
Prime Minister Tony Blair was questioned for a second time by police investigating cash-for-honours allegations, it has emerged. [...] Police are investigating whether cash was donated to political parties in exchange for honours.

(BBC News 1 February 2007)

Blair aide questioned in cash for peerages investigation
A SENIOR adviser to Tony Blair has been questioned under caution by police about correspondence that discusses the possibility of nominating Labour donors for peerages, *The Times* has learnt.

(Syal 29 June 2006 *The Times* Online)

Introduction

Anyone who hears the term 'legal language' thinks immediately of grammatically complex, sparsely punctuated, over-lexicalized, opaque written text. Is the characterisation accurate and, if so, how did it come to be so?

Tiersma (2001: 75) notes that in Anglo-Saxon times legal language was entirely oral, with written text, when it eventually came to be used, serving at first only as a record of what had already been performed orally:

What mattered was what was *said* by the participants, not what was *written* by
a scribe. The written documents were merely *evidentiary* of the oral ceremony,
rather than operative or dispositive legal documents in the modern sense.

Hence the expression 'An Englishman's word is his bond...'. However, over
time, the written document, instead of being simply a record of what had already
been accomplished orally, that is of the *performative* act, came to constitute the
performative act itself, although it took a long time and in some areas of the law,
like the British marriage ceremony for instance, the spoken word still retains its
pre-eminence. Tiersma notes a significant change in 1540, when the Statute of
Wills made it compulsory to bequeath 'real' property in writing; but, even so, it
was another century before the Statute of Frauds in 1677 made it compulsory to
bequeath goods and chattels by written will. So Shakespeare, in bequeathing his
'second best bed' to his wife in his will, dated 1616, was obviously being over-
zealous or overcautious. Contracts can still, even today, be purely oral, although
typically there must also be a written record, or *memorandum*, of the contract.
Even so, the memorandum may be nothing more than a sales receipt and legally
it is simply the written evidence that there was an oral agreement; it does not
constitute the contract itself.

Even in the area of legislation, the written text was originally primarily a report
of what had been said. Tiersma notes that Edward the Confessor's eleventh-
century laws were prefaced by *we cwaedon*, translatable as 'we have pronounced'.
He also observes that, although Parliament started to enact, or at least approve,
legislation towards the end of the thirteenth century, it was not until the fifteenth
century that written documents finally came to 'constitute the law itself', in other
words the text of the statute rather than the intentions of the law-makers had now
become 'authoritative' (2001: 77). The current situation, under what lawyers call
the *plain meaning rule*, is that:

> unless there is an ambiguity obvious from the text itself, anything that the
> legislature said or did outside of the text itself cannot be used to interpret it.
> (Solan 1993 quoted in Tiersma 2001: 77)

Because the crucial period for the textualizing of the law was during the period
when the king and the nobility standardly spoke French, legal language still
displays significant French influences. At first, French was the language of the
courts, though from very early on there were concessions to the fact that the
language of the majority of the population was English. One surviving lexico-
grammatical consequence of the two languages working side by side is the frequent
use of *binomials*; that is, pairs of originally synonymous words taken from the two
languages like *devise* and *bequeath*, *breaking* and *entering*, *acknowledge* and *confess*,
null and *void*. Indeed, binomials are up to five times more frequent in English legal
language than in most other prose genres. For centuries the law worked with a
strange mixture of the two languages, nicely exemplified from this extract from a
case report written by Mr Justice Hutton Legge in 1631:

[The prisoner] sudenment throwe ove grand violence un great stone al heade del it Seignior Rychardson quel per le mercy del Dieu did come close to his hatt et missed him ... et le stone hitt the wanescott behind them and gave a great rebound, quel si ceo stone had hitt le dit Seignior Rychardson il voet have killee him.

(Tiersma 1999: 33)

Gradually, the English language drove out the French and by the sixteenth century the number of French legal terms in active use had shrunk to under a thousand (Tiersma 1999: 32). However, it was not until 1650 that Parliament passed a law requiring that all case reports and law books should be in 'the English Tongue onely' and also that earlier reports of judicial decisions and other law books should be translated into English. Then, almost immediately, in 1660, the act was repealed and the old state of affairs reinstated, with many of the case reports being again written in French and some of the court records even being written in Latin. The use of French and Latin in legal proceedings was only finally and permanently ended in 1731 (Tiersma 1999: 35–6).

Legal style and register

Legal language has a reputation for archaisms and convoluted syntax, but as Halliday (1994) points out language is the way it is because of what it has to do. This is nowhere truer than in legal settings. Ritual openings of encounters such as the reading of the police caution or the Miranda Warnings at the beginning of an interview, or the reading of the indictment at a court hearing, use formulaic expressions, which signal the start of a formal legal process. On the one hand we can argue that such language is difficult to understand and therefore distances and disadvantages the lay participant, but an alternative functional perspective is that the formulaic formality is part of the way the participants orient to what is going on. It is a signal that a formal 'high stakes' activity is starting. Understanding legal style is therefore one of the many interpretative skills that needs to be acquired in order to make sense of legal texts.

> As we noted above, one of the comments most frequently made about legal language is that it is impenetrable. As Bhatia (1993: 101) puts it: legislative writing has acquired a certain degree of notoriety rarely equalled by any other variety of English. It has long been criticized for its obscure expressions and circumlocutions, long-winded involved constructions and tortuous syntax, apparently meaningless repetitions and archaisms.

Extract 2.1 (with instances of archaisms, repetitions, long-winded involved constructions and complex syntax italicised), which is taken from the British Theft (Amendment) Act 1996, demonstrates this very clearly.

Extract 2.1

Theft (Amendment) Act 1996
An Act to amend the Theft Act 1968 and the Theft Act 1978; and for connected purposes. *Be it enacted by the Queen's most Excellent Majesty, by and with the advice and consent of the Lords Spiritual and Temporal, and Commons, in this present Parliament assembled, and by the authority of the same,* as follows:–

Obtaining a money transfer by deception.
   1. -(1) After section 15 of the Theft Act 1968 insert- 'Obtaining a money transfer by deception.
   15A. - (1) A person is guilty of an offence if by any deception he dishonestly obtains a money transfer *for himself or another.*
   (2) A money transfer occurs when–
      (a) debit is made to one account,
      (b) a credit is made to another, and
      (c) the credit results from the debit or the debit results from the credit.
   (3) References to a credit and to a debit are to a credit of an amount of money and to a debit of an amount of money.
   (4) *It is immaterial (in particular)-_*
      (a) *whether the amount credited is the same as the amount debited;*
      (b) *whether the money transfer is effected on presentment of a cheque or by another method;*
      (c) *whether any delay occurs in the process by which the money transfer is effected;*
      (d) *whether any intermediate credits or debits are made in the course of the money transfer;*
      (e) *whether either of the accounts is overdrawn before or after the money transfer is effected.*
   (5) A person guilty of an offence under this section *shall be* liable on conviction on indictment to imprisonment for a term not exceeding ten years.

From the perspective of the legal drafter, that is of the professional whose job it is to convert legal intentions into unambiguous prose, the constructions in the italicised sections are either 'devices which bring precision, clarity, unambiguity and all-inclusiveness' or a 'ploy to promote solidarity between members of the specialist community, and to keep non-specialists at a respectable distance' (Bhatia 1993: 102). What these opposing views of legal language show is that the legal drafter is in an unenviable position, striving to use language to 'do justice to the intent of Parliament and, at the same time, to facilitate comprehension of the unfolding text for ordinary readership' (Bhatia 1993: 103). Equally importantly, s/he has also to protect the intended interpretation against uncooperative readings by skilful lawyers. Thus we can see that there is a major difference between insider and outsider views of legal language and what we hope to show is that an insider view is one that does give meaning to text that the outsider often thinks is deliberately obscure and at times totally impenetrable.

An analysis of the style of legal statutes reveals consistently used linguistic forms and syntactic features that contribute to characterizing the genre. These include the already mentioned binomial expressions (Gustafsson 1984) (*by and with the advice and consent*), complex prepositions (Quirk 1982: 302; Bhatia 1993: 107) (*in the course of*) and long, complex, multi-clause sentences with syntactic matching in the subordinate clauses (such as section (4) of the Act). These features make this text instantly identifiable as an example of the genre of a written legal statute.

If we ask the question 'What is it that characterizes a particular chunk of language as legal language?' we have to consider the selection of a particular vocabulary or register. This leads us to ask: 'What is meant by a legal register and which words are legal words or, rather, which are found more frequently in legal texts?' Crystal (2003: 374) points to the particular nature of legislative language by noting that it

> depends a great deal on a fairly small set of grammatical and lexical features. For example, modal verbs (e.g. *must, shall, may*) distinguish between obligation and discretion. Pronouns (e.g. *all, whoever*) and generic nouns (hypernyms, e.g. *vehicle, person*) help foster a law's general applicability. Certainty can be promoted by explicitly listing specific items (hyponyms): if a law concerns a particular category (such as birds), then its provisions may need to say what counts as a member of that category (does *bird* include *ostrich*, which does not fly?).

A concern with semantic precision is one of the things that characterizes legislation. In the research activities for this chapter, you are invited to investigate the lexical and grammatical nature of laws and statutes in relation to how particular choices are made to ensure inclusiveness, to make rules that are clear and unambiguous, to facilitate the understanding of obligations and responsibilities for action and to clarify what kinds of action transgress the law.

Grammatical words in legal contracts

In legal contracts the choice and frequency of particular grammatical and lexical items is distinctive. One of the ways in which we can answer the question of which words are legal words, or which words are used differently in legal texts, is to look at frequency lists across collections or *corpora* of texts selected from different genres. If we compare the British National Corpus (BNC), which represents a broad range of English genres and text types, with specialist legal corpora, which embody particular genres such as statements, interviews or contracts, we can see how legal language differs from language in general. The corpus of legal contracts, held at Projeto COMET (2007) in Brazil, gives us an opportunity to compare the frequencies of grammatical and lexical words with those in the BNC, obtained from Adam Kilgariff's (24 May 2007) comprehensive summary. A study of the two corpora reveals marked differences.

First, compare the ten most frequent words in the two corpora:

BNC:	*the, of, and, a, in, to* (infinitive), *it, is, was, to* (preposition)
COMET contracts:	*the, of, or, and, to* (preposition), *in, any, to* (infinitive), *shall, be.*

One of the interesting things about frequency lists is that it is differences between grammatical words that strike us first, since they are the most frequent items in all texts and usually account for nearly half of all the tokens. When we look at a legal text, though, we often pass over the grammatical items, unless they are especially distinctive (for example, complex prepositions), and focus on features of syntax or archaic lexical items in an attempt to isolate what is distinctively legal in character. In the group of the ten most frequent grammatical words in contracts, the distinctive ones are: 'or', 'any', 'shall' and 'be'. Also of note is that the preposition 'to' is more frequent than the infinitive 'to' and the preposition 'by' comes in eleventh place in COMET. By comparison, in the BNC frequency list these words occur in the following frequency places:

or = 32; *any* = 84; *shall* = not even in top 140; *be* = 15; *by* = 19.

All five words appear in the Theft Act (extract 2.1), but you probably did not notice them on first reading. On re-examination they combine with other characteristic syntactic, stylistic and lexically distinctive features. The higher frequency of *by*, for example, is a consequence of the much more frequent passive constructions, particularly in written legal language, such as in 'Be it enacted by' (Theft Act) or 'The legal services to be provided by Attorney to Client are as follows' (COMET). In our short Theft Act extract, consisting of a mere 273 words, there are five instances of constructions using 'or':

1 *himself or another; debit or credit; credits or debits*
2 *before or after; presentment of cheque or by other method*

The frequency of 'or' in legal texts is a direct consequence of the communicative task of ensuring the inclusiveness that is necessary to cover all eventualities in relation to actors and entities (line 1 above) and time and activity (line 2 above), although activity is not conveyed by a verb, but expressed instead by nominalizations: 'presentment', 'method'.

This distinctive and frequent use of *or* is not limited to contracts, but extends to many other legal sub-genres. For example, when a police officer has taken a statement under caution, s/he asks the suspect: *Do you want to correct, alter or add anything?* The joining of verbs and nouns in lists with an 'or' between the final pair, indicating completion, is extremely common – every possible alternative of action or state is covered. And questions with the alternative or inclusive *or* are also used in interviews and cross-examination. For example, in the police investigative interview with Shipman, questions featuring both alternative and inclusive uses of *or* occur (extract 2.2).

Extract 2.2

Q.   'So just, how many lines is actually on your main line then into your surgery?
     Is it just one telephone or does it feed the number?'

Q.   'Do you use that when you're on your rounds? **Is that what the use of it is, or is it a general pager for all your business?'**

Q.   'Is it **a message paper or numeric?'**

Q. ' How are **notes or records** maintained of what is said and what visits are arranged from them phone calls.'

Q.   'With regards to the calls that come into the surgery, and you're saying that the receptionist has to assess the urgency, **do they ever** have to come through to yourself and consider whether it is **urgent or non-urgent, or do you leave** the responsibility to themselves?'

Q.   'So when a patient is seen the person responsible for **administering treatment or dealing with that patient** should make a record **as soon as practicable or as soon as possible** after seeing the patient?'

                                                                    (Shipman Trial, Day 24)

By contrast, in the cross-examination of Shipman in court, alternative questions are infrequent but *or* is quite often used inclusively (extract 2.3).

Extract 2.3

Q.   'Why then, if somewhere between 5 and 7 milligrams was the appropriate dose, were you prescribing 30 milligrams for Lillian Ibottson, **some 4 times or 5 times your dose** for a naïve morphine patient?'

Q.   'Let's try to get one thing straight. When evidence is read out to the jury, do you remember, it will have been **either Mr. Wright or myself** at his Lordship's invitation, saying to the jury that when evidence is read out it is agreed evidence unless they are told to the contrary?'

Q.   'Right. Now that was **on the 3rd September or thereabouts**, was it not?'

                                                                    (Shipman Trial, Day 32)

Legal style, then, is related to use, function and activity. What is being done has a direct impact on word choice, and this in turn produces the distinctive register that can be measured and observed in frequency lists and analysis of extracts of legal text and talk. Lexical choice is a direct consequence of communicative activity and purpose.

Interpreting legal words

It comes as something of a surprise to the layman to discover that 'generally the words "or" and "and" when occurring in statutes may be construed as interchangeable when necessary to effectuate legislative intent' (McKinney's Cons. Laws of New York, Statutes §365, quoted in Solan 1993). Although Solan reassures us that in the vast majority of cases 'and' and 'or' are in fact read in their ordinary language meaning of additive and disjunctive respectively, he reports a case where 'and' was agreed to mean 'or'.

> A Californian man who admitted he had strangled his wife, while visiting her on a day pass from a hospital where he was being treated for paranoia, pleaded insanity. The definition of the defence of insanity the court had to apply was as follows:
>> This defense shall be found by the trier of fact only when the accused person proves by a preponderance of the evidence that he or she was incapable of knowing or understanding the nature and quality of his or her act **and** of distinguishing right from wrong at the time of the commission of the offense.
>> (Californian Penal Code §25(b)) (emphasis added) (Solan 1993: 48–9)

The court found that, although he was unable to distinguish 'right from wrong' at the relevant time, he was capable of understanding 'the nature and quality of his act' and therefore was not legally insane, so he was convicted of second degree murder. On appeal his lawyers argued that the 'and' should in fact be read as 'or' and therefore, as he did satisfy one of the criteria for insanity, he should be acquitted. The appeal court agreed that such a reading was consistent with the traditional insanity defence and therefore chose to 'effectuate legislative intent' by adopting the suggested reading. One wonders what would happen if students who registered for a university degree whose course description was 'Students take six taught modules and write a dissertation of 12,000 words' were to argue for the alternative definition of 'and' and simply submit a dissertation in complete fulfilment of the course requirements.

Potentially ambiguous constructions can cause all kinds of problems in the interpretation of statutes. For this reason lawyers have interpretive rules, derived from past struggles with texts, which they then apply to new and previously uninterpreted texts. For instance, *the last antecedent* rule states that the scope of a limiting clause has to be restricted to the immediately preceding antecedent, 'unless the context or evident meaning requires a different construction'. Solan (1993: 29–30) exemplifies from a bizarre case. Here are the basic facts. A Mrs Anderson met a Mr Larson at a county fair and they decided to go off to a restaurant in Mr Larson's car. After spending several hours in the restaurant Mr Larson said he was going to the toilet, but he never came back. After waiting for some considerable time, Mrs Anderson left the restaurant and drove off in what she thought was Mr Larson's car. In fact it was not and what was worse she had an accident. Her insurance company denied liability for the damage she had caused to the 'borrowed' car, and justified this by referring to the following part of her car insurance policy:

> Such insurance as is afforded by this policy ... with respect to the owned automobile applies to the use of a non-owned automobile by the named insured ... *and* any other person or organization legally responsible for use by the named insured ... of an automobile not owned or hired by such other person or organization *provided such use is with the permission of the owner or person in lawful possession of such automobile.*
>
> (Solan 1993: 30)

At first reading the insurance company's interpretation seems quite clearly correct – Mrs Anderson, 'the named insured', was certainly allowed to drive cars belonging to others, as indeed was 'any other person [for whom she was] legally responsible', but only *provided the owner had given permission* – and in this case there was no dispute that no permission had been given – indeed the owner did not even know her, let alone that she was in his car at the time of the accident. However, Mrs Anderson's lawyers argued for another, more favourable, interpretation of the policy as a result of applying the last antecedent rule. They argued that the correct interpretation of the text was that the requirement *with the permission of the owner* only applied to the immediately preceding *any other person or organization* and not to the *named insured*, who was therefore properly insured to drive the automobile. The court accepted their argument.

Interestingly, Solan cites an apparently similar case involving 'or' where the opposite interpretative decision was taken. A school teacher was threatened with dismissal, after being convicted of the felony of growing one marijuana plant at home. The school board was allowed to dismiss anyone who had a 'conviction of a felony or of any crime involving moral turpitude' (Solan 1993: 34). In this case the court did not apply the last antecedent rule, but found another rule which read:

> When a clause follows several words in a statute and is applicable as much to the first word as to the others in the list, the clause should be applied to all of the words which preceded it.

Using this rule they reasoned that growing marijuana, although a felony, was not a 'felony involving moral turpitude' and therefore argued that the teacher should be allowed to keep his job.

To the lay reader both of these decisions seem strained and the reader might like first to work out how, in both cases, linguistic analysis could support opposite readings to those reached by the court and then study Solan's own analyses. (2002: 31–6)

Lexical words in legal contracts

Let us now return to the language of contracts. We find that it is not just their grammatical vocabulary that displays distinctively different frequencies by comparison with a general corpus – the distribution of lexical items is different too. In the BNC all 56 most frequent items are grammatical – the first lexical item is *said* which occurs in fifty-seventh place; by contrast, the contract corpus has 15 lexical items in the top 57:

> *agreement, company, lessee, party, respect, agent, notice, property, time, provided, date, including, parent, guarantor, lessor.*

There is one word, though, that needs to be discounted from this list – *respect* – because each of its 433 occurrences in the corpus occurs as part of a complex preposition: *in respect of, with respect to, in respect thereof* and *with respect thereto*. *Respect* is never used as a lexical noun or verb, but its presence as a high frequency item nevertheless points to its distinctiveness as part of the different grammatical set in the contract corpus. It also highlights the distinctiveness of complex prepositions in the genre and in legal language as a whole. The greater number of frequent lexical words, implies that contracts are unusually dense lexically and for that reason alone they will necessarily be harder to understand. In addition, there is a great deal of vocabulary that is core in legal texts, which is not core in a general English corpus.

The majority of the words in the above list are nouns (*agent, agreement, company, date, guarantor, lessee, lessor, notice, parent, party, property, time*) and refer to the parties involved in the contract and to the contract itself as an entity (*agreement*) that is transacted by the parties. The two lexical verbs that are present in the list, *provided* and *including*, are important in relation to the function of the contract and the notion of selectivity and inclusiveness already noticed in the use of *or*. The verb *including* is generally used to introduce non-finite subordinate clauses that give provisions and inclusions, which hold important interpretative details. Some examples of the distinctive patterns among the 373 occurrences of *including* in COMET are:

1 *including* preceded by comma or enclosed in brackets:
    – *and manner of delivery, including the carrier to be used by SUPPLIER.*
    – *administrative and judicial proceedings (including any informal proceedings) and all orders,*
2 *including* + , *without limitation,* or , *but not limited to,*
    – *(including, without limitation, the Maturity Date)*
    – *including, but not limited to, the Securities Act of 1933*
3 *including* + list
    – *including fire, flood, strikes, labor troubles or other*
4 *including* + *all* or *any* + noun or list

– *including all common parts, the internal decorations and the fixtures and*
– *including any actual loss or expense incurred*

The verb *provided* occurs 389 times in COMET. It is used 224 times (58 per cent) as a verb in constructions like:

provided + prepositional phrase
– *as provided for in the Agreement,*
– *as provided in paragraph 10 hereof,*
to be provided herein/under,
noun + *provided to* + noun phrase
– *Investment Banking Services provided to the company*

Of the 165 (42 per cent) uses as a conjunction, *provided that* (expanded to *provided, however, that* in almost half the cases), the following patterns appear:

preceded by a comma or semi-colon
– *upon confirmation of receipt; provided, however, that any Funding Notice*
followed by a comma and another exclusion clause
– *provided that, subject to the following sentence*
provided that + noun phrase containing a party: *lessor, Company, Landlord, lessee, translator, tenant*
– *provided that the lessee shall have paid*

A final distinctive feature in the use of *provided* in COMET can be seen when we compare its frequency in the BNC. In COMET verbal use is 16 times and conjunctive use is 21 times more frequent than in the BNC. These patterns of inclusive use that surround the verb *including*, and its partner *provided*, which introduces provisos (in clauses *provided that…*), underline the dominance of these functions in contracts and show us clearly what contracts are about: everything that is covered with certain provisos. In addition, the repetition of lexical items (*landlord, lessee, company*), rather than the use of pronoun substitutes, produces frequency information that underlines the key semantic fields present in contracts.

Other marked features of legal English are latinisms, like *prima facie, bona fide*; archaic adverbs, *hereinafter, thereunder*; specific prepositional phrases *pursuant to, at the instance of*; a greater use of performative constructions, *X hereby agrees/confers*; a more frequent use of passives, conditionals and hypotheticals; and unusually long sentences. Hiltunen (1984), for example, found that the British Road Traffic Act of 1972 had a mean sentence length of 79.25, with one sentence being 740 words long. And then of course there is punctuation, or the lack of it, which can create problems.

Solan (1993) discusses a case (*Anderson v. State Farm Mut. Auto. Ins. Co.* (1969) 270 Cal.App.2d 346) which hinges on the use of a comma, and a similar case has recently come before the Canadian Radio-television and Telecommunications

Commission (CRTC). The story was reported in the Canadian newspaper, *The Globe and Mail*, in both its on-line (6 August 2006) and print (7 August 2006) editions. The print edition headline, 'The $2-million comma', highlights the cost of the decision to the losers, Rogers Communications. The on-line report starts:

> It could be the most costly piece of punctuation in Canada. A grammatical blunder may force Rogers Communications Inc. to pay an extra $2.13-million to use utility poles in the Maritimes after the placement of a comma in a contract permitted the deal's cancellation. The controversial comma sent lawyers and telecommunications regulators scrambling for their English textbooks in a bitter 18-month dispute that serves as an expensive reminder of the importance of punctuation.
>
> (Robertson 06.08.06)

The CRTC decision quotes section 8.1 of the contract, the Support Service Agreement (SSA), that was the subject of the dispute.

> Subject to the termination provisions of [the SSA], [the SSA] shall be effective from the date it is made and shall continue in force for a period of five (5) years from the date it is made, and thereafter for successive five (5) year <u>terms, unless</u> and until terminated by one year prior to notice in writing by either party.
>
> (para. 16 CRTC Decision 2006-45)

The Commission's decision related to the placement of the second comma (underlined) and, as Robertson states in his article, 'had it not been there, the right to cancel wouldn't have applied to the first five years of the contract'. The Commission's decision was that 'based on the rules of punctuation, the comma placed before the phrase "unless and until terminated by one year prior notice in writing by either party" means that that phrase qualifies both the phrases' (para.27 CRTC Decision 2006-45).

Ordinary and special meanings

With the exceptions noted above, the vocabulary used in a legal text will look very much like that of ordinary English and most of the time the words will have ordinary language meanings. However, a small number of the words in any given legal document will have a *legal definition*, which dictates how an otherwise ordinary language item must be interpreted in the particular contexts to which the document applies. Sometimes the 'defined' word appears in bold, sometimes it is spelled with an initial capital, both conventions being used to indicate that it is, at that point, being used in its defined meaning. For example, one early road traffic act redefined 'carriage' to include 'bicycle', while another had to define 'dusk' in order to be able to forbid people to remain in public parks after dusk. However, a candidate for the most amusing definition, though certainly not the easiest to remember, is quoted in Tiersma (1999: 118). Apparently a Florida ordinance, designed to control the amount of flesh erotic dancers were allowed to expose, required them to 'cover their buttocks'. In order to help these dancers comply with the law (and, of course, to make it easier for the poor law enforcement officers, armed with tape measures, to check that the dancers were indeed observing the law to the letter, or at least to the fraction of an inch), the crucial term 'buttocks' was defined as follows.

> the area at the rear of the human body (sometimes referred to as the gluteus maximus) which lies between two imaginary lines running parallel to the ground when a person is standing, the first or top of such lines being one-half inch below the top of the vertical cleavage of the nates (i.e. the prominence formed by the muscles running from the back of the hip to the back of the leg) and the second or bottom line being one-half inch above the lowest point of the curvature of the fleshy protuberance (sometimes referred to as the gluteal fold), and between two imaginary lines, one on each side of the body (the outside lines) which outside lines are perpendicular to the ground and to the horizontal lines described above and which perpendicular outside lines pass through the outermost point(s) at which each nate meets the outer side of each leg.

Bizarre though this may seem, any officer faced with the practicalities of judging how much flesh needs to be exposed to constitute 'uncovered buttocks' has a difficult task and a definition is therefore a necessary tool for the law enforcer. Similarly where lexical items are homonyms or polysemantic, a more specific legal term is important. One which Johnson remembers from her police days is the word *audible warning instrument* to mean *horn*. In British English *horn* is a homonym: the horn of an animal, as in *the bull had huge horns*; and a car horn, as in *he sounded the horn*. In American English *horn* is not polysemantic, since cars have *hooters*. The offence of sounding the horn after 11p.m. at night, which is a traffic offence in England and Wales, uses the term 'audible warning instrument' which includes a 'horn, bell, gong or siren'. General words or hypernyms like 'audible warning instrument' are clearly more useful as legal terms than taxonomic sisters such as 'horn', 'gong' or 'bell', where using one in a law would signal that warnings using other instruments were acceptable.

In her analysis of two versions of a contract for furniture removal, the second of which was rewritten according to principles of the Plain English Campaign, Davies (2004: 82) sets out to examine 'two different ways of saying the same thing' and to evaluate whether the second text preserves the meaning of the first, as the writers claimed. One of the features she looks at for comparison is 'field-indicative restricted senses of lexical items', or in other words ordinary words with special legal meanings. She finds that one text uses the word 'parties' whereas the plain English text uses the word 'sides'. Some words occur in both texts: *agreement*, *cost(s)*, but there is a number of words with special meanings that occur only in the first: *award*, *difference* (meaning 'dispute'), *question* (meaning 'dispute'), *parties*, *claim* (legal claim for money or damage), *calling* (in the phrase 'barrister of ten years calling' meaning experience, but coming from the phrasal verb 'called to the Bar'), *discretion, condition, subject of, precedent* (as an adjective). She concludes that this difference leads to 'a more formal tenor', which indicates a restricted field of expertise common to technical varieties of English (Davies 2004: 97). However, although the first 'is not easily comprehensible to the lay readership', she concedes that the second, 'which is much easier for the layman to understand, may not convey exactly the same legal content' (Davies 2004: 98). Special meanings are a necessary part of the work that legal language does in expressing content.

Specialized lexis can present particular problems, though, for law students in countries such as India, where, because of British colonisation, the laws are written in English, but where English is a second language for the majority of students studying law. Sandhya (2004: 137) discusses the challenges he faces as a language teacher in an Indian university with law students who need his help to understand legal English. He observes 'that students had to be sensitized to the dynamic, the problematic and the dialogic aspects of the law-language nexus … if they were to sincerely deliver justice to the laity' (2004: 137). His investigation with his students into legal language took him into special meanings:

> that if 'detriment' meant 'injury' or 'harm' in common parlance, 'legal detriment' did not necessarily mean harm or injury; that one could not only 'prefer coffee to tea' but could also 'prefer an appeal', that 'damage without injury' and 'injury without damage' had different legal implications and that 'damages' was not the plural form of damage, but 'compensation'.
>
> (2004: 137)

Since English is a world language in former colonies of the British Empire, the legacy of specialized meaning is a worldwide one. The Test of Legal English website (http://www.toles.co.uk/) lists test centres in 30 countries around the world in many countries where English was not exported as part of the Empire, including Argentina, Latvia and Thailand. It uses the phrase 'global legal English' in its website, indicating that legal English has a global market and a global set of learners and users.

On applying the law

Texts such as statutes, and talk in legal settings, are the way they are because they are situated in a multidimensional, real-world context that produces complex and dynamic textual and intertextual forces. These forces constrain and determine the nature, meaning and effects of those texts on individuals. We cannot simply interpret laws and statutes as texts, but rather need to consider their use in context. Taking the trial as an example, a defendant faces a charge, such as murder, which is read out by the Clerk of the Court as an indictment. At the heart of this process is the particular law or statute that specifies an offence, but the way that the statute is understood and applied is specific to each case and set of circumstances.

The judicial process is influenced by a whole range of prior texts and contexts (police interviews, statement making and taking, meetings with lawyers), both written and spoken, all of which centre on the law.

In the case of murder, in many countries, the US and Australia are two obvious examples, there are written statutes that define the offence, but in England and Wales it is an offence under Common Law (the law that existed before statutes started to be made by Parliament). Murder is defined by reference to cases, but a definition that is often referred to is that of Sir Edward Coke (1979: 47):

> When a man of sound memory and of the age of discretion, unlawfully killeth within any country of the realm any reasonable creature in *rerum natura* under the King's Peace, with malice aforethought, either expressed by the party or implied by law, so as the party wounded, or hurt, *et cetera*, die of the wound or hurt, *et cetera*, within a year and a day after the same.

This contains a number of conditions, all of which need to be proven in order for someone to be convicted of murder: sound mind, not a child below the age of criminal responsibility (under the age of ten), unlawfully (so not in wartime), any living person (therefore not a fetus), occurring in the countries of England or Wales (therefore of any nationality as long as they are in the 'Realm' at the time they do the wounding), intending serious injury and inflicting a wound or assault that kills the person. Coke's 'year and a day' rule has now been overruled by a law passed in 1996, so that someone can be charged with murder even if the victim dies as a result of an injury sustained more than a year earlier. A trial for murder will therefore concentrate on the evidence that demonstrates that the crime meets the above conditions.

In chapters 3 and 4 we look at linguistic aspects of the collection of evidence from the initial call to the emergency services, through the subsequent police interviews to the interaction in the courtroom. All of these situations create a complex collection of talk and texts: interviews, statements, consultations with lawyers, examinations and cross-examinations of witnesses in court and the judicial adjudication. At each stage, the law influences and determines the goals of the talk and the subsequent written record.

Where statutes exist, charges are written in accordance with the part of the Act of Parliament that specifies the offence(s), but before anyone is charged with an offence, there needs to be an investigation to establish whether any offence has actually been committed. In a news story that was current in the UK at the time of writing this chapter, the police were making inquiries into allegations that knighthoods or peerages had been given to individuals following gifts to the governing Labour Party. This story is referred to in the third epigraph.

At the heart of this particular investigation were two specific laws – the Honours (Prevention of Abuses) Act 1925 and the Political Parties, Elections and Referendums Act 2000 (PPER Act) – and a common law offence – perverting the course of justice, which includes fabricating evidence. An aide to Prime Minister Tony Blair was arrested and questioned and her case sent to prosecutors to decide whether she should face charges in relation to the PPER Act. Others, including the Prime Minister, were questioned as suspects or witnesses. The allegation against the aide was that:

> e-mails, written in 2004 and 2005, discussed which lenders might be placed on a list of nominees for peerages. The list of names was to be forwarded to the House of Lords Appointments Commission, the parliamentary body that recommended the names of individuals to be appointed on merit.
>
> (Syal 29 September 2006)

The Act in question specifies that:

> A person commits an offence if he (a) knowingly enters into, or (b) knowingly does any act in furtherance of, any arrangement which facilitates or is likely to facilitate, whether by means of any concealment or disguise or otherwise, the making of donations to a registered party by any person or body other than a possible donor.
>
> (PPER Act 2000, Section 60(1))

The Times (Syal 29 September 2006) reported that 'Police were trying to establish whether there was a conspiracy to give out honours in exchange for loans that could later be converted into gifts'. Therefore a series of connected actions, the giving of loans by a number of individuals that might be a way of disguising a gift, the placement of names of loan-givers on a list and forwarding a list by email to an appointing commission, could be seen as possible infringements of the written law that seeks to control donations.

In the Shipman Inquiry, already discussed in the Introduction, 37 different statutes are referred to as relevant, including the Births and Deaths Registration Act 1953, the Cremation Act 1952 and the Misuse of Drugs Act 1971. These are contained in a section of the inquiry entitled 'Generic Evidence', which 'contains information that provides general background to the matters being investigated by the Inquiry and evidence that may pertain to more than one area being investigated' (The Shipman Inquiry 2001). In addition, 85 different regulations, which have a legal status, are also listed. The extensive nature of this general background is an important part of the generic context and indicates the power of the legal statute as a context for text and talk.

Conclusion

There is some debate about the need for legal language, which we have not addressed here. On one side of the debate is the argument that legal language has a high degree of precision and inclusivity that is required by the genre. However, The Plain English Campaign (1996a, b) provides a counter argument that this language is 'unnecessary' (1996a: 22–7). Two articles which are written from these two positions (Prakasam 2004; Davies 2004) are suggested in the further reading for this chapter. For the moment, at least, we have to 'tak[e] legal language seriously' (Gibbons 2004: 11), since there are 'dangers inherent in the editing process [that revises a law into Plain English]' because simpler documents often lose something in translation, which Davies (2004: 98) herself notes. It is unlikely that major reforms in legal language will take place, since, as Gibbons (2004: 2) points out, 'lawyers exert much effort in finding loopholes and alternative readings of legal documents; so when these documents are produced, a major objective is to avoid leaving them open to hostile or unintended reading' and therefore this produces the need for 'maximal precision'. Coincidentally though, as this book was being completed, a legal reform story made the news in the United States. Rules governing procedure in federal trial courts have been rewritten according to Plain Language principles, the authors winning an award for legal achievement: 'Reform in Law' Awarded for First Plain-Language Rewrite of Federal Civil Court Rules in 70 Years (Munro 2007).

For the student or researcher setting out to observe and analyse talk or text produced in legal contexts, some knowledge of the legal determinants of activity is therefore important. Visiting a courtroom to observe cases from the public gallery, without some knowledge of the written laws and the professional genres that exist, presents the lay observer with some difficulty in understanding what is going on.

The claim that legal language is incomprehensible can be seen to be partly attributable to a lack of knowledge that leaves non-members of the discourse community without the interpretative resources to make sense of texts. As Crystal (2003: 374) says, legal discourse is

> pulled in different directions. Its statements have to be so phrased that we can see their general applicability, yet be specific enough to apply to individual circumstances. They have to be stable enough to stand the test of time, so that cases will be treated consistently and fairly, yet flexible enough to adapt to new social situations. Above all they have to be expressed in such a way that people can be certain about the intention of the law respecting their rights and duties. No other variety of language has to carry such a responsibility.

The words of the law and of legal statutes, whether plain or opaque, clearly produce an important intertextual context for any investigation and for the interactions that take place within it. There is an interdependency between written laws and speech in legal contexts that gives both spoken and written legal language its distinctive features, but it is the work that legal language does that truly characterizes it.

Further reading

Bhatia (1994); Davies (2004); Frade (2007); Gibbons (2003, chapters 2 and 5); Gibbons (2004); Gustafsson (1984); Kurzon (1997); Maley (1994); Prakasam (2004); The Test of Legal English website (<http://www.toles.co.uk/> – here you can look at sample exams and answers); Tiersma (1999).

Research tasks

1 Investigate some of the laws and statutes of your own country. How do the lexical and grammatical choices of the legal drafters aim to ensure inclusiveness and produce rules that are clear and unambiguous? To what extent do the lawmakers produce a clear document that means individuals understand their obligations and responsibilities for action and what kind of action transgresses the law?

2 Analyse some of the lexical and grammatical features of legal contracts in the COMET corpus, by exploring concordances of some of the distinctive vocabulary of contracts. Take as a starting point some of the lexical and grammatical items discussed in this chapter. Explain the use of the features in relation to the function of contracts and in contrast to a more general corpus or one from a different field. Legal contracts can be found at: Projeto COMET: http://www.fflch.usp.br/dlm/comet/

3 A Mr Jacober took out car insurance. He was killed while travelling as a passenger in his own car, which was being driven, with his permission, by a friend Mr Dell. Subsequently, Mrs Jacober sued Mr Dell to get compensation from the insurance company for the death of her husband, but the insurance company refused to pay on the grounds that, although Mr Dell was insured on Mr Jacober's policy as the driver, Mr Jacober himself as the policy holder was specifically excluded from injury insurance. On what *linguistic grounds* would you argue the case for and against an award of compensation? The relevant clauses in the insurance contract are presented below; (highlighting in bold has been added):

> [The insurer agrees] to pay on behalf of the insured all sums which the insured shall become legally obligated to pay as damages … because of bodily injury [including death] sustained by **other persons**

> The unqualified word 'insured' includes (1) **the named insured** … and (4) any other person while using the owned automobile … with the permission of the named insured

> Exclusions
> [Insurance does not apply] to bodily injury to the insured.

4 A nineteenth-century US statute made it a crime 'in any manner whatsoever, to prepay the transportation of [an] alien … to perform labor or service of any kind in the United States'. A church was convicted of violating this statute, by having pre-paid the transportation of its rector from England. In an appeal in 1892, *Church of the Holy Trinity* v. *United States*, the Supreme Court was

asked to reverse the conviction. What linguistic grounds can you see for them
to do this?

5   Before going to the Far East, a Dr Rowland and his wife made identical wills.
Both left their property to the other unless the other's death was 'preceding
or coinciding', in which case other relatives were to benefit. Both were on a
ship which disappeared without trace. The named beneficiary of the wife's
will claimed the whole estate on the grounds that if their deaths were not
coinciding she, being the younger, would be deemed by the Law of Property
Act (1925) to have survived him. On what grounds would you argue the case
that the deaths were not coinciding and how would you expect the husband's
family lawyers to respond?   You need to consider also how one can tell
what the testators meant by 'coinciding' and even if you think this might be
different from the literal meaning, how can you argue for this interpretation
in this case?

Note

Tasks 3 and 4 are based on Solan (2002) and Task 5 on Zander (1999).

3   Legal genres

Text A

Close friend the Rev Allan Ellershaw said: 'Everyone is very shocked. Ken and I were ordained on the same day in 1977. He was someone who loved people and liked to be with people'.

The churchman added: 'Ken was a former detective sergeant. He came to the faith during an inquiry into the murder of a girl many years ago. He left the force and went to college'.

Text B

And he saith unto them, Why are ye fearful, O ye of little faith? Then he arose, and rebuked the winds and the sea; and there was a great calm.

But the men marvelled, saying, What manner of man is this, that even the winds and the sea obey him!

Text C

'It's as plain as a pikestaff,' said Lestrade triumphantly. 'By purloining his wife's jewels while she was away he hoped to repay those debts. He had the only key to this room and to the strongbox: and the butler testifies he left him alone here after bringing his glass of Drambuie. The glass is still here, the door was not forced. Even if he claims to remember nothing, it's all most conclusive.'

'Why, then did you arrest the wrong man, pray?' demanded Holmes, with a twinkle in his eye. Lestrade was dumbfounded.

'Explain yourself, Holmes,' said I. 'Surely this is the glass?'

'Indeed it is, Watson my dear friend, but look closer. You will observe faint traces of the precious liquid on one small section of the rim.'

'So,' continued he, 'it was swallowed in one gulp …'

Text D

I said 'You gonna take something heavy, do you know what I mean, to make things easier in there.'

Bob said, 'No, fuck off, like that's too much, I'll just have a blade, that'll do.'

I said, 'Yeah okay.'

Bob said, 'I'm just a bit jittery like as its getting close like.'

I said, 'Yeah, okay but keep in touch.'

Introduction

Each of the epigraphs comes from an easily recognisable *genre*. Can you identify them? 'Of course', you say: a newspaper report, *The Bible* (King James version, Matthew 8 26–7), a Sherlock Holmes novel and notes made as a record of a conversation. But is that right? Well 'yes' and 'no'. Two of the texts are not what they seem. Text C is an advertisement for the Scottish alcoholic liqueur, Drambuie, using the genre of a Sherlock Holmes novel in which to embed the drink as an advertised product, and Text D is discussed in Chapter 6, as a disputed text. In this case the police claimed that it was a record of a conversation made from memory, but the defendant in the case claimed that the record was too accurate to have been made from memory and that it had in fact been covertly tape-recorded.

All of the extracts, though not complete texts, are distinguishable as coming from particular genres, which we can name. The extracts are also selected to demonstrate another feature of genre. Each text deals with reported speech, but the way the speech is represented differs according to the genre. Text D uses a very restricted set of reporting verbs – only one in fact, *said* – while Text C uses a much wider range, as is usual in novels, employing elegant variation for richness: *said, demanded, continued*, with the reporting clauses after the reported speech containing adverbs and adverbials of manner: *triumphantly, with a twinkle in his eye*, which would not be found in Text D. There are other contrasts to be made (you will be invited to do this in the tasks at the end of the chapter), but the point is clear: different genres do reported speech, as well as many other things, differently and in such distinctive ways that we can use them to identify a *genre* or text type.

Defining 'genre' – functional hybridity

In Chapter 2 we said that, when creating texts, the producer's lexical choice is a direct consequence of their communicative activity and purpose. This assertion makes *register* and *genre* inter-related aspects of textualisation. Lexical and grammatical choices, such as the use of a restricted set of reporting verbs in police statements and notes (*said, replied*), inclusive phrases and lists in legal texts (using *and* and *or*), passive constructions with *by* and phrases that contain the verbs *including* or *provided* in contracts, are made because of what needs to be communicated.

'Genre' can be defined simply: conventional, repeated and distinctive features of text that arise from its communicative purpose. Another way is to say that a text is an example of a particular genre. We are all familiar with the major *fictional* genres and their structures and interpretation. We can readily name them: novel, play, poem, film, and also their *subgenres*, such as horror film, romantic comedy or science fiction, and we know that in a romantic comedy a boy will meet a girl, fall in and out of love, struggle against obstacles placed in the path of true love, but we also know that everything will get sorted out in the end. However, when it comes to professional and spoken genres, naming and definition is much more difficult. The *Little Britain* extract, used in Chapter 1, draws our attention to genre, since satirical drama activates generic or schematic knowledge to produce humour. The literary genres noted here highlight the structural aspect of *genre*. They have an underlying script with a particular structure and usually specific lexical and grammatical features, some of which are compulsory and some of which are optional.

So, although genres are stable entities, that are repeated and understood through conventions and regularities that are consistent across texts, they do not occur in identical form in each textual realisation. As Gibbons (2003: 130) says (quoting Swales 1990), genres are 'prototypes' that can be followed or modified. We recognize the prototypical elements in them, but only if we are expert users of the genre. So, for example, when, as young science students, we were asked for the first time to write an account of a science experiment we had just conducted, we needed some help with the *report* genre. The way we learn genres is either through training by expert producers, in this case science teachers, or by inductive trial and error.

In the early stages of writing scientific reports we may not have realized why we were writing down information under headings such as *equipment*, *method* and *results*; we had to learn the role each of these sections plays in the whole job of communicating the purpose and nature of the experiment and the results. We learned that while a list might be appropriate in the *equipment* section, a sequence of declarative sentences with past tense verbs in logical steps is the typical way of constructing the *method* section. Genres are therefore domain specific; they have lexico-grammatical features associated with them; they have specific stages, often named and usually sequenced that contribute to a structural whole; while each stage has a purpose in the text as a whole, some of them may be optional, as, for example, diagrams and pictures in the scientific report genre.

Martin (1992) describes some fictional and factual macro-genres that exist in society: *report, procedure, exposition, narrative, recount*, but Gibbons also points out that in texts 'deeper' genre patterns 'may underlie more formalized and rigid "surface" genres that are used for specific social purposes' (Gibbons 2003: 131). Gibbons talks about the police interview genre as having a number of stages, and notes that the genre has within it an 'underlying narrative structure' (2003: 143), while Heffer (2005: 67), in addition to noting the importance of the narrative mode, makes a distinction between three phases of the trial and the principal genres found there: *procedural* genres such as jury selection, the calling and swearing-in of witnesses; *adversarial* genres such as opening statements, witness examinations, closing argument and *adjudicative* genres such as a judge's summation and sentencing. There can also be 'genres within genres' (Gibbons 2003: 131) or 'complex genres' (Heffer 2005: 65). Maley (1994: 16) provides a chart of legal genres, which is expanded by Gibbons (2003: 132–3) in relation to trials.

The many genres that pre-date the trial and occur within it can be both written and spoken. Written genres include 'pre-existing, codified' documents, such as legislation, contracts, precedents or judgments which inform the legal process, or records and law-making that form a part of the legal process after cases have been heard and which may be embodied in case reports. These contrast with 'dynamic pre-trial and trial' genres, which are primarily spoken, such as police interviews, consultations between lawyers and clients (see Maley *et al.* 1995 and Halldorsdottir 2006 in the follow-up reading) and instructions to lawyers, committal hearings and jury instructions. Hasan (2000: 29) takes the 'genres within genres' concept a step further when she discusses the 'uses of talk' in institutional environments. She notes that in such talk participants can make 'the talk move to suit [their] own purposes' in a way that signals the speaker's 'readiness to constantly reclassify discursive situations'. She refers to this as hybridity, which is 'the mixing of the recognized properties of different pre-existing genres' (Hasan 2000: 29; see also Sarangi 2000). Genres can thus be said to be hybrid and dynamic.

Johnson (2006), for example, demonstrates how in police interviews officers may switch between acting as a representative of the institution, as in turn 143 of extract 3.1 below, and adopting an almost therapeutic role, as in turns 149 and 163, in order to create a more productive context for disclosure.

Extract 3.1

143 We have to find out what's happened to the child. That's our major aim as police officers. If you wish to no-reply like your solicitor has advised, you can do. If you wish to talk to us and tell us what may have happened in reply to the questions that we ask then you have that right to do so also.
149 We're here to help you.
163 It's important to you, just for you, to tell us what's happened. You need to get it out of your system because at the moment from where we're sat you're quite screwed up really about it all.

Turns 149 and 163 move away from the institutional voice of turn 143 with its complex subordinated grammar of conditional *if*-clauses and its intertextual reference to the police caution, or right to silence, in the use of the verbs *wish* and *no-reply*, using instead a therapeutic voice that focuses on the interviewee's perceived need to talk, rather than on the institutional need to find out what happened. The institutional *we* (143) seems to change to a more personal *we* (163) and the verb changes to a more conversational *get it out of your system* from *talk* and *tell*, which is related to institutional aims and rights. This constitutes the dynamic shifting within a hybrid genre with the interviewer moving from one role to another within a surface genre that forms part of the questioning phase of an interview.

What is also evident here is an attempt to elicit storytelling and this narrative genre underlies the second of the three phases of the police interview genre, what Gibbons (2003) calls the *secondary reality core*, which involves orientation to the offence and questioning. This questioning phase is both preceded and followed by *primary reality framing*: at the beginning of the interview there are introductions and the reading of the caution and at the end of the interview there is closure and an explicit reference to the recording procedures.

Johnson (2006: 667) confirms the claims of interactional hybridity with an analysis of the closing stages of an interview with a woman suspected of stealing money. In extract 3.3, which on the surface sums up the content of an interview concerning an alleged theft of money and starts to bring it to a close, a number of lexical items are highlighted with bold. These are items that link the talk intertextually with the Theft Act 1968 (extract 3.2), which defines the offence. As you read the extract from the Theft Act (3.2), note the words in bold and bear them in mind when you read extract 3.3.

Extract 3.2

> *Theft Act 1968*
> A person is guilty of **theft** if he **dishonestly [cf. knowing] appropriates property belonging to another** with the intention of permanently depriving the other of it; and 'thief' and 'steal' shall be construed accordingly (section 1).
>
> Any **assumption** by a person of **the rights of an owner** amounts to an appropriation (section 3).
>
> **Property** includes **money** and all other property, real or personal including things in action and other intangible property (section 4).
>
> A person appropriating **property belonging to another** without meaning the other permanently to lose the thing itself is nevertheless to be regarded as having the intention of permanently depriving the other of it if his intention is **to treat the thing as his own** to dispose of regardless of the other's rights; and a borrowing or lending of it may amount to so treating it if, but only if, the borrowing or lending is for a period and in circumstances making it equivalent to an outright taking or disposal (section 6).

Extract 3.3

1	I	So is that the amount that you closed the account with –
2	A	Mhm. I think so.
3	I	**knowing** for a while that all the **monies** that you've transferred
4		from the date we've just gone through those transactions –
5	A	Mhm.
6	I	we're talking from the fourteenth of the second, the transactions
7		I've just done, all the **monies** there, **you knew wasn't your money?**
8	A	Yeah.
9	I	And you've actually stolen it from the Skipton Building Society
10		haven't you, that amounts to **theft**.
11	A	Why do you need –
12	I	You've taken – you've **taken money** which in effect –
13	A	Yes.
14	I	– is **property**.
15	A	Mhm.
16	I	And you've **assumed rights of ownership** and you've **used that**

17		**money as your own.**
18	A	Mhm. Yeah.
19	I	Is that right?
20	A	Yeah.
21	I	**Knowing** that that **money is not yours.**
22	A	Yeah.

A comparison of the two reveals the inbuilt generic hybridity present in many of the legal genres. On the surface, the talk in extract 3.3 appears to be summing up and closing the questioning phase of the interview, but it subtly incorporates the legislative genre (extract 3.2) within it, a fact which may be at best only partially understood by the interviewee. The effect is to produce a complex and powerful set of communicative actions that create interpretative challenges for the lay participant in the talk and also for observers and analysts.

Gibbons' (2003: 130) assertion that knowledge of genre 'is critical to both the construction and the comprehension of discourse' is relevant in the case of the interview above. He gives his own example (extract 3.4), taken from a marriage agreement in the United States, which is reported in the *Washington University Law Quarterly*, vol. 73. Non-lawyers find the writing of the agreement to be 'incompetent' and 'incomprehensible' but lawyers readily understand it, because of their knowledge of the genre. The relevant clause in the contract reads as follows:

Extract 3.4

> After this marriage in the absence of any agreement to the contrary the legal relations and powers as regards to property might, by reason of some change in our domicile or otherwise, be other than those of our present domiciles or other than those which we desire to apply to our relationship powers and capacities.
>
> (Gibbons 2003: 130)

Generic knowledge is, in part, knowledge of what texts and their constituents do, or, as Gibbons (2003: 130) expresses it, knowledge that involves the use of 'interpretive frameworks'. Lawyers were able to activate this knowledge to gloss this 'incomprehensible' clause and explain that it 'is inserted at the beginning of many such contracts to cover the contingencies of the parties moving to another state where the law is different' (Gibbons 2003: 130).

To some extent, then, professional genres are closed to lay interpretation, or at least lay interpreters have to work harder to derive meaning from these texts. For this reason, one of the things that forensic linguists have had to do, before working on texts from a particular legal genre, is to determine the scope and nature of the genre. This may involve some ethnographic fieldwork on a fairly small scale, such as observations in court, or a much more systematic ethnography such as that described by Scheffer (2006) in his micro-analysis of a trial, from an array of observations of the work of lawyers in meetings, notes on the file before and during the trial, consultations and examinations and cross-examinations of witnesses in the case. Scheffer demonstrates how lawyers' talk is closely oriented to the relevant legislative materials by using an example from a case of Wounding with Intent, an offence contrary to sections 18 and 20 of the Offences against the Person Act 1861. The indictment against the defendant was that he 'unlawfully and maliciously wounded (victim's name) with intent to do him grievous bodily harm [GBH]' (Scheffer 2006: 305). There are lesser offences under the act, which do not require malice and intent to be proven and where the injury suffered is less than grievous. This is therefore a serious indictment. Scheffer's ethnographic study traces the lawyer's pre-trial and in-trial notes in relation to the question of intent, since the defendant admits hitting the victim, but not intending to do him serious injury or GBH.

The defence case centres around this issue of impulse versus intent, which is crystallized in a short dialogue (extract 3.5) reported by Scheffer between the prosecution and defence barristers (PB and DB) 'minutes before they appear before the judge' to begin the case (Scheffer 2006: 320).

Extract 3.5

1 PB.   Is it a definite?
2 DB.   Yes, I guess so.
3 PB.   ... The only issue between us then is the question of intent.
4 DB.   Yes. ... Let's get it done.

In indirectly noting their agreement on most elements of the case (line 3) they distil the only remaining focus of the immediate legal contest into one issue. The question of intent is not evaded in the defence lawyer's questions to his client in court either. Scheffer (2006: 329) notes that, at the end of the friendly examination of the defendant, the defence lawyer confronts head-on 'the case's most vulnerable point ("I wasn't finished")' which are the words the defendant used to police in interview, concerning the assault, and which will certainly be exploited by the prosecution in terms of intent to do GBH. The relevant part of the friendly examination is shown in 3.6.

Extract 3.6

1 Q.   And then you were asked, 'Did you feel remorse for what you had
2   done, or anything?,' and you say, 'No, I wasn't finished.'
3   What did you mean by that?
4 A.   I don't know. I was still very angry. I just – I don't know.
5 Q.   And, when you struck with the glass, what did you intend to do?
6 A.   I don't know.
7 Q.   Did you think about the fact that you had the glass in your hand?
8 A.   No.

9 Q. Did you want to cause him really serious injury?
10 A. Not really serious injury, no.

In what Scheffer (2006: 329) describes as 'a forward defence' strategy, the defence view of intent is laid before the jury in advance of the prosecution cross-examination. It is returned to by the defence lawyer in his closing address to the jury, who have to decide the case in relation to intent (extract 3.7, italics for our emphasis).

Extract 3.7

> You might want to consider the circumstances surrounding what happened, and in general terms, you might want to consider whether anything did happen before the blow was delivered. Was there any physical contact between Mr ... and the defendant? Is it a case in which he did appear to *stop and consider* what he was doing? Or was it a *quick response* to something which *just happened* – perhaps a touching on the shoulder or perhaps, as he suggests, more physical violence?
>
> (Scheffer 2006: 334)

In 3.7 the jury is invited to consider two possibilities in relation to deciding intent: planning (*stop and consider*) and spontaneity (*quick response*), with the second of the two rhetorically prominent as end-focus and underlined by the agentless verb *happened* and the mitigating adverb *just*. Familiarity with these genres is therefore an advantage to professional speakers and forensic analysts, as:

> knowledge that makes sense of the text ... includes, in addition to textual knowledge, the awareness and understanding of the shared practices of professional and discourse communities (Swales 1990) and their choice of genres in order to perform their everyday tasks.
>
> (Bhatia 2004: 20)

One of the key defining aspects of legal genres is style, as we saw in Chapter 2 in our analysis of the use of legal lexis and syntax, which is motivated by function and purpose. So far we have looked at genre in terms of structure, function and style and we have suggested that legal genres are to some extent characterized by functional hybridity; that is, a constant awareness of and interaction with the legal statutes and laws to which they relate. Bhatia (2004) suggests that the study of professional genres has in recent years moved from a focus on form and structure to a focus on contextual factors in interpreting discourse. Context has always been an important consideration for sociolinguists and in the next section we look at how context affects the interpretation of legal genres.

Legal contexts

The study of context is vital to the understanding and interpretation of legal texts and forensic linguistic analysis. It is the focus of renewed and recent research among anthropologists and linguists (Duranti and Goodwin 1992; Hanks 2005), as well as having a history in the twentieth century, particularly in Hymes' (1974) 'speech situation', Goffman's (1967) 'social situation', Gumperz's (1982, 2003) 'contextualization cues' and Halliday and Hasan's (1989) 'context of situation'. Hymes' (1972) notion of the *speech community*, a 'community sharing rules for the conduct and interpretation of speech, and rules for the interpretation of at least one linguistic variety' (Hymes 1972 in Paulston and Tucker 2003: 36), is important, because these rules and norms generate some of the distinctive ways of speaking: the register (what Trudgill 1992 defines as the use of specialist vocabulary and syntax), generic features of openings and closings, norms for interruption and politeness and so on.

The legal community shares some ways of speaking at the level of register, as we have seen, but we might want to differentiate between different 'communities of practice' such as lawyers, judges and police officers who each use language in quite different ways and for different communicative purposes, thereby generating different genres of talk and writing. Hymes points out that the speech situation is multifaceted with speakers existing within differing situations according to the different combinations of the components of the situation, in relation to such things as setting, participants and norms. These change as the situation changes, between a police interview, a meeting with a solicitor and direct examination and cross-examination in court. In the next section we examine the police interview and courtroom contexts in some detail, to reveal the nature of context as a constituting force.

Context – interviewing and the courtroom

Imagine a bare room containing simply four seated participants and audio tape recording equipment. This is the environmental context for a standard British police interview. There will normally be two police officers, one an interviewer, the other a note-taker, and a witness or suspect, who may have an accompanying solicitor, parent or social worker. This constitutes Gibbons' primary reality, but it also implies other realities that are equally and sometimes even more important. These other realities can be illustrated with an extract from the early part of a police interview with a male suspected of stabbing his girlfriend during an argument. The extract (3.8) begins with the interviewer (I) interrupting the suspect's (S) storytelling.

Extract 3.8

117 I.   Can I can I just perhaps interrupt you there for moment just so I
            can get a full picture. What sort of a state were both of you in I
            mean were you drunk, happy?

118 S.   Well I was pretty happy.

119 I.   Drunk I'm talking about.

120 S.   Well it's quite true to say that I had been drinking. I was not
            paralytic. I was tired. I was wondering why why she was shouting
            and screaming and hitting me because I did not understand that. I
            knew [victim's name] was stoned as well as pissed. I knew that
            she'd drunk quite a fair amount and I knew that she was stoned.

121 I   You're you're saying to me that you knew that she was drunk and
            high on drugs. Is that what you're –

122 S.   – yes.

123 I.   I'm sorry you – everybody must understand exactly what you're
            saying er ok then. So she's banging your head against the wall did
            you say?

124 S.   Yeah I kept trying to walk away.

125 I.   Yes.

126 S.   And she's there shouting at me, don't walk away from me. And she
            was repeatedly like pushing me against the wall.

What extract 3.8 demonstrates is that there are three simultaneous realities of
the context operating here. Apart from the primary reality of the interview room,
there is also the secondary reality, the event that is being talked about, that is the
argument and subsequent fight that have resulted in his arrest. The transitions
between these two realities are indicated by shifts in tense: the interview is in
the present tense (*you're saying to me*) and the story in the past (*What sort of state
were both of you in?* (interviewer turn 117); *I kept trying to walk away* (suspect turn
124)). Sometimes the past is vividly in the present: *she's there shouting* (turn 126)
and then moves back to the past. A third reality also exists and is invoked by the
interviewer in turn 123, when he makes reference to *everybody*. With only four
people present, the referents for this pronoun are unclear, unless we consider the
wider context for the utterance, which is more complex than the blank room
with four occupants plus a tape recorder implies. The interviewer's invocation of
a wider audience for the talk, through the use of *everybody*, cues the future and
overhearing audience: a judge and jury in a courtroom. The use of *everybody* is
thus a 'contextualization cue' (Gumperz 1982, 2003), which signals and situates
the institutional meanings of the talk.

At the start of the interview in extract 3.8 the suspect was 'cautioned' or told
of his right to remain silent. In England and Wales the caution also refers to the
future courtroom audience: 'it may harm your defence if you fail to mention when
questioned anything you later rely on in court'. Using *everybody* draws attention
to the absent others and reminds the interviewee of their virtual presence, of the

need for shared understanding and of the future context in which his present words may be (re-)interpreted. The relexicalisation of *pissed* and *stoned* as *drunk* and *high on drugs* models the kind of talk that is appropriate for this wider audience and reminds the suspect that though the speakers in the interview room may share understanding of the terms he is using, others may not.

Gumperz (2003: 140) observes that the value of these signals 'depends on the participants' tacit awareness of their meaningfulness'. In his formulation of the suspect's talk with the preface *You're saying to me that* and the tag *is that what you're –* (turn 121), the interviewer makes explicit the meaning of the rewording, reshaping the context from the lay to the institutional and from informal to formal. It signals and cues a wider audience who *must understand* (turn 123) what is being said, but who are not present or visible. It reinvokes the caution with its warning about inferences that may be drawn if the accused chooses not to reveal some or all of what he knows and at the same time it signals the legal frame. This frame values precision, formality and standardness, signalled by the rewording of *pissed* as *drunk* and the use of *must* to convey the strong deontic modality of obligation.

Given all these cues and clues, the force of the obligation on the interviewee is not simply derived from the interviewer's presence, but from the wider legal context signalled by *everybody*. The suspect is positioned to draw inferences from the contextualisation cues and is invited to see the story recipient (the interviewer) as a representative of the *everybody* who, although absent in the present, will be present in the future. The relexicalization of the colloquial language disturbs the present and foregrounds the wider contextual frame of the institutional judicial system that comes into view against the background of the bareness of the interview room.

This future context for interview talk is a very important one, which is often only barely recognized by suspects and witnesses. Part of the interviewer's job, then, is to remind them of this context by references like the one above and also by reminders about the tape recorder, which symbolically represents the overhearing audience. Halliday and Hasan's (1989) model of context is useful here, containing the components of *field*, *tenor* and *mode*: the what and where, the who and the how of talk. The legal field, the present and future participants and their formal relationship with the interviewee along with the spoken channel that is recorded for future use, all create a complex contextual configuration.

Police interviews are goal-focused, frequently having an end-product: a statement and a future use in court. The norms that govern interviews are related to the genres that they contain: interrogation and storytelling, but, as Rock (2001: 44) notes in relation to witness interviews, interviewing involves 'multiple tasks' and 'multiple goals', tasks such as 'telling, listening, writing, formulating, analysing' and goals such as 'the extraction, communication and use of emotional and factual information'. We will return to these tasks in a moment, but first we must consider the goal and future context of the suspect interview. This is most plainly seen in the way that the police interviews with the accused are used in the Shipman trial. On day 22, the police sergeant who conducted most of the 15 interviews with Shipman takes the witness stand in the prosecution case. For an entire day the prosecuting counsel and the police sergeant re-enact the interviews for the court, with the lawyer reading Shipman's turns and the sergeant reading his own. Shipman himself, had not yet spoken in the trial, since the prosecution case is always presented first. He would only take the witness stand five days later on day 27.

In the trial transcript (extract 3.9) we can see how this scenario is staged, producing an even more complex context, one that now takes place in the present whilst referring to the past, a past that is dramatically re-enacted in the present, in front of the complete courtroom audience. Thus the written transcript of the interview (which has been edited) 'stands in' for the accused, Shipman, who has yet to speak (Rock 2001: 46) and for the other officer, who was present. In the transcript deictic expressions (e.g. *that, these, we, now*), temporal features that refer to present, future and past time (verb tenses and aspect), and the names of participants invoked as co-participants, are all highlighted with bold. In addition, some noun phrases that metalinguistically and deictically refer to the situation are also indicated in bold. We will explain their relevance below.

Extract 3.9

(Mr Wright is prosecuting counsel and Miss Davies defence. When the transcript moves to Q and A labels for speakers (question and answer) Q is Mr Wright and A is the police sergeant.)

MR WRIGHT: I am going to turn to **the interviews** now,

…

MR WRIGHT: **My Lord**, with **my learned friends'** approval, with **their** consent, may **I** invite **your Lordship** to consider that **the brother officer Detective Constable Denham**, who **was present** at **these interviews**, may sit in court **during examination-in-chief whilst the interviews are being read** to the **jury**?

MR. JUSTICE FORBES: That's agreeable, is it?

MISS DAVIES: My Lord, it is.

MR. JUSTICE FORBES: Very well, yes. Since there is no objection **that may be done.**

MR. WRIGHT: Thank you.

…

MR. WRIGHT: Thank you. (To the witness) **Sergeant, on the 7th September 1998 did you**, together with **Detective Constable Denham**, conduct **a series of interviews** with **the defendant Dr Shipman**?

A. Yes, I did.

Q. And **were those interviews in the presence of his solicitor Miss Ball**?

A. At all times, yes.

Q. **Were those interviews** tape-recorded?

A. Yes.

Q. And **have transcripts been made of the tape of the interviews themselves?**

A. Yes, they have.

Q. And **in due course those have been prepared** into **a file in edited form** for **the ladies and gentlemen of the jury?**

A. Yes.

Q. My Lord, **it is still a fairly substantial document** but I think **it is now** available for distribution. If I can just check one matter …Yes, thank you. If **those can be distributed to the ladies and gentlemen of the jury now.**

(Pause)

…

MR. WRIGHT: … (To the witness) **Now, sergeant,** so that **we** familiarise **ourselves with the bundle itself, the first interview, we see the formal contents of this document before us. It** identifies **the person interviewed, the place of the interview, the date of it, the time it commenced and the time it concluded, and then the duration of that interview,** together with **a tape reference number** because **each interview was,** as indeed are all interviews, **tape-recorded.** Yes?

A. Correct.

Q. **This document** also identifies **the officers [sic] present** and **any other person present. We see that Miss Ball of Hempsons [sic] solicitors was present,** as indeed **she was present throughout.**

A. Yes.

Q. As I say, **these interviews are a synopsis of that that took place** and so **there are occasions when you will see within the bundle of documents themselves** what appear to be **gaps.** There is nothing sinister in **that.** It is merely **the unnecessary detail** that has been edited out in an effort to reduce the amount of material that need necessarily go before **the jury.**

A. Yes.

Q. **Officer,** may **we** deal with **it in this** way, please? **You** ask the questions of **each individual officer** and I will give the replies that **Dr Shipman** gave.

A. Yes. I began **the interview by saying: 'This interview is being** tape-recorded. **It may be given in evidence if your case** is brought to **court. As you can see there's a note** explaining that **this interview may be the subject of remote monitoring.** When **the red light above the machine's illuminated this** means that **this interview is being monitored by other officers** to assist **the investigation.**

Q. **Now, can we just pause for a moment?** Of course, **these** are the formal aspects of **the interview** and **you** must have **done them many times.**

A. Yes.

Q. If **you** could slow down a little, please, **then we can all digest** what **you** are saying.

A. **The time presently is 9.43 a.m. on Monday the 7th September 1998. I'm Detective Sergeant Walker** and the other officer is Detective Constable

Denham. We're in the interview room at Ashton-under-Lyne police station on interviewing. If **you** could state **your full name**, please.

...

Q. (Harold Frederick Shipman.

(Shipman Trial, Day 23)

In extract 3.9 the most significant item referred to is the police interviews with the defendant. By tracing the references to the interviews, we can see how this interaction is transferred from a spoken and tape-recorded *interview* to a written *document*:

> *the interviews; these interviews; the interviews; a series of interviews; those interviews; transcripts; the interviews themselves; those*[transcripts]; *a file in edited form; it* [the file]; *those* [files/documents]; *the bundle itself, the first interview; the formal contents of this document; it [the* document*]; the interviewed; the interview; it* [the interview]; *a tape reference number; each interview; this document; these interviews; that* [activity]; *the bundle of documents; gaps; the unnecessary detail; it* [the interview]; *this interview.*

This chain of reference constitutes a continued focus on the same item whilst transforming it from being distant and removed from the current time and space, though being mentioned in it (*those* interviews that the officer conducted) to being distant but present in the current time and space (*those* documents or transcripts that are being distributed to the jury) to being finally near and present – *this document* – that the lawyer, police witness, judge and jury are now holding and which now makes *these interviews* present, tangible and a legally named and transformed object (*the bundle; formal contents*).

Prosecuting counsel, in performing these acts of deictic reference, 'take[s] up a position in the deictic field' (Hanks 2005: 193), one which powerfully objectifies and appropriates the object from the past and from another time and place and positions it in the current location to be held, handled, viewed and heard. At the same time the defendant, Shipman, the second interviewing officer, who has also been positioned by the lawyer in the courtroom, and Shipman's solicitor who was present during the interviews, are all referred to and therefore 'thrust into a position' (Hanks 2005: 193) by being brought forcibly into the current deictic field. In naming all the relevant listeners, through deictic reference, the lawyer positions all these further objects in the field and then includes them by reference: *then we can all digest what you are saying.* Now we can see the relevance of the reference to *everybody* in the police interview (extract 3.8), when in fact only three people other than the defendant were present.

When detective sergeant Walker begins to read the transcript of Shipman's interview, *This interview is being tape-recorded*, the deictic reference is simultaneously past and present. The temporal world becomes displaced and transferred to an immediate co-presence. This is part of the power of the legal setting and of the prosecution role. As Hanks (2005: 194) points out, when deictic expressions are used and embedded in a social setting, they gain meaning: '*embedding* converts abstract positions like Speaker, Addressee, Object, and the lived space of utterances into sites to which power, conflict, controlled access, and other features of the social fields attach'. Embedded in the judicial field, the re-enacted interview transcript becomes an evidential object for scrutiny and evaluation by the jury. It makes the defendant speak for the prosecution, whilst being positioned as a silent spectator. The official trial transcript underlines this position.

In the final line of extract 3.9 Shipman 'speaks' through the mouth of the prosecution and the turn is labelled Q for question. The questioner becomes defendant, a stance that is adopted for a whole day, with counsel stepping out of this stance from time to time to assume his prosecution function and comment on procedure, as for example when he asks the officer to *pause for a moment*. Thus the context shifts constantly from the primary reality of the courtroom to the other reality of the interview. This 'repertoire of stances' is part of the 'function of the field' (Hanks 2005: 210) and involves the lawyer managing the social reality that is presented to the jury. Hanks argues that 'the various stances that speakers adopt in practice impinge directly on how they construe the world through language'. What this extract shows is that the view inside the courtroom is carefully constructed and managed by the lawyer's appropriation, positioning and stance-taking in relation to his addressees, the jury, and his object, the evidential interview.

Conclusion

Legal genres, their styles and modes of interaction and the social practices, roles and participant relationships that they produce, constitute complex inter-relationships between text and context. Legal genres are the way they are because of the communicative practices that they employ and the functions that they serve in legal and world contexts. Police statements and courtroom discourse are rich in spatial and temporal expressions, because of the work they do in situating the talk. If we want to fully account for what the language is doing or what the speaker is doing through use of language, we have to take account of the context of use and the linguistic choices that are made. Holmes discusses the linguistic choices that reflect to a greater or lesser degree one or more of the following speech situation components:

1   The **participants**: *who* is speaking and
                                who are they speaking to?
2   The **setting** or social context of the interaction: *where* are they speaking?
3   The **topic**: *what* is being talked about?
4   The **function**: *why* are they speaking?

(Holmes 1992: 12)

These components, though essential to our understanding of the different situations in the legal and judicial system, are not always easy to define, as we have seen. The answer to 'Who is speaking?' and 'Who are they speaking to?' is not at all straightforward in the police interview or in the courtroom. An audience can be conjured up, seemingly from nowhere, through the use of the deictic expression *everybody*, but it only gains its full significance in the courtroom context.

One of the ways that those who are not members of the professional legal community can equip themselves with the necessary resources to make sense of such material is to engage in the study of legal genres, both through studying texts that are the product of legal contexts and through ethnographic research that involves observing the production and use of text in its context of production and use. Although gaining access to many of these contextual domains, such as police interviews or lawyer consultations with clients, is not at all easy, students and researchers can gain insights and understanding through vicarious involvement – that is by learning from the experiences of others, by reading ethnographically based research (such as Heffer 2005; Scheffer 2006), and also by analysing the fictional examples provided in films and on television. Television frequently gives viewers lengthy opportunities to get inside the mind of the real-life legal professional, whether it be police officer, lawyer or judge. 'Reality TV' shows also provide real situations for vicarious learning, as Linfoot-Ham (2006) demonstrates in her discussion of the American reality TV show 'Cops'. There are limitations to this kind of observation, however, since it can rarely be done without some degree of bias. Ethnographical research can also suffer from observer bias, showing widely different stances from admiration to censure of the professional activity under scrutiny. Whatever the limitations, direct or vicarious observation of professionals at work does allow linguists to move their research focus into understanding the legal context.

Further reading

Gibbons (2003, chapter 4); Halldorsdottir (2006); Hanks (2005); Levinson (1979); Maley *et al.* (1995); Maley (2000); Scheffer (2006); Sarangi (2000 – although this is not a forensic linguistic article, the frameworks and models applied to medical discourse have similar and contrastive uses in legal discourse. This article should stimulate thinking about the research tasks below).

Research tasks

1 Examine texts A to D in the epigraphs to this chapter. Identify generic features in each text, particularly in relation to reported speech. Look at other legal texts (see below) and identify other generic features.

2 Find a legal text from one of the genres or subgenres discussed in this chapter, such as opening speeches by prosecution and defence lawyers or an entire witness appearance. Identify generic features which contribute to the communicative functions of the text and consider the effect of the institutional context on the text's production and effect. Other text types you could analyse are interview, statement, legal statute, all of which can be found without too much difficulty.

US trials can be found at http://www.courttv.com/trials/
The OJ Simpson trial at: http://www.courttv.com/casefiles/Simpson/
President Clinton in Jones v. Clinton can be found at:
http://www.courttv.com/archive/legaldocs/government/jones/
In the UK, the Shipman trial can be found at:
http://www.the-shipman-inquiry.org.uk/trialtrans.asp

Consider whether some of the following are relevant to your analysis and discussion.

- generic structure;
- the relationship of the text to the context;
- the type of 'speech event' (Hymes 1972) or 'activity type' (Levinson 1979) and how this is embedded in the context. See Sarangi and Coulthard (2000):[4] and their model of activity analysis (figure 1.2). How can this framework be used to explain text and discourse features?;
- a sociolinguistic framework that involves analysing the social factors affecting linguistic choice (Hymes 1972) and Holmes' (1992) solidarity, status, formality and function;
- use of deictic reference relating to contextual factors: time, space, participants;
- communities of practice and common practices, for example, Sandra Harris' (2001: 451) claim is that in politics 'systematic impoliteness is not only sanctioned but rewarded in accordance with expectations of Members of the House' and that this 'can only be understood and interpreted in relationship to Parliament as an institution and the wider political context'. How do politeness and impoliteness work in legal settings?.

4 Collecting evidence

Calls to the emergency services and first encounters with witnesses and suspects

1968 in the US – call to the emergency services that R.F. Kennedy had been shot (CT is call taker and C caller)
CT. Police department ( )
C. Yes This is the Ambassador Hotel Em– Ambassador Hotel?
    ((echo: Hotel))
C. Do you hear me? ( )
CT. Yeah I hear you.
C. Uh they have an emergency=They want thuh police to the kitchen right away.

(Zimmerman 1992: 436–7)

1994 in the UK – arrest interview with Rosemary West (DS is Detective Sergeant Onions and RW is Rosemary West)
DS You were arrested by myself and other officers on suspicion of the murder of your daughter Heather, who disappeared about 1986/87. You were interviewed, but not about that. Can you just go over the circumstances of when Heather left your house?
RW You ask the questions, I'll try and answer them.

(BBC Crime 10 August 2006)

Introduction

The first epigraph illustrates the importance of talk in encounters with the emergency services, which can be the first stage in evidence gathering in criminal cases. Calls to the emergency services involve a conversation between a telephone operator and a member of the public. This encounter typifies the intersection between lay and institutional interaction and the sometimes conflicting goals of each party. The caller is seeking a rapid response from the emergency services, while the call-taker needs to make a decision about whether the incident deserves an immediate response. This call is often simply the first in a series of encounters with institutional decision-making. During interviews with suspects, as in the second epigraph, police officers have to make decisions about whether the reported actions and events constitute a legally defined offence. Then in court the role of evaluator falls to a magistrate or a jury, who have to decide whether a case has been proved 'beyond reasonable doubt' if it is a criminal charge or 'on the balance of probabilities' if it is a civil case. Thus once things get to court lay participants are firmly in control in the sense that the talk is performed for them, though in the recipient role, as what they receive is channelled through the legal experts.

We will first examine encounters between the public and the police or their representatives, in calls to the emergency services, when talk is a resource for negotiating help and action. We will then focus on the role of listening in emergency calls and in encounters with the police. Finally, we will look at the different uses of speech and writing as resources for recording interviews and statements.

First encounters – calls to the emergency services

As a result of examining first encounters between the public and police in telephone calls for help, Whalen and Zimmerman (1987: 172) note that 'conversation is a fundamental resource ... for achieving regular, recurrent patterns of action in the face of varying details and circumstances'. Callers and call-takers work towards a shared goal: the provision of appropriate help.

Calls to the emergency services are routinely recorded, because they often form part of a subsequent investigation, as was the case at the beginning of a call to the police reporting that Robert F. Kennedy had been shot (extract 4.1).

Extract 4.1

[CT. is call-taker and C is caller; ( ) indicates a pause; = indicates a contiguous utterance]

```
 1  CT.  Police department
 2        ()
 3  C.    Yes This is the Ambassador Hotel Em–
 4        Ambassador Hotel?
 5        ((echo: Hotel))
 6  C.    Do you hear me?
 7        ()
 8  CT.  Yeah I hear you.
 9  C.    Uh they have an emergency= They want thuh
10        police to the kitchen right away.
11  CT.  =What kind of emergency?
12  C.    I don't know honey They hung up I don't know
13        what's happening
14  CT.  Well find out, ( ) We don't send out without=
15  C.    =I beg your pardon?
16        ()
17  CT.  We have to know what we're sending on,
```

(Zimmerman 1992: 436–7)

Zimmerman (1992: 437) comments that

> while some embarrassment may have attended the subsequent public disclosure of delay in the dispatch of assistance to the scene, it is clear that the caller, a hotel operator relaying information from the hotel's kitchen, is initially not in a position to provide the required information

and that 'the mere characterization of an event as an emergency is, other things being equal, insufficient' to trigger a response. What is clear is that from the first moment, the call taker (CT) is assessing the caller's talk and therefore the caller has to be able to give sufficient information to warrant the dispatch of a police officer.

Garner and Johnson (2006), in their study of emergency call management in England, also emphasize decision-making and information gathering. They ask: 'Where are the critical decision-points for the handler in the call?' and 'How can critical information elements, such as the location of the incident and the caller's identity and reliability, be established rapidly?' (2006: 57). The call (extract 4.2) from an elderly female on New Year's Eve, demonstrates how the call-handler (CH) makes an early classification of the situation as 'non-serious' (line 5), but is nevertheless still involved in a long interaction to establish for certain that it is indeed not necessary to dispatch officers.

Extract 4.2

    1 C.   I want the police here
    2 CH. This is the police what's happening? (pause) What's happening?
           …
    3 C.   Well there's a some er er there's some banging going on outside we
    4   can't sleep. There (?)
 5 CH. Is it fireworks?
    6 C.   They're not fireworks no they're not fireworks
    7 CH. What is it then?
    8 C.   I – will you please send the police?
    9 CH. What's your name
   10 C.   Gibson
   11 CH. Gibson?
   12 C.   Gibson G-I-B-S-O-N Five Elms Farm Northerton
           [Several utterances to establish the precise location]
   13 CH. So what is it then? What's the banging?
   14 C.   What?
   15 CH. What is the banging?
           …
   16 C.   I (?) we can't sleep
   17 CH. Have you looked out your window?

18 C.   There there's banging going on outside really terrible
19 CH. Have a look out your window can you see fireworks?
20 C.   Not fireworks somebody kicking up a row out here
21 CH. Someone's having an argument?
22 C.   Will you please send the police up to inspect?

...

23 CH. You need to tell me you need to tell me what's happening. If it's
24   just banging then we're not going to come out because it's
25   probably fireworks.
26 C.   They're what? They're not fireworks these are not fireworks

...

27 C.   This is somebody kicking up a–a–a deliberate annoyance

...

28 CH. Are they having an argument?
29 C.   [cough] no [cough] no
30 CH. So what's the noise you can hear
31 C.   They're not speaking at all. All they're doing is banging
32 CH. What sort of banging is it?
33 C.   Just like bombs going off all the time
34 CH. Okay I expect it's fireworks

(Garner and Johnson 2006: 68–9)

Garner and Johnson note that in calls where the caller is 'argumentative, frightened or upset, it can be hard to reach a decision point' (2006: 70). In this call the decision is only finally made in line 34, after three attempts (lines 5, 19 and 23–5). The extract demonstrates what Garner and Johnson (2006: 63) refer to as the 'dynamic tension between natural conversation patterns and a range of overarching constraints ... [such as] aims, operating policies, strategic requirements and organizational culture'. Call-handlers have to take into consideration the resources available at the time and their own role in the prevention of unnecessary police deployment. It is clear that the call-handler makes an assessment that the caller needs reassurance rather than an emergency response to deal with a real threat to life.

Calls to the emergency services can become a crucial part of the evidence in a prosecution case, particularly if they are made by a caller who later becomes identified as a suspect. In the following extract from a police interview (extract 4.3), the suspect (S) identifies himself as the person who made a call to request an ambulance for his girlfriend, after he had stabbed her during an argument.

Extract 4.3

171 S   She said 'I'm bleeding can you get an ambulance'. I said 'I can't
         call an ambulance from here because the phone is out. I'll go and
         get you one'.
172 P   Yes.

173 S I went upstairs, got my jacket, put my jacket on, went out and got in my car. And I drove around the block and saw a phone box.

174 P Yes.

175 S And made the call from there.

176 P I think to clarify the position that the gentleman that did phone for an ambulance gave his – the same name as yours and I'm prepared to accept that it was you that made that phone call.

The police officer (P) converts the suspect's information (*made the call*) into an evidential fact (*clarify the position*) by tying this information to an item in the recorded call (*gave his – the same name as yours*).

Imbens-Bailey and McCabe (2000) report an American 911 call where failure to dispatch an officer may have resulted in a woman's death. In their study of emergency calls they found that callers used three strategies to elicit a response: a *demand* or a *request* for help or a *description* (or narrative) of the emergency, with the third strategy being the most frequent. They note that, during calls, the dispatcher and the caller can be 'at odds' with each other. Callers want to tell a story to elicit a response, whereas call-handlers need to elicit answers to questions that help them fill boxes on their computer screen and are not allowed to dispatch an officer until they have both a name and a location.

Garner and Johnson (2006: 66) also refer to the paradoxical constraints and benefits of technology that, on the one hand, 'can help to give structure to the interaction and useful guidance to the call-handler, but, on the other, the exigencies of filling in the slots can interrupt the flow of the call or distract the call-handler's attention from the subtle linguistic cues that may be crucial to the interpretation of what is being said'. Call-handling, like police interviewing and courtroom interaction, is characterized by the 'mutual influence of speech and text' (Garner and Johnson 2006: 66), or hybridity, and is therefore a skilled and complex discursive activity, blending features of service encounters with storytelling, interrogation for form-filling, decision-making and assessment. The success of the description of the event determines the level of response and therefore callers are being required to present their emergency event as worthy of a police response. The caller's definition of an emergency may not meet the institutional criteria that the call-taker has to fulfil in order to justify deploying a police officer.

The criteria that determine call-handlers' assessments of the level of emergency are generally known only to the institution and not to the caller. The lay participant can therefore be at a significant disadvantage, since they may not know the rules by which the CT is working, and worse, may not even have all the information required by the institution. In addition to being told that the call is being recorded, they could benefit from knowing more, but such an informative preamble would interfere with the speed of response expected from an emergency service. Internet websites and advertising campaigns can improve the situation. For example, many police force websites already give information about what for them constitutes an emergency, or what the British West Yorkshire Police label 'immediate incidents'; that is those that justify an immediate response. These include:

- danger to life, or violence being used or threatened;
- road traffic accident involving personal injury;
- crime in progress or likely to occur;
- suspect for crime present or nearby;
- witness evidence might be lost;
- especially vulnerable victim.

(West Yorkshire Police 1 March 2007)

Research shows (Garner and Johnson 2006; Imbens-Bailey and McCabe 2000) that callers are unlikely to identify many of these criteria for themselves, and therefore it is the success (or otherwise) of the interaction itself that determines whether sufficient, useful information is elicited to allow the call-taker to make an adequate assessment of the situation.

Policespeak, lawyerspeak and listening

Listening is as important to successful verbal communication as speaking, but it is often overlooked in the institutional encounter. We think of institutional discourse in terms of two channels: speech and writing, and expression and reception. Despite an overwhelming focus on the expressive mode in research to date, active listening and the valuing of talk is vital to good communication and the achievement of institutional goals. In Chapter 2 we looked at some of the defining features of legal language, but speech in legal settings is about much more than simply selecting a register. Discursive choices and competences are part of social interaction and, in interactive settings involving the police, lawyers and the public, resources of genre and register provide only a limited template for the complex socio-cultural needs of the situation, as we saw above in relation to call-handling.

'Policespeak' (Fox 1993) is the particular variety of speech that is reproduced in police dramas on the television and in films, and which often carries with it the negative associations of formality and circumlocution associated with other forms of legal language. It is produced not only by police officers, but also by lay speakers when interacting with the police. Extract 4.4 is from a webchat between members of the public and an English police inspector about legislation relating to the use of mobile phones when driving. The Inspector, M, is addressed by his first name and questions are posed by participants, here C, using their first names or Internet pseudonyms.

Extract 4.4

C. M, what are the implications for sat nav devices? They can be far more distracting and require removing eyes from the road.

...

M In response to C's question: 'M, what are the implications for sat nav devices? They can be far more distracting and require removing eyes from the road.' It's the same as using hands free. Regulation 104 of the Road Vehicles (Construction and use) regulations 1986 say the offence is failing to have proper control of the vehicle or have a full view of the road and traffic ahead. Therefore, using your sat nav could be classed in the same way.

(Avon and Somerset Constabulary Interactive webchat 27 February 2007)

We note that C, a member of the public, uses the complex noun construction *sat nav devices* and the complex verb construction and complementation *require removing eyes from the road*, producing the same kind of redundant, formal language apparent in policespeak. This use can be explained as C attempting to use the language of the legislation, even though he can't recall the exact wording, which M realizes, helping him out by producing it exactly: *have full view of the road and traffic ahead.* This kind of collaborative talk shows how policespeak can be a shared code, rather than a restricted one, in a setting like this which is designed for egalitarian talk. It also embodies a high level of hybridity, fusing informal conversation with a professional register, which results in sentences such as: *I don't watch The Bill, I never have albeit that friends tell me that it does portray police officers as fairly aggressive individuals which generally we are not* (Avon and Somerset Constabulary 9 February 2007). The conjunction *albeit* and verb *portray* mark this sentence as not simply chat in an informal setting.

This distinctiveness can be used forensically, as Coulthard (2002) and Fox (1993) have shown, to identify the author of a given text as belonging to a particular community of writing or speaking practice – the police or legal professionals. Both Coulthard and Fox comment on the distinctive writtenness of postposed *then*, as in, for example, *I then walked to the rear of the building*. Professional speakers and writers do this in a consistent manner that is distinguishable as a professional competence, unusual in texts produced by lay speakers and writers. However, as in the webchat, when professional and lay speakers speak together, there is an inevitable degree of convergence, as lay speakers attempt to move their linguistic choices towards those of the professional. In extracts 4.5 and 4.6 we see lawyer and witness interaction from the examination-in-chief of two different witnesses. The lawyer and lay witnesses both display this grammatical feature.

Extract 4.5

[Lawyer and witness A]

Q. And what did **he then say**?

A. He said, I think he said he had been seeing another patient on the Wych Fold Estate so he was able to arrive at my mother's very fast and when he answered the door, sorry when my mother answered the door she remarked, 'What are you doing here?' Dr Shipman made a point of telling us this because he felt she made the comment because he had arrived there very early after receiving the message.

Q. Did he go on to explain your mother's condition?

A. He said that when she answered the door she was very grey, she was sweating. He helped her up the stairs and, he helped her up the stairs and took her pulse which was very low so **he then phoned** for an ambulance. **He then went downstairs** to his car to get his bag. When he returned my mother had died so **he then cancelled** the ambulance.

Extract 4.6

[Lawyer and witness B]

Q. Did he go on to explain **what had then occurred**?

A. **He then said**, 'Unfortunately while I have been here she has taken a turn for the worst.'

Q. And did **he then explain** anything?

A. **Then he said**, 'And she has since died.'

(Shipman Trial, Day 17)

However, as witness B shows, although the lawyer is consistent in his usage, the witness is not; he also produces the more common '*then* before pronoun' construction in sentence initial position, *Then he said*. This topic will be treated in much more detail in Chapter 8; suffice it to say for the moment that speaking and writing like a police officer (or in a police register) is something we can recognize stylistically, and statements by the police have their own distinctive style, motivated by the need for precision and accuracy. So, for instance, police statements are full of time and place adjuncts (*on Monday 1ˢᵗ September, at 11.50 a.m., at* + named place) and the stylistically motivated testimonial *I* is foregrounded over narrative sequence producing *I then said*, rather than *Then I said*. This reflects the activity that is being done.

Listening like a police officer also has linguistic hallmarks, as Royce (2005) shows in his fascinating case report on 'the role of active listening by a police negotiator in New South Wales, Australia, in the process of serving a "high-risk warrant" on an armed and dangerous man who was expected to resist' (2005: 5). Royce demonstrates that 'the use of active listening in the early stages of the negotiation was a critical factor in the resolution' of the crisis with the man referred to as 'the bomber', since he 'was allegedly regularly entering a nearby town carrying loaded weapons and wearing a live body-bomb, ostensibly for his own protection against perceived threats' (2005: 6). Royce notes the importance of active listening in establishing rapport, so that the bomber developed trust in the negotiator. This kind of listening is important at all levels of police interaction with the public, as we have seen with call handlers and will see with child complainants and adult witnesses and suspects. Active listening develops a context of trust, although this can be criticized as being synthetic, rather than real.

Royce (2005) notes that active listening involves both 'semantic and verbal skills': minimal responses and backchannel signals, paraphrasing and mirroring of the other speaker's turns and the use of pauses. All these encourage the other to speak. In addition, 'emotion labelling' demonstrates insight into the person's feelings and emotions and 'I messages' by the negotiator emphasize to the other person that the negotiator is a real person, rather than an amorphous institution. In extract 4.7, the negotiator is talking to the bomber via a phone that has been set up at a road block. The bomber was first addressed by means of a megaphone and then directed to the telephone to talk more intimately with the negotiator. The extract is taken from the beginning of the encounter, when the negotiator is trying to get the bomber to divest himself of his body-bomb and lay down his guns. The negotiator, O'Reilly, has already told him that he knows that, although he has been into the local town wearing the body-bomb, he has not hurt anyone.

Extract 4.7

[Mirroring, *I* messages, paraphrases and other active listening features are italicised]

1	Bomber.	No one will be either unless you decide to *declare war on me*.
2	O'Reilly.	No, *we* don't want to *declare war on you*, not at all, not at all, but *I*
3		*do* need you to take off the bomb and to leave the guns on the
4		roadway there.
5	Bomber.	Well, certainly I'm going to keep my weapons: I've had them most
6		of my life.
7	O'Reilly.	*I know* that, *I know* that, but *police* have to make sure that the
8		bomb is disarmed.
9	Bomber.	Yes.
10	O'Reilly.	And *they* can't let you go with the weapons, *they* are going to have
11		to take the weapons from you now. You are under arrest, O.K?
12	Bomber.	Now listen, *this is absolutely ridiculous*.
13	O'Reilly.	*I know* from your perspective *it may seem ridiculous* but *the*
14		*people in town* are very worried about it and *the police* are
15		obligated to act, as you can understand.

(Royce 2005: 18–19 and 22)

Royce (2005: 25) suggests that O'Reilly was able to disassociate himself from the 'police' and build a relationship with the bomber partly through his adaptive use of personal referential pronouns (lines 2, 7, 13). He was also able to create, by using the 'reflective empathizer' *I know* (lines 7 and 13), the impression that he was empathizing and this was supported by other active listening techniques such as mirroring (lines 1 and 2; lines 12 and 13) and tag questions (line 11). Interestingly, the bomber makes explicit reference to O'Reilly's listening role, *Now listen* (line 12), indicating that he is coming to see the negotiator as separate from the police and in the role of what Royce describes as 'rescuer' (Royce 2005: 19–20).

Rapport, in the context of a crisis negotiation, or indeed in an abuse interview, means more than simply 'getting on' and is not really about getting to know the other person in the usual social sense. For the professional negotiator it involves the development of an environment for talk, which successfully leads to surrender and arrest. For the interviewer in a child abuse case, it involves the development of a context for disclosure, in which reticence is overcome and honest, open, free and frank talk is achieved. Leo (1996: 260–1) takes issue with this position, arguing that police interrogation (of suspects) is a 'confidence game' in which the interviewer exploits the powerful relationship, resulting in a 'betrayal of trust'. In this confidence game, Leo argues, 'the suspect's ignorance [is exploited] to create the illusion of a relationship that is symbiotic rather than adversarial' (1996: 284–5). Rock (2001), too, talks of 'simulated concern' by an interviewer when taking a statement from a witness who is struggling to remember details of the event. Thus, a conflicting picture of the professional listener emerges. For both negotiators and interviewers trust is vital for them to achieve their goals, but, at the same time, since this is not a social relationship, the activity can be viewed as exploitative, manipulative and an abuse of power.

This pretty much sums up a major tension in the criminal justice system as a whole, between, on the one hand, prevention and detection of crime and, on the other, the protection of human rights and social justice. While in many institutional interactions participants readily and positively submit to questions and authority (a job interview or a therapeutic session for example), in legal interaction, power and authority is continually negotiated, gained and lost, and much more is at stake: individual liberty, freedom, incarceration and categorization as a criminal or valuable witness, as aggressor or victim. The fleeting and often adversarial nature of the relationship is a constant element in talk, which needs to be dealt with in dynamic and fluctuating conditions. As Raymond (2000: 355) points out in relation to live news interviews, authority is 'tenuous' and is something that speakers must continually strive to achieve and then sustain, or else risk losing.

Police interviews – from talk to text and text to talk

Police interviews are goal-focused events, the primary aim of which is the collection and synthesis of evidence into a written statement for use in any subsequent court hearing. This means that written statements frequently have more evidential value than the spoken interviews on which they are based, although, as we saw in Chapter 3, the interview itself can also be converted into a written text that becomes an evidential object in the courtroom. These written documents are easy to collate into a written case file and so they are much easier for lawyers, juries and judges to refer to during a case than are tape recordings. The statement or interview transcript can literally speak for the witness. Any statements that are undisputed are simply read out in court and accepted as primary evidence, thus sparing the witness(es) from making a personal appearance and also saving the time of the court that would otherwise be spent on examination and cross-examination. So, for example, in the Shipman trial the 'Index of Proceedings' for day 17 shows that more evidence was read out than given in person: ten statements as opposed to only seven witnesses who gave oral evidence (Shipman Trial, Day 17).

The end goal for all interviews and statements is their use in court, when they become primary documents. It is the written statement, though, that is most valued for its efficiency. As both Rock (2001) and Komter (2006) show, statements are inherently intertextual and dialogic and, although they come to be seen as authoritative versions of the memory of a witness or suspect, they are in fact the result of multiple tellings of the same story in which some details are lost, some transformed and some, it must be admitted, created. The final telling – the statement – is 'moulded through those previous texts' (Rock 2001: 45).

Witness testimony moves between spoken and written a number of times on its journey from first telling to presentation in court. Rock (2001) identifies at least three stages from interview to statement: witness monologue, questions and answers based on the monologue narrative and then the production of a written version. And also, as she acknowledges, the witness will often have told their story several times before they even start to tell it to a police officer. By the time the story becomes embodied in a statement it has been transformed into the voice of the institution and is 'dialogic' in that it bears traces of the underlying dialogue. It is 'another's speech in another language' (Bakhtin 1981: 324) or monologue transformed through dialogue into dialogic monologue. The oral becomes written in the statement and is then either retold or read out from the written version in court. These texts become a vital part of the evidential journey that transforms witness and defendant stories during the judicial decision-making process. Komter (2006: 196) defines this process as 'a chain of events where encounters of spoken interaction are "wedged in" and informed by written documents and where written documents are treated as [the] official basis for decision making on the assumption that they "represent" the spoken interaction'.

Talk and writing can be seen to be complementary and intertwined modes in the criminal law process. Rock (2001) shows how a witness statement originates in talk, though, as Scheffer (2006: 305) points out, text and talk are given different degrees of primacy in the courtroom, through a complex process that takes place over many months. A case file prepared by a solicitor is passed to a court lawyer who, after analysing the materials, transforms them, in the course of an all too short pre-trial preparation, by means of marks, notes and maps written on the documents, into an outline script for his opening address. Scheffer goes on to explain how the interplay between the various texts and oral entities produces another 'presence' in the legal encounter. It is the lawyer who puts together all these parts into a courtroom performance which involves him

> modulating written and oral, old and new, friendly and hostile statements. From the process of modulation unfolds a homogeneous analytical field of presence that [he] can exploit to perform the [prosecution or] defense in court.
>
> (Scheffer 2006: 305)

The real-time interaction of talk with pre-existing text is therefore a defining and crucial part of the development of a criminal case, from the first oral report through interviews with witnesses and suspects, written statements and notes on file, all the way to a court hearing. What all these genres have in common is a shared orientation, on the part of the institutional participant, to collecting evidential facts for legal decision-making, decisions such as: 'Do the facts constitute an offence?' 'Should the suspect be charged with an offence?' and later: 'Is the defendant guilty of that offence?'

Police interviews and social interaction

Watson's (1976, 1983, 1990) ethnomethodological research into police inter-viewing practice focuses on the construction of 'reality' through social control in the interview, and, within this context, Atkinson *et al.* (1979) argue for the 'standardization of interrogation procedure' in their report to a Royal Commission. Linell and Jönsson (1991: 97) also focus on the asymmetry of the interactional floor, arguing that reports written by police officers for presentation to the Swedish court, following interrogation of the suspect, by and large have only the police perspective, despite being produced as a result of a dialogical interview. They argue that the suspect has 'limited influence' on the police report, although they concede that the story in the final report incorporates the voices of both suspect and institution.

Linell and Jönsson (1991: 75) examined the interview and statement stages of eliciting and recording the narrative of a crime. Their interviews were with 'middle-aged or elderly first-time offenders accused of shop-lifting' (1991: 93) and provide clear examples of 'perspectivity conflicts'. For the suspect:

> the triviality of the legally crucial action – leaving a supermarket without paying for a few articles – may lead [them] to say little about it. Moreover, the majority of them admit the offence, which, from an everyday perspective, may mean that there is no point in wasting more words.
>
> (1991: 93)

However, the police have 'long traditions of professional practice' behind them and much of their institutional role is invested in collecting minute details surrounding the commission of alleged offences. This produces 'an empiricistic, almost behaviouristic, touch to the policemen's concentration on technical details' which 'seem to square well with what is otherwise accepted as legal evidence, such as fingerprints, signatures ... and eye witnesses' testimonies' (Linell and Jönsson 1991: 93–4). As we saw in Chapter 3, such detail is also intertextually linked with the wording of the law or statute that determines the offence of theft. Leaving without paying constitutes theft, if it can be proved that the 'shopper' intended to deny the supermarket payment. The combined acts of choosing goods, passing the till without payment and leaving the store with the goods, constitute a theft story, rather than a shopping one. The police perspective is the version of events that is written up in the statement or report and the interrogation therefore 'becomes an arena for the authorization of one version of the suspect's alleged criminal conduct' (Linell and Jönsson 1991: 97), although there is a 'dialogicality underlying the police report' that originates in the two perspectives of the interview. Thus competing narratives are articulated in the course of the interview, but the statement only presents a single, if dialogized, version of events.

Linell and Jönsson contrast the police's rational perspective with the suspect's more emotional, psycho-social one, which for elderly shoplifters follows a similar script:

> The background deals with psycho-social circumstances, some complications in the suspect's everyday world. Then comes a train of events in which these complications get condensed or aggravated. Some unlawful behaviour is part of this process, but it tends to be pictured only as a peripheral aspect. A fair amount of space is allotted to the resulting attitudes and emotional reactions (shame, guilt, contrition and finally relief).
>
> (Linell and Jönsson 1991: 95)

However, in the end the suspect's socially 'normal' perspective is dominated by the institutional one, as the necessarily narrow prosecution-biased, legal perspective filters out the emotional and psychological perspectives that are not factual evidence, and foregrounds the details of the offence, which are often glossed over in the suspect's story and therefore have had to be elicited through questioning.

Heydon's study of police interviews in Victoria, Australia, builds on the work of Linell and Jönsson and of Auburn *et al.* (1995), who also examine how the police use language to steer the interviewee towards a 'preferred version' of the allegedly criminal events (Heydon 2005: 33). She explores the range of 'discursive practices that construct a police version of events and the role of such interactional resources as accusation-denial/acceptance adjacency pairs, "my side" tellings, topic management tools and formulations' (2005: 117). For example, an accusation-denial structure (extract 4.8) presents a possible version, which the suspect can accept or deny.

Extract 4.8

Police.   **I put it to you** that you actually went into the kitchen and helped drag in Wayne Gibson one of the bouncers
Suspect.   **no way**

(Heydon 2005: 117)

However, using evidence to challenge a suspect's version of events presents a competing version and attempts to move the suspect towards the police perspective (extract 4.9).

Extract 4.9

Police.	**all our witnesses say that** you slammed it
	[a shop door, breaking the glass] the second time again
Suspect.	aw well (0.3) I **that's what they say**
Police.	you've got nothing to say to that
Suspect.	nup

(Heydon 2005: 130

In terms of topic management she found that suspects introduced fewer new topics than interviewers and that their topics 'were less likely to obligate the recipients to respond to the topic', while interviewers 'initiate new topics disjunctively and even interruptively' in order to construct their version of events (Heydon 2005: 131). Furthermore, the suspect's version was frequently 'formulated' (Garfinkel and Sacks 1970) by the police interviewer in a way that summarized or 'glossed' it, by including some aspects and missing out others, thereby 'fixing' (Heritage 1985) the version in an institutional voice (as in extract 4.10).

Extract 4.10

Police.	uh **you saw the glass shatter to the ground**
Suspect.	I just kept walking
	I just got in the car
	and Rob me friend said what the hell's going on
	whadcha do
Police.	**so you didn't bother saying anything to them**
	that the glass was broken or

(Heydon 2005: 136)

Heritage and Watson (1979: 123) say that in normal conversation a 'formulation enables co-participants to settle on one of many possible interpretations of what they have been saying', but, as a practice, this is overwhelmingly restricted in police interviews to the interviewer. Indeed, it is a key feature of the asymmetry and a powerful way of transforming the story. It underlines what is being talked about as a key evidential fact in the alleged offence and converts action from event to criminal behaviour. Heydon draws attention to the suspect's non-confirmation of the first formulation (extract 4.10 – *you saw the glass shatter to the ground*) leading to the officer repeating the formulation, which provides a gloss on the suspect's action of walking away. Heydon says of the formulation that the investigating officer

> formulates [the suspect's] prior turns about walking directly to his car after the glass door broke as demonstrating that *he didn't bother saying anything to them*. In this way, [the police officer] constructs a version of events where [the suspect] is remiss firstly in evading the suggested course of action by

leaving the scene, and secondly in failing even to consider that such a course of action may have been appropriate.

(Heydon 2005: 137)

In this way the content of these turns – summarizing the gist of what has been said before – constitutes a micro-narrative, a minimalist reconstruction of the longer narrative detail that the interviewee has contributed, or that the interviewer has inferred from what the interviewee has said. As Heritage and Watson (1980: 247) point out, this activity 'is rarely seen by members as "description for its own sake"'; it 'may be (and very often is) part of some wider conversational activity oriented towards the achievement of an end, e.g., persuading, justifying, making claims'. These activities are part of the institutional goals of the police interview and make them central to the turn and its nature.

Komter (1998, 2003, 2006), too, looks at formulations in police and courtroom interaction and argues that they are an important resource for the professional in stating 'the record-thus-far' (Komter 2006: 201). Holt and Johnson (2006) argue that these turns are part of 'a freeze-frame effect' in the interview where 'the narrative is frozen and, in that moment of productive paralysis, is examined, reformulated and restated'. This is therefore one of the institutional resources at the heart of the process of 'formulating the facts of the story, being important fact-making moments that distil and encode a version of reality, which will play an important part in any future legal case: an authorized-authoritative version' (Holt and Johnson 2006). Holt and Johnson also note that formulations are often *so*-prefaced, as in fact extract 4.10 illustrates. Drew (1979: 298), in a comparative analysis of formulations, finds that they are infrequent in mundane conversations, but frequent, indeed core activities in a range of institutional settings, as an analysis of police interviews and lawyer and client interaction confirms. Interestingly, there has been little analysis of formulations in the fact-establishing settings of examination and cross-examination in the courtroom.

Invitation to narrative and resistance to storytelling

The Fred and Rosemary West case (the second epigraph for this chapter) is very well-known in the UK. The Wests were convicted of killing their own daughter, Heather, and Fred was convicted of killing 11, and Rosemary 9, other women over a period of 20 years from 1967 to 1987. The police investigation came to the notice of the press in February 1994, when police obtained a warrant to search the garden of the Wests' house. Both Fred and Rosemary were questioned. Detective Sergeant Terence Onions' second interview with Rosemary West begins conventionally, with DS Onions' invitation to Mrs West to narrate her own story of how her daughter, Heather, came to leave the family home: *Can you just go over the circumstances of when Heather left your house?* Mrs West abruptly declines: *You ask the questions, I'll try and answer them.* Such invitations are intended to allow a witness or defendant to give their own version of events first, uncontaminated by the inferences and institutional overtones that will be encoded in later questions.

It is the customary opening for police interviews and is sometimes responded to, as West does, by a rejection, although not usually in such a terse way.

If the invitation is accepted, this long narrative turn redresses the otherwise asymmetrical balance of a largely question-and-answer focused interview. Drew and Heritage assert that one of the asymmetries in institutional talk 'arises from the predominantly question-answer pattern of interaction' where 'there may be little perceived opportunity for the lay person to take the initiative' and where the professional may therefore 'gain a measure of control over the introduction of topics and hence of the "agenda" for the occasion' (1992: 49). However, giving the interviewee the initiative can also be seen as unwelcome freedom to take control of the talk and the topic. Nevertheless, topic management and movement is generally controlled by the interviewer, particularly in the interrogation section of the interview. Johnson (2002) examines the distinctive use of *and*-prefaced and *so*-prefaced questions in police interviews and the role of these questions in topic connection, topic marking, summarizing and movement. In extract 4.11, an interview with a child witness, topics are introduced and developed.

Extract 4.11

[Child is W; P is police].
```
 1  P.    Right. So are A and B your brothers?
 2  W.    Yeah.
 3  P.    And how old are they?
 4  W.    A's two and B's eight.
 5  P.    That's right. And you're the middle one then aren't you at five?
 6  W.    (Nods head).
 7  P.    Right. And can you tell me what your house is like? Can you
 8        describe your house to me?
 9  W.    Erm.
10  P.    What's it look like? Could you draw it?
11  W.    (Nods head).
12  P.    Do you want to draw the house then?
13        [... Dialogue continues prompting drawing the house and its rooms.]
14        Right. So can you tell me who sleeps in what bedroom then?
15  W.    My mum and my dad sleep together, and A and B sleep together
16        and I sleep on my own.
```

So-prefaced questions (lines 1 and 14) indicate topic movement and *and*-prefaced questions (lines 3, 5 and 7) continue the first topic and connect questions together in a sequence. *So*-prefaced questions as well as summarizing what has been said are also strategically used to formulate 'the facts' of the story in interviews with witnesses and suspects (extract 4.12).

Extract 4.12

[P is police; S is suspect]

1	P.	How – I mean what did th– what impression did he give, what was
2		he going to do with the stool.
3	S.	He were going to hit him he had it above his head and he were like
4		going for him.
5	P.	What did your brother do?
6	S.	He like he'd stopped and were going to grab it going up like that
7		but I had already hit him so he fell down before he had a chance
8		to hit him.
9	P.	**So you** thought that he were going to hit your brother with a stool.
10	S.	Yeah.

In this way, it is often the interviewer who tells the story, so the invitation and opportunity for interviewees to take the initiative through an extended narrative turn right at the start of the interview is an important opportunity that is rejected by West at the start of her interview. One assumes that she sees the opportunity to tell her own story as a disadvantage, since it necessarily involves disclosure; so, in rejecting the storyteller role, West assigns the role of questioner to the interviewer and puts herself in the role of interviewee. We should therefore be wary of assuming that the interviewee's asymmetrical position is entirely due to powerlessness. Adopting this role allows West to discover what information and suspicions the police have and her unwillingness to supply information voluntarily gives her some control of the situation.

In their analysis of one police interview with Shipman, Newbury and Johnson (2006) show how he resists powerful moves by the police questioner in four ways: through contest, correction, avoidance and refusal. Contest is when the suspect answers 'no' when the question expects 'yes'; correction occurs in denial and correction sequences like: *No. This happened/is the case.* Avoidance is realized through responses such as *I don't remember, It's a rhetorical question* or *Continue the story* and refusal through *[I have] nothing [to say], There's no answer* or by remaining silent. Since it is in the interviewee's interests to present himself as a cooperative interlocutor, resistance has potentially significant costs, presenting, as it does, a challenge to the consensus of power and control, although the right to silence means that even refusal to answer a question is acceptable.

Vulnerable witnesses – on interviewing children and rape victims

At the start of Mark Haddon's Whitbread prize winning novel, *The Curious Incident of the Dog in the Night-time*, the narrator, a boy of 15 with Asperger's syndrome, is arrested for assaulting a police officer, after he has been discovered with a dead dog, which he claims was already dead when he found it. This fictional interrogation illustrates some of the problems that are encountered by the police when questioning a child, and in this case a child with communication difficulties, as well as some of the difficulties for a child in communicating with the police.

> He [the police officer] said, 'I have spoken to your father and he says that you didn't mean to hit the policeman.'
> I didn't say anything because this wasn't a question.
> He said, 'Did you mean to hit the policeman?'
> I said, 'Yes.'
> He squeezed his face and said, 'But you didn't mean to hurt the policeman?'
> I thought about this and said, 'No. I didn't mean to hurt the policeman. I just wanted him to stop touching me.'
>
> (Haddon 2003: 22)

For the police officer, accurately assessing his interlocutor's ability to process questions is not straightforward and posing them in such a way that makes the intention clear is equally difficult. The child needs 'to possess socio-cultural knowledge about question-answer sequences' and needs to 'make assumptions about their interlocutors' intentions, knowledge states and beliefs' (Kremer-Sadlik 2004: 190). In the novel extract the child's response to the question about whether he meant to hurt the policeman requires thought followed by selection of relevant details from those thoughts. The child finds the questions too numerous and too rapid; the policeman allows insufficient time for processing and one of the questions, *I've spoken to your father and he says you didn't mean to hit the policeman*, is not even framed as a question.

Ochs and Capps (2001) studied interaction in 16 families with a child suffering from high-functioning autism or Asperger's Syndrome. They classified responses to questions as *adequate, inadequate* or *ignored*. A response was classified as adequate if it contained a sufficiently relevant response to the question, inadequate if it failed to respond to the question relevantly and ignored if the question was ignored and not treated as a question (as in the Haddon example above: 'I didn't say anything because this wasn't a question'). They found that 10 per cent of the time responses were inadequate and 15 per cent of the time the question was ignored showing that only 75 per cent of the time were the children 'able to detect their interlocutors' communicative intentions and produce relevant answers that were marked as acceptable' (Kremer-Sadlik 2004: 192). And this was in interactions when the children's interlocutors were their own parents, who had a deep understanding of their communicative needs. This emphasizes how difficult it is for an adult to pose questions and for a child to answer them and why interviewing children or anyone with communication difficulties is challenging to say the least.

One of the first difficulties is the institutional legal voice, which, as we saw in Chapter 2, contains words that have specific meanings not found in everyday conversations. Very young child witnesses have little experience of legal language, even in fiction. They are unlikely to have watched reality TV shows involving the police or crime dramas. Police officers and other professionals involved in the judicial process have 'not just a specialist vocabulary, but a special way of conceiving and construing the world' (Gibbons 2003: 36). The meanings created through lexical selection by the interviewer are generic and can be alien to any lay interactant and certainly to a child. Sometimes these words are familiar – in that they are known to the layperson – but still feel foreign, because of their use in the interview context. For example, in an invitation to an adult to tell their narrative, an interviewer says:

'Can you **say in your own words** what **happened**?'

The words *say in your own words* and *happened* are familiar but they require some explanation for a child, and maybe also for an adult, because there are particular generic meanings attached to them in the police context. In the following example, the invitation to a teenage rape victim is long and explanatory, indicating some of the meanings implicit in the shorter version.

> Okay you said that you're up here today to **speak** to us about erm this – to catch this person who raped you. Yeah? What I need you to do is **tell me what happened**. I know that you've **told other people what happened**, okay. But **I don't know what's happened**, right. What I want you to do is, **like in a story tell me from say Friday night**, Friday was it four o'clock. **Tell me from Friday four o'clock, all right, evening time. Until Sunday morning. What has happened to you over those – those couple of days. Give me as much detail as you can because obviously I'll go over it again er and– and get as much as I – I need from you, but if you can tell me as much as you can yourself, all right, and I'll just let you talk.** All right, so off you go.

In the explanation to the teenager, we can see that the officer means much more than simply telling what happened. The meaning of *in your own words* is 'tell me yourself in as much detail as you can without me interfering'. What *happened* means the relevant details at the material times. Thus the invitation is an attempt to elicit 'undialogized' and individual speech (*yourself ... let you talk*). What the interviewer wants is the newly 'created' individual monologue authored by the child that is free of the interviewer's 'accented' style and 'given' meanings (Bakhtin 1986: 119–20). Importantly, the storyteller is aware of the active listener – we described the important role of listening ealier – and while telling her story she makes her utterances referentially relevant in terms of literally drawing a picture for the interviewer (lines 12–13 in extract 4.11; turn 447 in extract 4.13, for example). The interviewer's presence will determine the storyteller's choices of events and of the words to narrate them. This 'addressivity' (Bakhtin 1986: 95) is part of the process of story creation.

In interviews with adult suspects we said that *so*-prefaced questions can be used to summarize and formulate the facts in the case. With child witnesses or complainants these questions are important too as a way of arriving at an institutional version of events. In an interview with a teenage rape victim the complainant introduces the information that the suspect had a knife:

414   W He had a knife and he was slitting down the side of the tarpaulin.

The interviewer establishes through questioning that the witness was quite a distance away from the suspect when she saw this and a challenge comes in turn 435 (*So how far away were you from the lorry?*), signalled by the discourse marker *so*, and is made explicit in turn 441 (extract 4.13) by the metalinguistic verbal group *trying to get at*. The challenge unfolds in turns 443, 445 and 447 and culminates in a reformulation from the officer in 449 where the earlier claim made by the witness (turn 414) is re-presented by the interviewer for agreement.

Extract 4.13

441   Okay. **What I'm trying to get at is if – if you're
       a distance away, how do you know he had a knife
       in his hand** and what w–

443   Right. **So** you didn't actually see the knife. You just saw what he'd
       actually done.

445   Okay. **Did you see the blade at all?**

447   Right. **'Cause I'm talking about from here.** [using map drawn by witness to
       indicate position]

449   Right, okay then. **So** you assumed that he was cutting it with a
       knife at that time?

Challenging the witness is necessary in interviews to gain accurate and robust facts that will stand up to unfriendly cross-examination in the court. In this exchange the officer probes and challenges the witness account, accurately identifying a problem and more reliably establishing the point at which the child could see the knife, confirming that it was not at the distance the child first indicated. This takes place over a span of 35 turns. Slightly later (in turn 472) in the complainant's story she says *He put the knife to my throat and says get up* and shortly afterwards the interviewer says *So can you see what kind of knife it is now?* (turn 479), accepting that this is an appropriate point for the witness to describe the knife and inviting her to draw it.

There is therefore a tension in interview interaction, between collecting robust facts and avoiding intimidation. Witnesses are not best placed to evaluate their own talk as evidence, and it is therefore the job of the interviewer to assess the adequacy of the details they are given and to elicit enhanced versions. A further tension is the need for the evidence to be in the witness's own words, a tension between creation and given-ness. In 4.13 we can see that it is possible to challenge the witness account without entirely discrediting it. Through sensitive challenge, the fact becomes more robust, and the officer's use of power is in the service of the witness. To this end, in the UK, a whole section of the interview is allocated to establishing rapport, a practice recommended by the Crown Prosecution Service (2002).

The interview can be seen as restricting or empowering for the child, depending on one's view of the process. For the child it is important that the interviewer provides information in questions that children can respond to. In extract 4.11 above the interviewer asks *So can you tell me who sleeps in what bedroom then?* This question gives a clear vocabulary and structure for the answer, with the child only needing to supply the 'who' and the 'what'. However, the interviewer has to avoid leading the witness or putting words into their mouth. This can result in lengthy exchanges in which the interviewer attempts to elicit narrative in the child's own words and involves patient persistence. Aldridge and Wood (1998) give a long example of one such exchange with a seven-year-old, where the interviewer is trying to elicit her own word for 'vagina' [I is interviewer and C is child]:

Extract 4.14

I. So what part of your body are we talking about?
C. I don't want to tell you 'coz it'll embarrass me, that's why.
I. Well I tell you what, say it really quickly.
C. No.
I. What about if we do it another way. Do you go swimming?
C [Nods]
I. Right, what do you wear when you go swimming?
C. A cossie.
I. Right. On your body, where does your cossie cover? Which parts of you?
C. All from here.
I. And what does [name of child's brother] wear when he goes swimming?
   [9 intervening turns]
I. Right, so you know all about that. All we've got to do now is decide names for those parts of the body isn't it?
   [11 intervening turns]
I. What's on a boy then?
C. A long thing.
I. A long thing. Right, what's that long thing? What do you call it at home?
C. I don't want to say.
I. You don't want to say. OK, what does [name of child's brother] call it?
C. Sometimes a jimmy.
   [6 intervening turns]
I Ok right so what does daddy call it? …
C. Well, he calls it a different name.
I He calls it a different name. What's that?
C Which is spelt W.E.L.Y
I. Is that, if I say it welly?
C. No.
I. What is it then?
C. W.I.L, two Ls, yeah. W.I.L.L.Y.
I. Right, is that willy? Is that the word you don't want to say?
C. [Nods]

                                   (Aldridge and Wood 1998: 159–61)

This protracted process involves the interviewer and child engaging in adaptive strategies to achieve success. It is the child that comes up with the spelling solution w.e.l.y., even though the first attempt is unsuccessful. The child cannot understand fully why the interviewer cannot supply the word, even though she explains that some children call body parts different names and she needs to know the specific name the child has. The child is unable to overcome her embarrassment, whatever the reason, so this is something that the interviewer has to try to overcome. The interviewer role is therefore restricting, goal-focused and challenging, but also potentially enhancing in a way that establishes more credible and evidentially powerful facts.

Not all interviewees are compliant though, as our fictional example of Vicky Pollard in the *Little Britain* example in Chapter 1 demonstrates. Fairclough (1995) discusses a similarly resistant youth, in a police interview over an incident where an upper-deck bus window was broken (extract 4.15). The youth (A) is non-compliant in a number of ways. He interrupts twice (lines 2 and 7); he challenges the interviewer's questions, rather than answering them and questions rather than answers (line 7) and marks his different social 'orientation' through peer group lexis (*coons*) (Fairclough 1995: 51).

Extract 4.15

([indicates interruption)
```
 1  B.   so why did [you get the other fellows to come up with
 2  A.   [some went up first
 3  B.   you as well
 4  A.   I'm not getting on the bus with a load of coons me sitting
 5       there jack the lad d'you know what I mean ...
 6  B.   why's [that
 7  A.   [get laid into what do you mean why's that ...
 8  B.   well they weren't attacking any other white people on the bus were they
 9  A.   no ... that's coz there was no other skinhead on the bus that's why ...
10       if there was a skinhead on the bus that was it they would lay into him
11  B.   so there's a feud is there
12  A.   yeah
```
(Fairclough 1995: 50)

We can see too how the interviewer formulates the facts in summarizing and transforming the gist of the youth's story, in a way that suggests a more socially divisive version of events for agreement (11) than the youth has articulated.

The interviewing of rape victims is an area that has received considerable critical attention. Fairclough (1995: 28–30) discusses an example from an interview between two male officers and a female alleging rape and shows how 'ideologically-based coherence' which is based on ideologies that are seen as 'naturalized' creates conditions in which the woman's story is devalued. The interviewer says *you're female and you've probably got a hell of a temper,* implying that the woman could have done more to signal her lack of consent (1995: 30).

A recent UK Home Office Report (February 2005) states that:

> Home Office data on reported rape cases in England and Wales show a continuing and unbroken increase in reporting to the police over the past two decades, but a relatively static number of convictions, thus increasing the justice gap.
>
> (Kelly *et al.* 2005: x)

The authors report that 'all UK studies of attrition in rape cases concur that the highest proportion of cases is lost at the earliest stages, with between a half and two thirds dropping out at the investigative stage' and that 'withdrawal by complainants is one of the most important elements' (Kelly *et al.* 2005: x). There are four key points, the report says, where attrition occurs: 'the decision to report; the investigative stage; discontinuance by prosecutors; and the trial' (Kelly *et al.* 2005: x). Of these, the first two are the points at which most attrition occurs, resulting in a recommendation 'that a shift occurs within the CJS [Criminal Justice System] from a focus on the discreditability of complainants to a concentration on enhanced evidence gathering and case-building' (Kelly *et al.* 2005: x, xii). This recent study suggests that there are still lessons to be learnt about the investigation of offences in relation to collecting evidence through interviews with rape complainants.

Conclusion

In this chapter we have followed the collection of evidence from initial calls to interviews with suspects and witnesses. We have focused on some of the norms of language in these contexts and described usual and common features. We have not looked at disputed interviews. That is reserved for Part II. Here we establish norms against which deviation can be viewed. In the further reading you can find a range of interpretations, some of which take a more critical stance to the interpretation of interviewing practices.

Further reading

Emergency calls: Edwards (2007).
Police interviews and statements: Leo (1996); Shuy (1998 – chapters 2, 10 and 11); Johnson (2006); Komter (2003, 2006); Linell and Jönsson (1991); Rock (2001); Gibbons (1996).

Research tasks

1 Go to the Harold Shipman or Rose West police interviews referred to in this chapter, or other interviews that you can find. Investigate regular features

of interviewing, using features described here and identified in your further reading. Find guidelines for interviewing, for example the PEACE model in England or the law from the Police and Criminal Evidence Act (1984) and its Codes of Practice. How are the features you have found influenced by the Codes of Practice governing the talk?

2   Using features you have identified in your own study of interviews, or from your reading, contrast them with those found in the disputed interviews in chapters 6, 8 and 9.

3   Follow Rock's (2001) 'Genesis of the witness statement' model and ask a witness to tell a story of a 'crime' that has happened to them. To replicate similar conditions, your witness should not be a close friend, since you will collaborate more. Find a younger or older person, who you do not know very well. Tape record the whole process, including the statement-taking and produce a transcript of the exercise. See if you managed to avoid leading questions and investigate how the story becomes transformed, referring to Komter (2003, 2006) and other reading.

5 Order in court

1995 in Australia – Crawford v. Venardos and Ors, *Brisbane Magistrates' Court, 21 February 1995 (DC is defence counsel; W is child witness; PROS is prosecutor; M is Magistrate)*

DC   You got <u>in</u> the car (2.1) without being forced – you went <u>out</u> there without being forced – the <u>pro</u>blem began when you were <u>left</u> there?

W   (1.5) [Mm.

PROS   [With respect Your Worship – there are <u>three</u> elements to that question and I ask my friend to break them down.

M   Yes – just break it up one by one Mr Humphrey.

(Eades 2002: 170)

Mary Albert Sexual Assault Trial in the United States, 1997
Judge: Now, you're going to have the benefit of some very skilful and very, very good lawyers. But let me caution you now. What the lawyers say in the opening statements and the closing arguments is not evidence. And you shall not receive their statements as evidence. The only evidence that you will consider in this case is evidence that you hear from the witnesses who testify before you in open court under oath and any exhibits that are introduced through various witnesses.

(Cited in Harris 2005: 221)

Introduction: into the courtroom

The first thing that strikes any visitor to the public area of a British Crown courtroom is the strangeness of the setting. Everything about it produces a sense of nervous excitement and hushed voices: the layered space with the judge supreme, routines of standing to the call of 'All rise!', lawyers in wigs and robes, no windows, witnesses looking nervous and dressed up for the occasion. One feels almost like an intruder in a private space, a feeling intensified by the fact that cases often originate in the private domain of domestic matters, but the spectator is aware that they are witnessing the lived experiences of their neighbours in a way that they have not seen them before.

In this chapter the research we focus on mainly looks at courtroom interaction from trials in Crown Courts (England) and Supreme Courts (United States), rather than interaction in lesser Magistrates' courts. In particular, the data extracts here are from The Shipman murder trial transcripts (The Shipman Inquiry 2001). Shipman was found guilty in January 2000 of murdering 15 of his patients and forging a will. The Inquiry that followed the trial investigated the deaths of many of his patients and concluded that he had killed a total of 215.

The trial as a complex genre

Heffer (2005: 71) describes the jury trial as a 'complex genre' which contains a number of key events formed from sequential speech acts. These events include: jury selection, the indictment – the offence(s) with which the trial is concerned being read out to the court – opening address, prosecution and defence evidence, closing speeches, summing-up and deliberation, judgement and sentencing. Cotterill (2003: 94) notes that these highly structured events involve two modes of address: *monologic,* where one speaker is addressing the court, as in opening and closing statements by the lawyers, or the judge instructing the jury; and *dialogic,* where two speakers are interacting, as during the examination and cross-examination of witnesses.

Speech events involve a large number of participants (judge, jury, clerk, recorder, two lawyers and their teams, the accused, witnesses, ushers, the press and the public), although the extent to which they speak and listen is different depending on their role and the stage of the trial. Much of the trial involves the *appearance* of witnesses, as the second epigraph indicates. Whether they appear for the prosecution or defence the genre conforms to the following four or five-part structure (Gibbons 2003) – the item in brackets is optional.

Opening
   Calling in by *court officer/usher*
   Swearing in with *court officer/usher*
Examination-in-chief by *friendly counsel*
Cross examination by *opposing counsel*
(Re-examination by *friendly counsel*)
Dismissal by *judge*

Thus a witness for the prosecution, for example a police officer, will be first examined by his own 'friendly' counsel, the prosecution lawyer, and then cross-examined by the defence, and may be re-examined by his own counsel. Likewise, a witness for the defence, such as the defendant, is first examined by defence counsel, his friendly lawyer, then cross-examined by the prosecution and finally re-examined by the defence. This conversation that alternates between two competing 'sides' constitutes the adversarial system of trials that are found in most parts of the English-speaking world.

In Britain, the clerk, who reads the indictment, also invokes an absent participant, the Crown. For all the participants speaking is strictly controlled by rules and norms which, for everyone except lay witnesses and the defendant, are part of their daily work. Heffer notes that a single question and answer sequence between a defence lawyer and witness

> involves at least four principal speech participants who remain 'online' during the examination, but with different speaking rights and participant roles. Examining counsel initiates with a question, a right shared by the judge, but not the witness or jury. The witness is obliged to respond. The judge listens and may interrupt at any time. The jury … listen but may not interrupt, though they are allowed to ask questions indirectly via written notes to the judge. Opposing counsel has the right to interrupt, though this occurs surprisingly infrequently in English courts … At the same time, non-verbal communication can take place between all four participants in such forms as gaze, gesture, facial expressions, prosodic features and other non-verbal vocalizations.
>
> (Heffer 2005: 47–8)

At the same time, the clerk and recorder are making notes and members of the public and the media are listening, but with no right to speak or even whisper audibly. There are many more listeners than speakers in the courtroom, with side conversations constrained and censored. Members of the public will be chastized if they talk and, as Cotterill shows, even lawyers can be censored in their speech by the judge. When the lawyers in the O.J. Simpson trial spoke *sotte voce* close to the jury, Judge Ito disciplined them, as the jury's overhearing could influence their decisions: 'Counsel, if I have to warn you to keep your voice down one more time, it's going to cost you 250 bucks' (Cotterill 2003: 97).

Two discourse types: narrative and question–answer

Narrative

A good deal of courtroom interaction is conducted by means of narrative. Stories are central to legal cases. Cotterill (2003: 24) suggests that Labov's (1972) features of *abstract, complicating action, evaluation, resolution* and *coda* can be directly mapped at a macro-level to the structural components of the trial. Opening statements relate to *abstract* and *orientation*; witness examination and cross-examination to *complicating action*; closing arguments to *evaluation* (although examples of *evaluation* are in fact omni-present throughout the trial), verdict to *resolution* and release or sentencing to *coda*.

We referred earlier to the importance of narrative in evidence collection. Bamberg's (2004) work on master narratives and counter narratives gives narrative an even wider significance in the social and cultural world. Master narratives exist in culture and are oriented to and recognized by both speakers and writers. Newspaper headlines about injured children in the care of relatives often draw on a master narrative of what is involved in good and normal parenting, particularly mothering. Bamberg discusses the 'normalizing' and 'naturalizing' tendencies of master narratives to engulf speakers and subject them to grand récits and meta-narratives, in which cultural expectations are embedded. He points out the tendency of speakers to situate their narratives within these master narratives which are therefore socially and culturally constraining (2004: 359–60). Master narratives position social actors, but counter-narratives can create spaces for them to reposition themselves, although articulating a counter narrative is not at all easy and master narratives often remain unchallenged. For Bamberg, master narratives are hegemonic and counter narratives are individual – they orient the individual to who they are, not what society wants them to be.

Prosecution and defence cases work within such master narratives, but also work to counter them. Criminal prosecutions centre around socially deviant behaviour and the work of the prosecution is to prove that the accused behaved according to individually defined rules and norms which are outside the 'normal' social script. Master narratives can, therefore, provide defence scripts for suspects who seek to appear socially normal. Thus Shipman's defence narrative was that he was a caring doctor, who assiduously attended to his elderly, infirm patients. He resisted the culturally deviant counter narrative, presented by the prosecution, that he was an evil murderer who had cynically abused his position of professional trust. For Shipman, accepting this counter narrative could only lead to a guilty verdict.

Harris (2001: 72) discusses the wider cultural context of narrative and makes a distinction between 'the over-arching trial narratives of guilt and innocence' and the 'even more wide-ranging social and cultural narratives which are refracted through (and further constructed by) the media' and which trial narratives reflect. On the first day of the Shipman trial the judge refused a pre-trial submission by the defence that, as widespread media coverage had obviously made a fair trial impossible, the trial should be definitively abandoned. The prosecution counter-argued that media narratives are erased from the minds of the jury by the immediacy of the courtroom experience and the judge appeared to accept this.

Cotterill (2003: 223) refers to some of the 'prejudice triggers', or in our terms master narratives, that are identifiable in the O.J. Simpson trial and that could predispose towards conviction or acquittal verdicts. Successfully triggering the African-American wife-beater script in relation to the defendant might lead to a decision to convict, whereas triggering the young, white, promiscuous woman script in relation to the victim, Nicole Brown Simpson, could produce an acquittal. And overshadowing both scripts was the master narrative of the police as institutionally racist. For this reason it took weeks to select the jury, with the prosecution wanting a majority of women and the defence a majority of blacks.

In court, the work of lawyers centres on eliciting narratives and asking questions, although there are many other things going on, most notably the adversarial activities of testing and challenging the story, which is central to the trial genre. Heffer (2005: xv) notes 'a strategic tension between two markedly different ways of viewing the trial: as crime narrative or as legal argument', and Harris (2005: 217) notes that trials are hybrid genres with 'the intermingling of narrative and non-narrative modes of discourse'. The explicit narrative mode of opening statements in trials can be contrasted with the argument and debate of cross-examination. Harris (2005: 221) highlights the difference between 'narrativity' and narrative fact and evidence with the judge's quote used in the epigraph for this chapter: *What the lawyers say in the opening statements and the closing arguments is not evidence.* Harris contends that 'opening statements are in the narrative mode, oriented to how speakers tell their stories; and the testimony of witnesses is in the paradigmatic (or non-narrative) mode, oriented to evidence, fact, truth' (2005: 220–1). The judge tells the jury that 'the purpose of this opening statement is to give you an idea of what he [the lawyer] thinks or intends the evidence to be presented to you will be' (Harris 2005: 221). Presenting it in the narrative mode makes it fictional not factual, a distinction that the judge has to explicitly 'warn' the jury about. There is a distinction then between fictional and factual narratives, between narrativity and factual recount of memories.

Lawyers question witnesses to elicit factual recount for the benefit of the jury. The organizing and 'embedding' of these facts into a courtroom narrative is a powerful determinant of the way jurors 'recognise and analyse the vast amounts of information involved in making a legal judgement' (Bennett and Feldman 1981: 5, cited in Harris 2005: 215). In some ways jurors are like 'readers of a detective novel or watchers of a mystery movie'. In opening and closing statements, and the subsequent directions given to the jury by the judge at the close of a case, these 'narrativised schemas' (Heffer 2005: 206) come significantly into play.

Cotterill (2003: 65ff) discusses 'the role of strategic lexical choices in constructing the prosecution and defence narrative frameworks' in opening statements. She reveals how analysis of lexical selection, which represents actors and actions in positive or negative ways, frames prosecution and defence stories. In the O.J. Simpson trial, the prosecution case was that he was violent to his wife and the defence case was that Nicole Simpson was manipulative and promiscuous. Cotterill suggests that the prosecution's choice of words such as *encounter* and *control* with their negative 'semantic prosodies' (Louw 1993) realized by collocates such as *prejudice, problems, opposition, risks, hazards* is central to the conceptualization of O.J. Simpson as a violent man capable of murder. The defence, on the other hand, seek to diffuse this image by presenting the violence as 'verbal rather than physical' (Cotterill 2003: 80). This was achieved through lexical choices with much more neutral or positive semantics like *incident, dispute, discussion* and *conversation* as ways of lexicalizing talk in the Simpson household, thereby paving the way for a defence narrative that refutes physical violence and the capacity for murder. This framing of the witness evidence to follow is, as Cotterill suggests, a powerful tool in orienting the jury 'towards their side's version of the trial narrative' (2003: 90).

If opening statements frame the evidence of witnesses, the closing statements evaluate the validity, reliability, value, truth and significance of witness stories following examination and cross-examination. This constitutes what Harris (2005 quoting Labov 1972) calls 'the point' of the story, that is its significance for the trial in relation to the defendant's guilt or innocence. In addition, the judge, in his direction to the jury, evaluates the work of the prosecution and defence counsels in presenting facts to enable them to come to a verdict; then, in his judgement, if there is a guilty verdict, he evaluates the crime(s) and decides on a fitting sentence.

In the Shipman trial, the prosecution closing statement was 34,922 words long and the defence statement 51,620. Let us compare the openings. In extract 5.1 the prosecution lawyer's vocabulary emphasises the contrast between the trust expected by the patient and the actual breach of trust resulting in murder: *entrust, trust, trusted* (3), *entrusted, honesty, integrity* versus *breached that trust, killed, duped, falsified, save his own skin, cover his tracks, misled, deliberate misstatements.*

Extract 5.1

> MR. HENRIQUES: Ladies and gentlemen, the 15 **ladies** whose names appear as **victims** in this indictment, they had all chosen or at least accepted **Dr. Shipman** as their **doctor**. In doing so, they **entrusted** their **health**, indeed they **entrusted** their **lives** to him. They **trusted** him to **care** for them. Their **relatives trusted** him to tell the truth about the circumstances in which his **patient** [sic] died. The **community trusted** him to keep records and to complete documentation with **honesty** and **integrity**. We submit that he has **breached that trust**. He did **not care** at all for those 15 **patients**: he **killed** them. He **did not, with truth, relate** the circumstances of their death to their **grieving relatives**. He **duped** them in order to **save his own skin**. His medical records were **falsified** in order to **cover his tracks**, and the **community** was **misled** by **deliberate misstatements** on formal documentation.
>
> (Shipman Trial, Day 40)

By contrast, the defence speech (extract 5.2) opens with positive statements about Shipman's *care* of his *patients*, referring to him many times as a *doctor* and as *Dr. Shipman*, where the prosecution speech had only referred to him once as *Dr. Shipman* and *doctor* and had labelled the *patients* as *ladies* and *victims*.

Extract 5.2

> MISS DAVIES: Members of the jury, the **man** before the court, charged with 15 Counts of murder and one of forgery, is **Harold Shipman**; a **doctor**; specifically **a general medical practitioner**. A **doctor's** primary objective is to **care** for his **patients**. A **doctor's** training, the knowledge he acquires, is directed to that one aim. **Doctors** are there to **care** for their **patients**, not **kill** them. And this particular **doctor**, **Dr. Shipman**, has been in general medical practice since the 1970s. He is a **doctor** whose following in the Hyde area was such that when he left his old practice, the Donnybrook practice, and set up as **a single handed practitioner** in 1992, many **patients** went with him; **patients** – one of whom was Kathleen Grundy – who had previously been **patients** of other **doctors** at the practice. At the time of his arrest in 1998, his list size, that is his list size of **patients**, was 3,100.

He wasn't the only **doctor** in that area. You have heard, for example, from those **other doctors** who would fill in form C on the cremation certificates, that their practice was just across the road. You know that not too far away was his old practice, the Donnybrook practice. No **patient** had to register with **Dr. Shipman**, but the fact that so many did, must be something upon which inferences can be drawn. It is not an unreasonable inference to draw, from the size of that list, the fact that **patients followed him and were satisfied with the care** which he provided; the **care** which is at the very core of **the medical profession: the doctor's duty to care for his patients**.

(Shipman Trial, Day 41)

The judge, after the guilty verdicts had been given, addressed Shipman using a sentence which combines both evaluative angles in a paradox:

None of your victims realised that yours was not a healing touch. None of them knew that in truth you had brought her death, *death which was disguised as the caring attention of a good doctor.*

(Shipman Trial, Day 58, our emphasis)

Cotterill (2003) discusses the way that the differing storytelling abilities of the lawyers in the O.J. Simpson case affected jurors. In that case jury members were explicitly authorized by the judge to tell their stories after the trial ended and Knox, one of the jurors who applauded the defence lawyers' storytelling abilities, said that 'what both lawyers have in common is their ability to give you a story, an interesting narrative wrapped around their facts'; while the defence 'Dream Team' constituted 'a show' with 'power and charisma', the prosecution 'never knew how to present [their case], they couldn't keep it sharp and simple' (Knox 1995, cited in Cotterill 2003: 222). As Cotterill observes, jury deliberation is a complex process, involving both joint evaluation of narratives and individual use of 'internalised story schemata' (2003: 224).

In many of the post-trial writings and interviews, jurors spoke of the individual and collective process of *narrative typification* (Jackson 1995: 419) which went on in the jury room, whereby they attempted to 'make sense' of the evidence. Through a process of trying the various stories on for size, the jurors attempted to reach a consensus on the most acceptable 'fit' of the story, given the evidence presented.

(Cotterill 2003: 223)

These story schemata can be linked to master narratives in social and cultural beliefs to produce a scenario in which powerful social forces act on juries by combining argument and storytelling within the trial with that which they themselves bring to the trial as socially constructed and constituted citizens.

Styles and goals of friendly and unfriendly questioning

A friendly lawyer will use his institutional role to produce questioning turns that often simply require confirmation, leading witnesses through straightforward parts of their stories. These questions, which constitute shared knowledge that is gained from a prior statement or consultation, are punctuated with information-seeking turns to elicit more evaluative and evidentially important detail. This activity is supportive of the witness, providing a routine that co-produces authoritative evidence with minimum effort. Of the first 19 questions put to Shipman by his friendly counsel (extract 5.3), 15 require only confirmation responses (bold), although Shipman chooses to answer two of them with additional information.

Extract 5.3

Q. What is your full name please?
A. Full name is Harold Frederick Shipman.
Q. And what qualifications do you hold?
A. I hold a Bachelor of Medicine, Bachelor of Surgery degree. I also, sorry, I also have obtained Diploma in Child Health and Diploma in Obstetrics and Gynaecology.
Q. Dr. Shipman, you were born on the 14th January 1946 in Nottingham?
A. That's correct.
Q. You grew up in the area, went to school in the area and thereafter went to Leeds Medical School?
A. That is also correct.
Q. From there you studied medicine and qualified, obtaining your primary medical qualifications in 1970?
A. That's correct.
Q. Having obtained your primary medical qualification did you thereafter carry out a series of training house jobs in hospitals essentially in the Pontefract area?
A. Yes.
Q. And did you there move into the field of general practice certainly in the 1970s, such that by September 1977 did you move into general medical practice in Hyde at Donneybrook House?
A. I did.
Q. On a personal level in fact did you marry in 1966 whilst still a student?
A. I did.
Q. And your wife, Primrose, is in court today, and of that marriage are there 4 children?
A. There are.
Q. By September 1977 you took up your position at the Donneybrook House practice. You were there with a number of other doctors?
A. I was.
Q. How many?

A. 6.

Q. And after one year in practise did you become a partner at that practice?

A. I did.

Q. In addition to your work at Donneybrook House did there come a time when you worked as an area surgeon for St. John's Ambulance but you gave up that position in order to devote more time to your general practice in 1988?

A. That's quite right.

Q. In respect of your practice at Donneybrook House what was your patient list?

A. I set up with a list of just over 2,000 patients.

Q. Did you maintain that list through the 1980s?

A. The list grew and became nearer 3,000.

Q. And in respect of your work at the Donneybrook House practice first of all the patients, in respect of age are we talking about a cross-section?

A. My practice had virtually the national figures for age, sex and so on.

Q. So we are talking a cross-section both as to age and gender?

A. We are.

Q. And in respect of the type of medicine that you carried out at Donneybrook House, again did it represent across the board of work of a general medical practitioner?

A. It did.

Q. You remained in that practice in the 1980s and can I move on now please to the early 90s. Did there come a time when you decided to leave that practice?

A. Yes, that's correct.

(Shipman Trial, Day 27)

In extract 5.3 the straightforward evidence of Shipman's work practice is dealt with through many *and*-prefaced questions forming a narrative series that emphasises the 'routine elements' of the questioning activity (Heritage and Sorjonen 1994: 5). However, by strategically placing information-seeking questions between those merely requiring confirmation, the lawyer can foreground evidentially important information and facts for the jury.

In extract 5.4, where Shipman is giving evidence about his patient, the victim, Mrs Grundy, the questions alternate between those that are straightforward, though evidentially important to his general defence of being a caring doctor, rather than a murderer (1, 3, 4, 5, 6, 9), and those that are strategically important to his defence, that the victim abused drugs, in particular codeine, which accounts for the fatal overdose (questions 2, 7, 8, 10). These latter questions and their answers are highlighted in bold. Only 3, 5 and 10 are designed as straightforward confirmation questions, and even 5 and 10 are different from the questions in extract 5.3 in that they only become shared knowledge for confirmation after Shipman had given evidence. They summarize the recent activity rather than being presented as already established facts prior to the examination. Here we can see the distinction between representations of *established in examination* and *displayed in examination*.

Extract 5.4

1 Q.   The first 3 entries relate to the year 1993 and then we can pick up an entry there, 12.10.96. In whose hand is that entry?

1 A.   That is in mine.

2 **Q.   Could you read it out please?**

2 **A.   'Irritable bowel syndrome again. Odd. Pupil small. Constipated. Query drug abuse. At her age. Query codeine. Wait and see.'**

3 Q.   Now in fact produced for the Court has been the appointment sheet for the 12th October 1996 and it does not appear from that appointment sheet that Mrs. Grundy visited the surgery on the 12th October 1996. Did she so visit?

3 A.   Yes.

4 Q.   Can you help as to why there is no entry on the 12th October 1996 in the appointments book for her visit?

4 A.   As a general practitioner I occasionally saw people who just wanted a word. I would take them into my room. Sometimes it just was word and sometimes it took a long time.

5 Q.   So in respect of this entry for the 12th October 96 you saw Mrs. Grundy on that day?

5 A.   I did.

6 Q.   Can you please tell the Court what occurred at the consultation between the two of you?

6 A.   Once we were in my room she sat down, I sat down. She talked about the problem of IBS.

7 **Q.   The irritable bowel syndrome?**

7 **A.   Irritable bowel syndrome. We had tried every NHS medicine and she had tried a lot of herbal remedies. She gave me the history that she was constipated and I noticed her pupils were very tight, small hole. Codeine can constipate and can make the pupils become smaller. Abuse of drugs in the elderly is becoming recognised. I couldn't offer her any other medication and I let the matter go.**

8 **Q.   Did you raise with her any question of abuse of drugs as you described it?**

8 **A.   Not at that time.**

9 Q.   Why is the entry in the Lloyd George card as opposed to the computer record?

9 A.   Here I was using it for confidentiality but also as an aid memoir [sic] to think about her when she next attended.

10 **Q.   And was that as far as you took it on that day?**

10 **A.   Yes.**

(Shipman Trial, Day 27)

Friendly counsel's goal is therefore to establish agreement on clear and precise facts, whereas the cross-examiner seeks to test the reliability of those facts and present alternatives (extract 5.5). Agreement and lack of contest in examination-in-chief is confirmed by a quantitative analysis of *and*-prefaced questions in Shipman's examination, cross-examination and re-examination, which spanned 11 days. Using *Wordsmith Tools* (Scott 2006) we looked at the number of occurrences of utterance initial *And* (as in extract 5.3). They were almost twice as frequent in friendly examination as in cross-examination (0.63 per cent versus 0.35 per cent) and generally followed agreement tokens such as *yes, that's correct, that's right, yes I did, yes it is, after the visit yes, it does, it was, I was, there was* or negative agreement *there is no visit slip, no* or a simple *no. And*-prefaced questions are used differently in cross-examination after disagreement (as in the questions at the end of extract 5.5), but since the unmarked use of such questions is in sequences that are uncontested and expect agreement, this marked use after disagreement functions to signal rejection by the cross-examining lawyer of the witness's version of events. It also signals the lawyer's continuing goal in pursuing his own side of events.

Cross-examining counsel manage to build negative evaluation into their questions to attack the defendant's character and/or to undermine their story. Note in extract 5.5 *quite deliberately, false, the purpose of which, drug abuse/habit, quite wicked, fabricated* and, specifically related to the claim that Mrs Grundy was a drug abuser, *real sign, really said to you.* Combining these evaluations with deictic reference to the speakers' here and now – *I, me, you, we, us, now, them* [the records], *these entries* – contributes to the lawyer's deconstruction of the defence. These linguistic choices mark a 'social attitude that is "wide awake"' and 'discerning' (Hanks 2005: 210) and which evaluates, for the jury, through judgement of the defence story.

Extract 5.5

Q. Now I am going to now suggest to you that you **created quite deliberately** 3 **false** written records, the purpose of which was to **suggest** that Mrs. Grundy had a **drug habit**. Did you?
A. Did I what, I am sorry?
Q. Create 3 false written records?
A. No.
Q. Let us look at them please. ... 'IBS (irritable bowel syndrome) again. Odd pupils small. Constipated query. Drug abuse at her age. Query codeine. Wait and see.' The 12th October 1996 was a Saturday, you recollect that fact?
A. I am informed that it was a Saturday.
...
Q. Tell me, was there **some real sign of drug abuse** there to be seen in Mrs. Grundy, visible?

A. She had episodes of irritable bowel syndrome. She had also got small pupils and with irritable bowel syndrome you get diarrhoea and constipation at times.

Q. We have read that. Was there something that **really said** to you, 'Here is a lady, 81 years of age, with a drug problem?' She would have been 79 then.

A. People don't have small pupils for no reason and her IBS was not absolutely typical of everybody else's.

Q. Let me **suggest** your **attributing a drug habit** to Mrs. Grundy is **quite wicked**?

A. If that's what you want to do then that's fine. I tell you that these recordings were made at the time, apart from one, and were accurate.

Q. These 3 entries were made at a time when you contemplated facing trial in relation to one deceased only, Mrs. Grundy, that's right isn't it?

A. What is right, I am sorry?

Q. **You fabricated** these entries at a time when you contemplated being tried in relation to Mrs. Grundy only?

A. No I didn't.

Q. And if you had been tried in relation Mrs. Grundy only your defence would have been that **she died from drugs she took herself because she had a habit**?

A. I am sorry again, no.

(Shipman Trial, Day 33)

This cross-examination of the evidence already given in examination-in-chief, casts doubt on the veracity and reliability of the defence story that the possible drug habit had not been recorded in the normal way, in order to preserve confidentiality. It counter-proposes the prosecution version: that records were fabricated as part of a defence against a charge of murder. As Heffer (2005: 135) notes in relation to negative judgements in cross-examination, at such points 'the counsel's subjectivity begins to appear', reinforced by the use of first-person pronouns. He looks at the 'I-clusters' produced by cross-examiners (2005: 136), noting that the two verbs *suggest* and *going to suggest* are the most distinctive collocates. In extract 5.5 *suggest* and *tell* also collocate with the object pronoun *me*, *tell me, let me suggest*. Heffer (2005: 137) characterizes these clusters as 'spotlights' that 'throw light on the lawyer's subjective intentions', which in extract 5.5 are to attack the defence account and suggest an alternative. Heffer tentatively, but convincingly, argues that, when counsel use *suggest* with the witness, they are also indirectly addressing the jury and offering them this version of events. Deictic markers such as the inclusive second-person pronoun *we/us* (*let us look at them please; we have read that*), also explicitly draw the jury into the dialogue and into a jointly produced negative assessment of the evidence. This continually competing and contested evidential perspective epitomises the nature of the adversarial system.

Questions are highly constrained and constraining in courtroom interaction. Lawyers are constrained by the genre and prior texts in terms of what and how they can elicit, while witnesses are doubly constrained: first, by the inbuilt constraints of the lawyer's framing and second, by how the questions are designed to constrain their answers to produce a particular kind of evidence.

As we saw earlier, each witness appearance has a generic structure and the styles and goals of the interaction within the different activities of examination and cross-examination will determine the kind of questioning – straightforward versus contest – and finally the pre-trial statement(s) of the witness will determine what the friendly lawyer asks and what the cross-examining lawyer deconstructs. In extract 5.6 from a statement given to the police by one of the witnesses in the Shipman trial, we read his evidence about what he saw, heard and did in Shipman's surgery while witnessing Mrs Grundy's signature:

Extract 5.6

> I am a single man and live at the address shown overleaf with my family. I have been a patient of Dr. H.F. Shipman, 21 Market Street, Hyde, throughout my entire life. On the 9th June 1998 (090698) I had an appointment at 4.10 p.m. (16.10 hrs) with Dr. Shipman. I attended the surgery about that time and to the best of my recollection there was only one other woman in the waiting room. Dr. Shipman then came out of his surgery and asked me and the other woman if we wouldn't mind witnessing a signature. The woman and I then followed Dr. Shipman into his surgery. Sat down in the room already was an elderly lady. I did not really see her as she had her back to me. Dr. Shipman then spoke to the elderly lady. I cannot remember what he said, but I recall that whatever it was, it was to suggest to me that the old lady was aware of what was happening. The old lady replied, 'YES'. I was then shown a piece of paper that was folded over so that only the bottom couple of inches were showing. The only thing I saw on the form was K. GRUNDY. I had not seen this being written.

Extract 5.7 comes from the examination of the same witness in court and we notice how closely the prosecution lawyer follows the script of the statement when posing his questions:

Extract 5.7

ANTHONY PAUL SPENCER, sworn
Examined by MR. WRIGHT
(The six opening introductory questions and answers have been omitted)
Q. And on the 9th June 1998 did you have an appointment at Dr. Shipman's surgery?
A. Yes.
Q. Ladies and gentlemen, if you turn to page 73 which is in fact 2 pages towards the front of your bundle, you see the surgery appointments diary there. ... did you go to the surgery that day Mr. Spencer?
A. Yes.

Q. And did you go into the waiting area?

A. I did.

Q.   And did you see Dr. Shipman that day?

A. Yes.

Q. Did you have any sort of conversation with Dr. Shipman in the waiting room area at any time that day?

A. In the waiting room area, Dr. Shipman came out of his surgery and asked me if I would not mind witnessing a signature.

Q. And so what happened then?

A. I obliged.

Q. So where did you go?

A. Into his surgery room.

Q. Did you go in alone or in company with anyone?

A. In company with the person who was in after me.

Q. In company with the person that was in after you?

A. Yes.

Q. You mean after you as far as any appointment is concerned?

A. Yes.

Q. When you got into his room was there anyone else in the room?

A. Yes.

Q. First of all, male or female?

A. Female.

Q. What sort of age, any idea? Young, middle aged, elderly or what?

A. Old.

Q. Pardon?

A. Elderly.

Q. Did you have much of an opportunity of looking at this lady?

A. Yes.

Q. Did you have much of an opportunity of looking at her face at all?

A. Not really, no.

Q. What were the seating arrangements like?

A. She was sat with her, I was looking at this side of her, at the left-hand side of her.

Q. And by that do you mean the profile?

A. Yes.

Q. A little like the way that I am looking at you now, you mean, that way round?

A. Yes.

Q. Was she introduced to you at all?

A. No.

Q. Did you ever get to discover at that time what she was called, at that time, that afternoon?

A. Until I saw the signature, no.

Q. What then happened?

A. Dr. Shipman folded over a piece of paper with a couple of spare lines on it and asked me if I wouldn't mind writing my name and my address and putting my signature and my occupation on the piece of paper.

Q. So was the paper handed over to you?

A. No, it was kept on the desk.

Q. It was kept on the desk. Did you see anything on the piece of paper?

A. K. Grundy as a signature.

Q. Could you see anything else on the paper at all?

A. Dotted lines.

Q. So far as that name or signature K. Grundy on that piece of paper, had you seen that being entered on to that particular piece of paper?

A. No.

Q. So you had not seen who had written that?

A. No.

(Shipman Trial, Day 6)

Extract 5.8 is from the cross-examination of the same witness about the same events. Note how the defence lawyer summarizes and offers simply for agreement those aspects of the story that she takes as unproblematic and then produces information-seeking questions for the parts that she disputes. She also switches from collaborative narration to challenging questioning (indicated in bold).

Extract 5.8

Cross-examined by MISS DAVIES

Q. Mr. Spencer you were waiting in Dr. Shipman's surgery, he came out and asked if you would witness a signature?

A. Yes.

Q. You went into his consulting room. There was a lady who you described as elderly. She was sitting at the side of his desk and you went in with another lady who was also a patient?

A. Yes.

Q. When you went into the surgery was there a short conversation between Dr. Shipman and the lady sitting at the desk?

A. Yes.

Q. **Was it in terms that Dr. Shipman was telling the lady that yourself and in fact Claire Hutchinson as we now know, were going to witness the signature?**

A. No.

Q. **What was the conversation?**

A. Something along the lines of, 'Is this okay,' or, 'Are you sure about this?'

Q. I am sorry?

A. 'Is this okay,' or 'Are you sure about this?'

Q. And she agreed all was well?

A. Yes.

Q. And went ahead?

A. Yes.

Q. On the desk was a document?

A. Yes.

Q. Was a document that was folded?

A. Yes.

Q. Because it was folded you could not actually see what was on the document itself, could you?

A. No.

Q. That document was already folded when you went into the surgery, was it not?

A. Yes.

Q. So therefore when you told the Court that Dr. Shipman folded over the piece of paper that is not correct, it was already folded over. The only bit that was free was where the signature was and where you were to sign?

A. Somebody had folded it.

Q. But could you not say who?

A. No.

Q. The position is that when you went into that surgery it was already folded over?

A. Yes.

Q. And all that you could see was the space where you were to sign and the signature that you have already told us was K. Grundy?

A. Yes.

(Shipman Trial, Day 6)

This switch from collaborative narration to challenging questioning signals the point at which the lawyer disputes the evidence the witness has just given in examination-in-chief. This is consistent with her goal of discrediting the witness or at least demonstrating that some of his evidence is unreliable. Nevertheless, she is constrained by the prior statement as to what she can safely ask the witness – trainee lawyers are warned 'never ask a question to which you don't know the answer'. The witness too is constrained by the ways the questions are put to him. His friendly lawyer (extract 5.7) has made answering easy by leading him through his statement. In cross-examination, however, he is given his story back in summary form for confirmation only, before being challenged with tag and declarative questions which compel agreement. Gibbons (2003: 101) says that tag questions are 'strengthening devices, which make the demand for compliance greater than that of a simple question' and so the tag form is 'more coercive' than simple polar questions. After extracting the admission that the evidence given in examination-in-chief, *Dr. Shipman folded over a piece of paper*, was incorrect, the lawyer is able to follow-up with declarative confirmation questions that force the witness to agree with the defence story that *when you went into that surgery it was already folded over*.

O'Barr (1982: 120–1) discusses a series of 'effective strategies for lawyers and witnesses', one of them being to 'restrict the opportunity of witnesses under cross-examination to short, direct answers to the specific questions asked'. It is clear that in extract 5.8 this strategy is being used, although the witness occasionally successfully overrides this restriction with one of O'Barr's 'effective strategies': 'blurt out relevant facts and opinions ... even though the opposition lawyer may attempt to limit your answer' (1982: 121). So, for example, in line 36 the witness observes *Somebody had folded it*, when the preceding question had attempted to limit his answer to a simple confirmation of the lawyer's assertion that his evidence was *not correct*. In this way the witness attempts to limit the damage to his credibility.

In monologue, as in their opening and closing speeches, lawyers can narrativize the evidence to represent a particular version of events, but in examination and cross-examination, their job is to elicit evidence from the witness. Nevertheless, as we have seen, it is possible to create implications and suggest unreliability through the question and answer mode. What this means is that questions can be used to achieve different goals, depending on the activity in which the speaker is engaged – examination, cross-examination – establishing agreement or disagreement and restricting response. It is not the form of the question, but rather its function within a particular activity that determines how questions work in the courtroom.

As Toolan (2001: viii) observes, 'narratives are everywhere' and research on narratives in courtroom discourse is extensive, since 'the law is awash with storytelling' (Amsterdam and Bruner 2000, cited in Harris 2005: 215). But we have seen that narrative can be disrupted and fragmented in the courtroom context by that other dominant discourse type, question and answer. The 'fragmentation ... [is] as a consequence of the question/answer mode of information exchange, which invariably involves lengthy interrogating sequences' (Harris 2001: 71). In addition, further fragmentation occurs, since 'narrative accounts usually involve multiple tellers, and shifts between "teller" and "knower" are common and often strategically initiated by lawyers' (Harris 2001: 71). In extract 5.8 we saw how the defence lawyer moved between storytelling and questioning the witness for strategic effect. We also saw how the same event is examined and cross examined, but what the extracts do not show is that these stretches of talk are not immediately sequential. Extract 5.7 is taken from page 3 of the transcript for day 6 while extract 5.8 is from page 8. Narrative disjunction is therefore as much a part of courtroom discourse as is narrative construction and so it is not surprising that jurors report on jury-room deliberations that involve making sense and (re)-constructing coherent narratives. Indeed, Hans and Vidmar (1986: 99) report a case 'where the jury *physically* re-enacted a shooting by role-play in the jury room, in order to assess the credibility of the evidence and plausibility of the story' (cited in Cotterill 2003: 224). Such role-play would not have been possible without a filtering of evidence through a story schema that is capable of replay.

Witnesses and evidence in trials

Not all witnesses are equal. Most of the evidence will be given by lay witnesses, ordinary people caught up in the crime, but occasionally experts, such as doctors or linguists, will be called. Expert witnesses present their evidential findings and explain technical aspects of the evidence to the jury, to enable them to evaluate its importance. We look at this in more detail in Chapter 10. The testimony of police witnesses is concerned with the procedures of collecting evidence: arrest, interview, searching premises, storing and examining evidence and giving the court information that the evidence was lawfully collected, in relation to legally determined procedures, such as cautioning suspects prior to interview in order to explain their rights to silence and representation by a lawyer. Lay witnesses present their involvement in the story of the alleged crime and the lawyers' questions centre on their memory of what they saw, heard, said and experienced.

When prosecution or defence lawyers call expert witnesses, such as doctors and toxicologists who need to explain complex science for the jury, they have to achieve a difficult 'balance between credibility and comprehensibility' (Cotterill 2003: 196). A juror in the O.J. Simpson trial recalled her exasperation with one expert, who got the level of accommodation wrong, and the consequent oversimplification made the jurors feel that she was talking down to them.

> Unfortunately, there's no way to let people know that you got it. You can't just raise your hand and say 'Dr Cotton, I understand what you're talking about. Move on.'
>
> (Second juror in Cooley *et al.* 1995: 115, cited in Cotterill 2003: 197)

Jurors are silent receivers of evidence, but all the talk is directed at them. One of the most important ways of managing what jurors hear is through questioning. We will now look at how difficult questions posed to children can influence what the jury hears.

Child witnesses – examining children and vulnerable witnesses

Children, who attend court as witnesses or victims of abuse or in sexual crimes, have also to endure cross-examination. Lawyer practices have been severely criticized, particularly for over-aggressiveness and unfair use of complex questioning (Brennan 1994a, b; Drew 1992; Ehrlich 2001; Levi and Graffam Walker 1990). Brennan and Brennan's (1988) and Brennan's (1994a, b) research into children's experience in Australian courtrooms suggests that children giving evidence in abuse cases are 'doubly abused' by hostile questioning. Brennan describes some of the effects and explains how questions in cross-examination are deliberately 'aimed at not admitting the experience of the child'. He demonstrates (extract 5.9) how questions are designed to be unanswerable and to elicit *I don't know* answers from the child, and then points out that 'the response "I don't know" can stand for a variety of states of knowledge, but the purpose of the cross-examination is well served as the response reduces the credibility of the witness' (1994b: 207).

Extract 5.9

Q. And where was your mother?
A. I don't know.
Q. You do not know, but she was in the house when you went to bed was she not?
A. I think so.
Q. Yes. Sorry, you think so.
A. Yes.
Q. Can you not remember?
A. Yes.
Q. Where would she have been if she was not in the house?
A. I don't know.

(Brennan 1994b: 206–7)

Brennan (1994a) suggests that the 'strange language' used in courts, particularly in cross-examination, adds up to 'a discourse of denial' of the child's world. He identifies 15 problematic constructions that have the effect of constraining, limiting and confusing the child. These range from negative rhetorical questions (*Now you had a bruise, did you not?*) to the lack of grammatical or semantic connection between questions and the use of the passive voice. Gibbons (2003) and Maley (2000) both report on the manipulative in-built constraints in professionals' questions. These are coercive for adults, but for children this experience can put them at an even greater disadvantage. Eades (2002 and in the epigraph) reports on a case in the Australian courts where Aboriginal children are witnesses and shows how multi-faceted questions are inappropriate; children are unable to respond adequately and presented with questions that are not interrogative and frequently also multiple, children can only fail.

Although the lawyer obviously needs to maintain control of such things as topic and event structure and cross-examination is by its very nature unfriendly, limiting the opportunities for children to give their evidence adequately is contrary to the spirit of the criminal justice system. Trials are places where the witness's story is exposed to public and hostile legal scrutiny, and children are particularly vulnerable in adversarial systems, since cross-examination is so probing and critical. The rape victim in extract 5.10 experiences destructive cross-examination.

Extract 5.10

1 Q. Your aim that evening then was to go to the discotheque?
2 A. Yes.
3 Q. Presumably you had dressed up for that, had you?
4 A. Yes.
5 Q. And you were wearing make-up?
6 A. Yes.
7 Q. Eye-shadow?

 8 A. Yes.
 9 Q. Lipstick?
10 A. No I was not wearing lipstick.
11 Q. You weren't wearing lipstick?
12 A. No.
13 Q. Just eye-shadow, eye make-up?
14 A. Yes.
15 Q. And powder presumably?
16 A. Foundation cream, yes.
17 Q. You had had bronchitis had you not?
18 A. Yes.
19 Q. You have mentioned in the course of your evidence about wearing a
20   coat.
21 A. Yes.
22 Q. It was not really a coat at all, was it?
23 A. Well, it is sort of a coat-dress and I bought it with trousers, as a trouser
24   suit.
25 Q. That is it down there isn't it, the red one?
26 A. Yes.
27 Q. If we call that a dress, if we call that a dress you had no coat on at all
28   had you?
29 A. No.
30 Q. And this is January. It was quite a cold night?
31 A. Yes it was cold actually.

(Levinson 1979: 82–3)

These questions start to build up a picture of a teenage girl who paid more attention to making herself attractive than to taking care of herself, despite having been ill. This episode is followed by questioning about her previous sexual experiences (extract 5.11).

Extract 5.11

 1 Q. … you have had sexual intercourse on a previous occasion haven't you?
 2 A. Yes.
 3 Q. On many previous occasions?
 4 A. Not many.
 5 Q. Several?
 6 A. Yes.
 7 Q. With several men?
 8 A. No.
 9 Q. Just one.
10 A. Two.
11 Q. Two. And you are seventeen and a half?
12 A. Yes.

(Levinson 1979: 83)

Levinson comments that 'careful juxtaposition [with what has gone before] does the job of suggesting that a girl of seventeen who has already slept with two men is not a woman of good repute'. Over the course of the cross-examination, the questions

> build up to form a 'natural' argument for the jury ... that goes something like this: the victim was dressed to go dancing, she was heavily made up – something of a painted lady, in fact – and, despite the fact that she had been ill, she was wearing no coat on the cold winter's night. The implicit conclusion is that the girl was seeking sexual adventures.
>
> (Levinson 1979 : 84)

Cross-examination is necessarily constrained by needing to be carried out in question and answer form – what Atkinson and Drew (1979) call 'turn-type pre-allocation' – and by inference, it can construct an argument for the jury, a story that is woven from the juxtaposition of questions and answers and is built up over time as a central goal of the cross-examination. Levinson argues that our understanding of what is going on in the questions

> rests on our knowledge of the kind of activity that the talk occurs within. We know that in a rape case it is the job of the defendant and his lawyer to show that the girl asked for it ... and the goal of the victim and her counsel to resist this and establish that the defendant committed the crime intentionally and against the girl's resistance.
>
> (Levinson 1979: 85)

Within a cross-examination genre, cleverly phrased and sequenced questions can organize a rape complainant narrative to be interpretable as implying consent rather than resistance. It is the activity within the genre, rather than the genre itself, that produces a narrative of blame rather than victimhood. The power of the cross-examination lies in the lawyer's skill in assigning blame and responsibility to the victim and presenting this as 'natural' (Fairclough 1989). Two particular sequences from extracts 5.10 (lines 27–30) and 5.11 (lines 7–11) can be analysed in terms of how the lawyer uses conjunctions to present unrelated events as 'naturally' connected. In extract 5.10 (lines 27–30) a connection is made between the witness having *no coat* and the month being *January* and in extract 5.11 the connection is between number of sexual partners (*two*) and her age (*seventeen and a half*). The connections provided by the lawyer through the conjunction *and* links material provided in the witness's answers with additional lawyer material which has inferential value. The implication in extract 5.10 is that the woman was dressed for display rather than comfort and in extract 5.11 that she had loose morals. Both connections are evaluative too with evaluation of recklessness and promiscuity supplied by juxtaposition that produces inference, rather than by surface features of lexical choice. A critical discourse analysis view of this cross examination extract therefore reveals 'how power and discriminatory value are inscribed in and mediated through the linguistic system' (Caldas-Coulthard and Coulthard 1996: xi). In addition, the master narrative of promiscuous young female looking for adventure produces a context of blame for the victim, rather than a narrative of victimhood.

Conclusion

The competitive and competing goals of interaction that characterize talk in courtroom interaction produce distinctive patterns of lexis and structure. Lexical selection creates semantic contrast between prosecution and defence accounts of the same events and narrative accounts are juxtaposed through challenging questioning that produces inferential meaning. As we saw here and earlier in Chapter 1 and Chapter 3, the courtroom produces a complex context for interaction, with the silent and overhearing audience having a major impact on turn design. Listeners are indexed in the talk through deictic reference, and particular modes of elicitation indicate the presence of audience design in conscious attempts to accommodate the jury as addressees, particularly in cross-examination. The highly ordered, yet fragmented nature of talk makes the courtroom a rich linguistic domain for study.

Courtroom research produces some of the most critical writing on linguistic issues in the justice system: Ehrlich's (2001) examination of the representation of rape, for example, or Atkinson and Drew (1979) and Drew's (1990, 1992) focus on the strategies used by lawyers to undermine witnesses and discredit testimony. O'Barr (1982), as well as looking at lawyer strategies, focuses on what witnesses can do to resist the powerful control of lawyers' constraining questions that Gibbons (2003: 100–12) outlines. Kurzon (2001) examines another of the participants in the courtroom in his study of the linguistic behaviour of judges and Cotterill (2003) and Heffer (2005) both discuss the language used by and with expert witnesses. The language of all these courtroom participants is extensively researched, but in this chapter we have recognized the central importance of juries and it is perhaps surprising, given their importance, though not given the secrecy that necessarily surrounds much of their talk, that juries are the least researched group. They have a largely silent and invisible role, despite the fact that they are the primary addressees for the vast majority of the linguistic work done in the courtroom.

In this first Part of the book we have examined legal language in a wide range of contexts, from the texts that constitute the law to the way that the language and discourse processes of the law are played out in real settings. We have considered how professional and lay speakers interact in institutional settings from initial calls to the emergency services to interview and court. In Part II we move from the language that characterizes the legal process to look at language which is used as evidence in cases where institutional practice is disputed and where discourse analysis is employed in expert reports and evidence to uncover what might have happened.

Further reading

Aldridge and Wood (1998); Atkinson and Drew (1979); Cotterill (2003); Ehrlich (2001, 2002); Heffer (2005); Jacquemet (1996); O'Barr (1982).

Research tasks

1 Compare the questioning strategies of two lawyers in examining and cross-examining mode in the same trial. To what extent are their strategies the same? Is the cross-examining strategy of lawyer A more similar to his own examining strategy or to the cross-examining strategy of lawyer B?

2 'The default requirement is for the witness in court to provide as answers to the lawyer's questions *preferred* second-part responses – which adequately satisfy all four Gricean maxims' (Cotterill 2003: 104). How far is this true in examination and cross-examination? Is this desirable but constantly resisted? Harris (1991) writes about evasion by politicians in broadcast interviews. She creates three categories of response on a scale of evasiveness: (i) *direct answer* (e.g. *yes, no, of course, that's correct*); (ii) *indirect answer* (e.g. *well if you say so*, where either *yes* or *no* can be inferred or where neither can be inferred, because some cohesion or coherence is missing); (iii) *challenge* where the interviewee challenges one or more of the presuppositions in the question. Apply her categories of evasive answers to a set of witness responses taken from both examination and cross-examination. What do you find?

3 Look at the evidence given by two expert witnesses. How are questions posed and responded to? Does the lawyer's examination enable the expert to make his or her expertise comprehensible for the jury? Cotterill (2003: 180) examines lawyer turns that use the phrase *When you say* as simplification questions. Are there other questions like this and if so what do they do? Can you find any occasions when the lawyer lays claim to as much expertise as the expert?

4 O'Barr (1982: 120–1) lists some effective strategies for lawyers and witnesses. Can you find examples of these being used in examinations and cross-examinations. Which strategies are most common in examination and which in cross-examination? Can you identify any additional strategies that are not on O'Barr's lists?

Part II
Language as evidence

6   The work of the forensic linguist

Have you any impairments?.... Loss of sight or hearing?.... Loss of arm or leg?...
Are you crippled or deformed?... If so explain....

(from insurance proposal form)

Introduction

Over the past 20 years there has been a rapid growth in the frequency with which courts in a number of countries have called upon the expertise of linguists. In this chapter we will give examples drawn from a large number of cases to illustrate the kinds of problems they have been asked to address and the wide range of tools and techniques they have used in their work. All cases require a different selection from the linguist's toolkit – phonetic and phonological, morphological, syntactic, lexical, discoursal, textual and pragmatic – and in what follows we have tried to group them according to linguistic criteria.

Morphological meaning and phonetic similarity

Shuy (2002b: 95–109) reports his contribution to the case of *McDonald's Corporation* v. *Quality Inns International, Inc.*, which revolved around whether McDonald's could claim ownership not simply of the name McDonald's but also of the initial morpheme 'Mc' and thereby prevent its use in other trademarks. The case began in 1987 when Quality Inns announced they were going to create a chain of basic hotels and call them McSleep, claiming, when challenged, that they hoped the 'Mc' prefix would evoke a Scottish link and with it the Scots' well-known reputation for frugality. McDonald's, who had previously successfully prevented the use of the name McBagel's, when a judge had decided that the prefix could not be used in conjunction with a generic food product, decided to challenge the McSleep mark, claiming it was a deliberate attempt to draw on the goodwill and reputation of the McDonald's brand.

In supporting their case McDonald's pointed out that they had deliberately set out, in one advertizing campaign, to create a 'McLanguage' with Ronald McDonald teaching children how to 'Mc-ize' the standard vocabulary of generic words to create 'McFries', McFish', 'McShakes' and even 'McBest'. Fanciful as this linguistic imperialism might seem to be to ordinary users of the language, particularly to those of Scottish or Irish descent, who would seem to be in danger of losing their right to use their own names as trademarks, the lawyers took the claim very seriously. Quality Inns' lawyers asked Shuy to help with two linguistic arguments: first, that the morpheme 'Mc' was in common use productively, in contexts where it was not seen to be linked in any way to McDonald's and second, that such examples showed that the prefix, originally a patronymic and equivalent in meaning to the morpheme *son* in John*son*, had become generic and thus now had a meaning of its own, which was recognizably distinct from both of the other major meanings, 'son of' and 'associated with the McDonald's company'.

Shuy chose to use a corpus linguistics approach and searched to find real text instances of what one might call 'Mcmorphemes'. Among the 56 examples he found were general terms like McArt, McCinema, McSurgery and McPrisons, as well as items already being used commercially such as the McThrift Motor Inn, a budget motel with a Scottish motif, and McTek, a computer discount store which specialized in Apple Mac computer products. On the basis of such examples, Shuy argued that the prefix had become, in the language at large, an independent lexical item with its own meaning of 'basic, convenient, inexpensive and standardized' (2002b: 99). Rather than resort to corpus evidence themselves, McDonald's hired market researchers to access the public's perception of the prefix directly and to do so through interview and questionnaire. Their experts reported that their tests confirmed that consumers did indeed associate the prefix with McDonald's, as well as with reliability, speed, convenience and cheapness. Faced with this conflicting evidence, the judge ruled in favour of McDonald's, thereby giving them massive control over the use of the morpheme.

Of course, the successful defence of a trademark may occasionally have unwanted consequences. In March 2007 McDonald's went to war against the Oxford English Dictionary after it described a McJob as 'an unstimulating, low-paid job with few prospects, [especially] one created by the expansion of the service sector'. The company's chief people officer for Northern Europe suggested they should change the definition to make it 'reflect a job that is stimulating, rewarding and offers genuine opportunities for career progression and skills that last a lifetime'. In fact this is one further skirmish in the constant battle to maintain the mark, because it is insisting that the word 'mcjob' can only have one meaning – 'a job at McDonald's – which is patently not what it is taken to mean by the general population (Stern and Wiggins 2007).

Trademark owners sometimes feel the need to defend their mark against other marks which are thought to be phonetically confusable. Tiersma and Solan (2002) list several pairs that have been found to be confusingly similar, including Beck's Beer and Ex Bier; Listerine and Listogen; Smirnoff and Sarnoff, while Gibbons (2003: 285–7) discusses in some detail an Australian case about the names of two drugs, Alkeran and Arclan, which at first sight seem quite distinct. He explains why some possible pronunciations of the words could be confused, in a country where 'a substantial proportion of the ... population speak English as a second language'.

Shuy (2002b) reports in detail on two cases in which he was involved: in one the dispute was over the name of two contraceptive pills, OVRAL and B-OVal; in the other it was over the names of two versions of a 'gooey tactile substance' which had been developed as an activity toy for young children and labelled GUK and GAK respectively. In both cases Shuy argued that the items were sufficiently dissimilar so as not to be in conflict. In the case of the contraceptive pills, one realizes that there is a marked phonetic difference between the two names when one is told that the manufacturers of OVRAL recommended a pronunciation with syllable final stress. This would produce a full final 'a' vowel and distinguish it clearly from B-Oval which has penultimate stress and consequently a reduced final schwa vowel – provided, of course, the salespeople and the users follow the manufacturer's instructions for pronunciation! For the GUK/GAK case you might like to pause at this moment and consider whether you actually agree with Shuy that the two words are sufficiently distinct phonetically so as not to cause confusion. What counter-arguments could you advance if you were asked to write a report for the other side, arguing that the marks are indeed confusingly similar? Then you can read Shuy's own detailed analysis and reasoning on pages 118–9 of his *Linguistic Battles in Trademark Disputes*.

In one of the earliest trademark cases involving phonetic similarity, *Pathfinder Communications Corp.* v. *Midwest Communications Co.*, the dispute was over the names of two radio stations – WMEE and WMCZ (those who do not have North American accents may need to be reminded that the letter 'z' is pronounced 'zee'). Dinnsen (ms, quoted in Levi 1994b) reports that he gave evidence in court that the typical pronunciations of the two sets of letters were 'overwhelmingly similar … and moreover likely to be confused' and he adds that the judge granted an injunction.

Syntactic complexity in a letter

Levi (1993) reports a case in which she acted as an expert witness, testifying on syntactic complexity. The plaintiffs' claim was that a letter sent to them with information about how to claim benefits was so badly written that it had actually failed to inform them of their rights. In supporting their claim Levi identified a series of syntactic features which, she argued, were likely to interfere with understanding; for example, 'multiple negatives, complex embeddings, nominalizations … passive verbs without subjects and difficult combinations of logical operators like *and*, *or*, *if* and *unless* (pp. 7–8). She quotes the following extract from the letter as an example of the syntactic problems encountered:

> If your AFDC financial assistance benefits are continued at the present level and the fair hearing decides your AFDC financial assistance reduction was correct, the amount of AFDC assistance received to which you were not entitled will be recouped from future AFDC payments or must be paid back if your AFDC is cancelled.

This 'translates' or rather produces the following equivalent reformulation:

> If X happens and then Y happens then either Z will happen [expressed in very complex terms including a negative with a relative clause] or – if R has also happened – then Q must happen.

(p. 8)

She then characterizes the syntactic complexity as consisting of 'a complex internal structure built out of seven clauses, six passive verbs without subjects' ... and several complex compound nouns (for example, 'financial assistance reduction'), which themselves contain nominalized verbs without expressed subjects (pp. 8–9).

Sadly she does not report the outcome of the case, nor give any indication of what the judge thought of her evidence, but at least she was admitted as a witness on syntactic meaning, which is by no means always the case – indeed one judge in the United States explicitly refused to admit the linguist Ellen Prince as an expert on the grounds that it is the function of the court to decide on meaning. Certainly, it is more difficult when the texts involved are legal texts, because lawyers and judges usually see themselves as the guardians of and adjudicators on such meaning. Stubbs (1996) reports an English Appeal Court case where he wrote an expert opinion arguing that the language of the judge's summing-up in the original trial could have pre-disposed the jury to convict. The Lord Chief Justice refused to consider his evidence arguing that:

> what the meaning is of the language used by a learned judge in the course of his directions to the jury is a matter for this Court and is not a matter for any linguistic expert.

(Stubbs 1996: 239)

However, even in this area linguists are occasionally allowed to express a professional opinion, although it does help if they are lawyer-linguists and/or have a lawyer as co-author, as happened in the next case.

Lexico-grammatical ambiguity

Kaplan *et al.* (1995) report on an appeal which went to the Supreme Court in 1994. The facts are as follows: a certain Mr Granderson pleaded guilty to a charge of destroying mail, for which the maximum custodial sentence was six months in prison, although there was the option of a fine plus probation. The judge chose the latter; he fined Mr Granderson and put him on probation for five years, that is 60 months. Subsequently Mr Granderson violated his probation by being caught in possession of cocaine. In such cases the law instructs the court to 'revoke the sentence of probation and sentence the defendant to not less than one third of the original sentence'. This presented the court with a problem because, if it took 'original sentence' to refer to 'probation', imposing a sentence of 'not less than one third' that is 20 months probation, could in fact reduce the penalty, as he had not yet served 40 months of his probation. In the end it was decided to sentence him to 20 *months* in *jail*, that is a prison sentence which, rather than being 'not less than one third', was more than three times greater than the original maximum prison sentence.

Kaplan *et al.* (1995) argued that this particular interpretation of the crucial clauses was inadmissible on linguistic grounds, because one cannot allow an admittedly ambiguous item to have both of its meanings simultaneously – they pointed out that the court had interpreted the phrase 'original sentence' as referring to 'imprisonment' for the purpose of determining the *type* of punishment, but to 'the initial imposition of five years' (of probation) for the purpose of determining the *length* of the sentence. One of the authors observed that what the court had done was the linguistic equivalent of a Frenchman taking the phrase 'Pierre a fait tomber l'avocat' to mean, 'Pierre did something to the lawyer [l'avocat$_1$] and caused the avocado [l'avocat$_2$] to fall'.

This case was methodologically interesting because Kaplan *et al.* had not even been invited to write an expert opinion. What they did was to write an academic article, concerned with the Granderson appeal and three other appeals to be considered by the Supreme Court, published it in the *Yale Law Review*, and then sent copies to the judges. The Supreme Court judges not only read the article and took note of the linguistic arguments, they also 'cited, and to an extent tracked, the team's analysis' (Kaplan *et al.* 1995: 87) in their judgment. They changed the interpretation to 'a sentence of not less than two months in prison' and, as the accused had by this time already been in prison for 11 months, almost double the original maximum sentence, he was released immediately.

Lexical meaning

In some cases the linguist's contribution can be restricted to the meaning of a single word. Eades (1994) reports a case in which the expert testified that the verb 'killem', as used by a Torres Strait Islander, has a much wider semantic range than the Standard English word 'kill', which the uninformed might think was an obvious equivalent. In fact, apparently, the range of meanings for 'killem' can include 'hit' and thus the use of this word by the accused, when he was describing a fight with a man who subsequently died, could not be used to claim that he had necessarily confessed to manslaughter.

The accused may be even more vulnerable when the incriminating word(s) are in an unrelated language. In 2004 an Iraqi Kurdish refugee in the US was arrested after a sting operation and accused of having been willing to launder money in order to buy a shoulder-fired missile that was to be used to assassinate the Pakistani ambassador to the UN. It was said that the accused had links with an Islamist terrorist group, because his name was listed in an address book found in a terrorist training camp in northern Iraq where he was referred to, according to the Defense Department, with an Arabic word meaning 'commander'. Late in the day translators at the FBI got to see the relevant page and announced that the word, although written in Arabic script, was in reality Kurdish and a common honorific 'kak', with an innocuous meaning, which, depending on the level of formality, ranged from 'Mr' to 'brother'.

In another case, Sinclair (ms) was asked to give an opinion on the ordinary man's understanding of the word 'visa'. Apparently in law a visa is not in fact an 'entry permit' as most people think, but rather 'a permit to request leave to enter'; in other words, even with a visa, a traveller can legitimately be refused entry to a country. Sinclair was asked to provide evidence that this is not the commonly understood use and meaning of the word. In such cases judges traditionally turn to dictionaries, but Sinclair, who had revolutionized the making of dictionaries in the 1980s by creating vast databases, or corpora, of 'real language' from which to derive evidence about how words are actually used to mean, chose to use corpus data.

He based his evidence mainly on a five million-word corpus of *The Times* newspaper, although he supplemented this data by reference to the whole of his Bank of English corpus, totalling at that time some 28 million words – the Bank of English is now over 450 million words and still growing (see http://www.titania. bham.ac.uk/docs/svenguide.html). *The Times* corpus included 74 instances of *visa* and *visas* in the sense under consideration, of which over 50 co-occurred or, to use the technical corpus linguistics word, *collocated* with common verbs like 'grant', 'issue', 'refuse', 'apply for', 'need' and 'require', Sinclair noted that, although the commonest modifier of 'visa' is 'exit', it also co-occurs with 'entry' and 're-entry' as in the following examples:

- you cannot *enter* an Arab country with an Israeli visa stamped in your passport...
- British passport holders *do not require* visas...
- non-Commonwealth students who *require* an *entry* visa will *need* a *re-entry* visa, even if you only *leave* the country for a couple of days...

On the basis of evidence like this he concluded that:

> the average visitor, encountering everyday English of the type recorded in the corpus, would deduce that a visa was a kind of permit to enter a country. ... There is nothing ... in these examples to suggest that a person who is in possession of a valid visa, or who does not require a visa, will be refused entry. The implication is very strong that a visa either ensures entry, or is not needed for entry. The circumstances of someone requiring 'leave to enter' in addition to having correct visa provision does not arise in any of the examples, and the word 'leave' does not occur in proximity to 'visa(s)' except in the meaning 'depart'.

> (Sinclair ms)

This is an example of what can be achieved with a fairly common word and a reasonably small corpus and demonstrates very clearly the usefulness of a corpus-based approach, which is becoming growingly more popular with forensic linguists as you will see below. (It is rumoured that some judges are now beginning to search legal databases.) This example also shows that it is essential to have a substantial number of instances of the word in question and is therefore in itself a justification for the collection of very large corpora – if, for instance, one were interested in a word which occurs on average only once every two million words, one would ideally consult the whole of the 450 million word Bank of English corpus.

There are times when linguists are asked to give evidence on special vocabulary, perhaps coded drug words, occurring in otherwise non-incriminating utterances, but Gibbons (2003: 294–5) reports a much stranger case in which he was faced with apparently incomprehensible phrases embedded in otherwise normal language in a tape-recorded conversation – for example, 'I'm just so nervous of gepoeping epinsepide'. What the speakers were doing in fact was using a disguise well-known to many children a generation ago and often called 'pig latin' where an encoding nonsense syllable is inserted between every syllable of the word to be communicated. In this case the nonsense syllable used was 'ep' and once the expert had explained how the code worked the jury were in a position to decode the message for themselves and hear 'gepoeping epinsepide' as 'going inside'.

Sometimes the lexical problem may involve the meaning of a series of key terms. McMenamin (1993) reports a case which hinged on the meaning of the words *accident*, *disease* and *syndrome*. A child was certified to have died from Sudden Infant Death Syndrome (SIDS) and his parents subsequently made a claim against an accident and life insurance policy. Their claim was refused, however, on the grounds that the policy did not cover deaths from illness or disease. McMenamin successfully demonstrated, using medical dictionaries and publications, that a *syndrome* is not professionally regarded as a disease. Apparently a disease is 'a temporally bounded state between health and death' and those who have a disease either recover or die, whereas a syndrome is something a healthy child has or does not have and a child who does have it is either healthy or dead – there is no in-between 'diseased' state, so it was irrelevant for the insurance company to point out that the policy did not cover 'deaths from illness or disease'. In addition, McMenamin demonstrated that SIDS is treated linguistically and collocationally like an accident; so, for instance, the expression 'near miss' co-occurs regularly, and, of course, the parents were claiming against an *accident* and life insurance policy. The insurance company eventually paid out.

Levi (1993) reports on a lexical analysis of a set of jury instructions concerned with imposing the death penalty, which she undertook as part of an expert report in the case of *US ex rel. James P Free Jr* v. *Kenneth McGinnis* et al. She was asked to express an opinion on the question 'How well could [the language of the jury instructions] have served its purpose in communicating clearly to the jury the legal concepts they needed to understand for sentencing in a capital case?' (p.10). The instructions in question were (emphasis added):

> If you unanimously find from your consideration of all the evidence that there are no mitigating factors *sufficient* to *preclude* the imposition of a sentence of death then you should return a verdict imposing a sentence of death.

If, on the other hand, you do not unanimously find that there are no mitigating factors *sufficient* to *preclude* the imposition of a sentence of death then you should return a verdict that the sentence of death should not be imposed.

In considering 'sufficient' Levi focused on the inherent vagueness of the word. She pointed out that 'sufficient' has only a contextually derivable meaning and that the instructions themselves did not give an individual juror any help on how to decide what would count as a sufficient mitigating factor in the particular situation of sentencing someone to death. In addition there was real doubt as to whether a single factor that was perceived to be 'sufficient to preclude', but only so perceived by one juror, would in itself be 'sufficient' for the whole jury to be able to 'preclude'. According to the law, it would, but would it according to the text?

In considering 'preclude' Levi chose a different approach; she pointed out that, while this word did have a context-independent meaning, most of the jurors were unlikely to have known the meaning. She supported this assertion by testing some 50 undergraduate students who happened to be attending one of her courses; only three of these students were able to provide the correct definition. Her conclusion was that there were grave doubts about the comprehensibility of the instructions. Unfortunately, she does not report how the court evaluated her evidence.

Pragmatic meaning

Some cases require reference to the pragmatic rules which govern the production of coherent interaction. Grice (1975), in his seminal article entitled 'Logic and conversation', observed that one of the controls on speakers' contributions is the *quantity maxim*, which he summarized as

1 make your contribution as informative as is required (for the current purposes of the exchange);
2 do not make your contribution more informative than is required.

What Grice is concerned with here is the fact that all utterances are shaped for a specific addressee on the basis of the speaker's assumptions about shared knowledge and opinions and in the light of what has already been said, not only in the ongoing interaction, but also in relevant previous interactions. This appeal to what Brazil (1985) called 'common ground' makes conversations frequently opaque and at times incomprehensible to an overhearer, as we can see in this question/answer sequence from a police interview:

Policeman.   Why did you do it?
Accused.   Well he told me if I didn't do it it would be even worse for me.

It is for this reason that it is impossible to present truly 'authentic' conversation on the stage, because the real addressee of any stage utterance is, in fact, the overhearing/audience, who needs supplementary background information. Thus, there has arisen the dramatic convention of over-explicitness, which allows characters to break the quantity maxim and to say to each other things they already 'know', even things that are strictly irrelevant, in order to transmit essential information economically to the audience. This is a convention which the dramatist Tom Stoppard parodies at the beginning of *The Real Inspector Hound*:

> Mrs Drudge (into phone) Hello, the drawing room of Lady Muldoon's country residence one morning in early spring … Hello! – the draw – Who? Who did you wish to speak to? I'm afraid there is no one of that name here, this is all very mysterious and I'm sure its leading up to something, I hope nothing is amiss for we, that is Lady Muldoon and her houseguests, are here cut off from the world, including Magnus, the wheelchair-ridden half-brother of her ladyship's husband, Lord Albert Muldoon, who ten years ago went out for a walk on the cliffs and was never seen again – and all alone for they had no children.

When we come to consider a person who sets out to fabricate a text in a legal context, we can see that s/he is in a situation directly analogous to that of the dramatist – s/he is creating a text with the overhearer, such as a jury, in mind, and for this very reason is anxious to make the incriminating information that is being transmitted as unambiguous as possible. Thus, at times, the fabricator, just like the dramatist, will break the maxim of quantity, though rarely as extremely as in utterances B3 and A4 in extract 6.1, which is taken from the beginning of a fabricated telephone conversation, sent to the police after his trial, by the convicted defendant, Mr B. The purpose of the fabrication is to discredit one of the witnesses, Mr A, who had given evidence against him.

Extract 6.1

A1. Hello.

B1. Hello, can I speak to Mr A please?

A2. Speaking.

B2. Are you surprised I've phoned you instead of coming down and seeing you as you asked in your message over the phone yesterday?

A3. No, I'm not surprised. Why are you phoning me here for? Why don't you come in to see me if you want to see outside?

B3. Well you've dragged me through a nightmare and I don't intend to give you an opportunity to set me up again for something else or beat me up again and abandon me miles away as you did outside Newtown prison with the two detectives; and for your information, as you may know, I've filed an official complaint against you and the two CID detectives.

A4. The detectives and I beat you up and the CID they denied, they didn't beat you up but you can't do anything because you got no proof.

The over-explicitness in this case is comical, and it would have been comparatively easy to demonstrate that in court, but unfortunately there was no need for a linguist to explain Gricean maxims to the court, because there were audible clicks at the end of each utterance, where the tape recorder had obviously been switched on and off between speakers.

Over-explicitness can also be realized in the choice of noun groups. In a disputed confession attributed to William Power, one of the six Irishmen who later came to be referred to collectively as the Birmingham Six, who were accused of carrying out a series of pub bombings in Birmingham in 1975 (see Coulthard 1994a), there was frequent reference to 'white plastic (carrier) bags':

> Walker was carrying *two white plastic carrier bags* ...
> Hunter was carrying *three white plastic carrier bags* ...
> Richard was carrying *one white plastic carrier bag* ...
> Walker gave me *one of the white plastic bags* ...
> Hughie gave J. Walker his *white plastic bag* ...

Our knowledge of the rules of conversational composition tells us that it is unlikely that Power would have used the combination, *numeral* + *white* + *plastic* + *carrier* + *bag* even once, let alone three times. First, it is a noted feature of speech that speakers do not normally produce long noun phrases of this kind; rather they assemble complex information in two or three bits or bites. Second, this phrase represents a degree of detail we do not see in the rest of his statement. Finally, these particular details do not seem to have any importance in the story as *he* tells it and it is very unusual for narrators to provide details which have no relevance to *their* story. Let us compare the way similar information came out in Power's interview with the police, which has a ring of authenticity:

Power: He'd got a holdall and *two bags.*
Watson: What *kind of bags?*
Power: They were *white,* I think they were *carrier bags.*

It takes three clauses to convey the information and even then nothing was said about 'plastic'. Extract 6.2 taken from cross-examination during the trial, confirms clearly that, once a full form of a referring expression has been used, a speaker's normal habit is to employ a shortened version on subsequent occasions:

Extract 6.2

Barrister: And did you say '*two white plastic carrier bags?*'
Power: Yes sir.
Barrister: Whose idea was it that Walker was carrying *two white carrier bags?* Were those your words or the Police Officers' words?
Power: They were the Police Officers'. They kept insisting that I had told them that they carried *plastic bags* into the station.

Barrister:	Does *the same* apply to what Hunter was carrying?
Power:	I don't know what you mean sir.
Barrister:	I am sorry. Whose idea was it that you should say that Hunter was carrying *three white plastic bags*?
Power:	Well, sir, I said that.
Barrister:	But was it your idea?
Power:	No. They kept saying that I had already told them that they were carrying *plastic bags* into the station. When I said that, they said 'who was carrying *them*? who was carrying *them*?' They threatened me. I said 'They were all carrying *them*.' They asked me how *many* were they carrying and I just said *one, two, three, one and one*.

Thus the conclusion must be that, at the very least, the police officers expanded what Power said to make it fully transparent to another audience.

Tiersma (2002) uses similar concepts to shape a general discussion of the linguistic features of product warnings, on which the legal requirement is that they be 'adequate' and then uses Gricean maxims to evaluate the adequacy of some of them. He reports a case, *American Optical Co.* v. *Weidenhamer*, where safety glasses, despite being marketed under the labels *Sure-Guard* and *Super Armorplate*, came with a warning 'lenses are impact resistant but not unbreakable'. The manufacturers were sued on the grounds that this warning was not adequate. The jury sided with the plaintiff and deemed the warning to be inadequate on the grounds that it was written in small letters. Tiersma explains the decision saying that, given the nature of the warning, the labels were breaking the maxim of *relation*, because it is natural for a user, when faced with apparently conflicting messages, that is:

> the contradiction between the name of the product in larger print – [*Super Armorplate*] – and a warning in much smaller letters that the product is not unbreakable … to try to treat each as relevant [and] therefore conclude that [the] glasses will guard the eyes under all normal circumstances.
>
> (Tiersma 2002: 58)

While this might be a natural and justifiable Gricean-based conclusion, in this case it was not a true conclusion in the real world and hence the manufacturer lost the case.

Tiersma (2002) looks at the applicability of other Gricean maxims. In discussing one of Dumas's (1992) cigarette packet examples – 'Cigarette Smoke Contains Carbon Monoxide' – taken from a case where smokers were suing tobacco companies for not warning them adequately about the dangers of smoking, Tiersma suggests that this warning can be seen to be breaking the maxim of *quantity*. By not providing sufficient information to the smoker/reader, it not only presupposes that the reader knows that carbon monoxide is dangerous in small quantities, but also that the reader has the ability to work through an inferential chain to reach the 'real' warning, which is now expressed explicitly on British cigarette packets – 'Smoking kills'.

Prince (1981) reports possibly the earliest forensic application of a pragmatic analysis. It is a case where a 58-year-old cement worker sued an insurance company. They were refusing to pay his disability pension because they asserted that he had lied when he responded to four of a long series of questions on the original proposal form. One of the questions read as follows:

> Have you any impairments? ... Loss of sight or hearing? ... Loss of arm or leg? ... Are you crippled or deformed? ... If so explain ...

The insurance company argued that the man had lied when he wrote 'no' in answer to the question, because 'he was overweight, had a high cholesterol level and occasional backaches', even though they did not dispute his assertion that none of these conditions had ever caused him to take time off work (Prince 1981: 2). In her report, Prince approached the document from the point of view of an imagined co-operative reader who was genuinely trying to make sense of the meaning of the document. For the question quoted above she focused on the vagueness of the word *impairment*, and argued that any 'co-operative reader' would reasonably infer, given the content of the three phrases which follow the word 'impairment' and which in fact constitute the only textual clues to the meaning of 'impairment' in the proposal, that the word was being used in that particular specialized context to mean a relatively severe and incapacitating physical condition. The typical reader, faced with an unknown or unclear word, does not go straight to a dictionary, but tries to work out the meaning from the context. Given that 'impairment' was not specifically defined and that the examples helpfully provided in the question suggest a meaning for it of 'major physical problem', the examples are at best unhelpful, if not downright misleading, when one knows the meaning the insurance company insisted the word was supposed to have in that context. Therefore Prince argued that the man had indeed answered 'no' 'appropriately and in good conscience' to the question he understood them to be asking (Prince 1981: 4). The judge ruled in favour of the plaintiff.

The recording of interaction in written form – police interview notes

Some cases revolve around disputes about the accuracy of the written record of an interaction between the police and the accused. Converting the spoken to the written, as anyone who has attempted it is well aware, is not an unproblematic task, but, even so, most police forces have no explicit guidelines about the procedures to use and what could or should legitimately be omitted, even when the aim is to produce a verbatim record in the interviewee's own words. In this context it is useful to consider Slembrouck's (1992) observations about the production of Hansard versions of proceedings in the British Parliament, where scribes, who are similarly linguistically untrained, are charged with the creation of highly important verbatim records of what was said. Slembrouck (1992: 104) notes that:

> there is filtering out of 'disfluency' and other obvious properties of spokenness (e.g. intonation, stress). Repetitions, (even when strategically used ...), half-pronounced words, incomplete utterances, (un)filled pauses, false starts, reformulations, grammatical slips, etc. are equally absent.

In the typical police record the same rules seem to apply. For this reason the appeal of Robert Burton, *R* v. *Robert Burton*, in the English Court of Appeal in 2002 was fascinating. Burton was captured red-handed with several companions, trying to steal trailers loaded with £250,000 worth of whisky from an overnight trailer park. Until he was arrested he did not realize that his companions were in fact all undercover police officers. Burton's defence was that he had tried to call off the operation on several occasions, but the undercover police officers, who he had thought were real criminals to whom he owed a lot of money for drugs, forced him to go through with the robbery. Thus his defence was that the undercover police officers had been involved in an illegal action, 'incitement to commit a crime'.

When the case went to court, the police submitted, as part of their evidence, several records of telephone calls, which they claimed an undercover officer, using the codename Charlie, had written down from memory immediately after each of the conversations with Burton had ended. Paradoxically, part of Burton's defence was not that these records were inaccurate and therefore unreliable, as one would expect them to be if someone had been writing down what was said from memory; rather Burton claimed that the records were too accurate and therefore could not have been produced from memory. This would have to mean that the conversations had been transcribed from tape-recordings. He claimed that the police had denied the existence of such tape-recordings because they did not want to submit them in evidence, as they would have revealed that in these same conversations police officer 'Charlie' was indeed pressurizing Burton to commit a crime.

A linguistic analysis confirmed that either the police officer had an amazing ability to recall conversations verbatim or there had indeed been tape-recordings. This opinion was based on the occurrence of two sets of features. First, the appearance in the records of a set of spoken discourse items which are regularly produced by speakers, although they carry little or no significant content and which are therefore typically forgotten or at least not reported by those producing remembered accounts of what was said. For example:

1   discourse markers – items which typically occur at the beginnings of utterances – 'well', 'right', 'so';
2   acknowledgements of replies to questions – what some call *third parts of exchanges* – realized by 'yeah', 'okay', 'alright' and repetitions of whole phrases from the preceding utterance;
3   other kinds of cross-utterance repetition and reformulation;

4   fillers such as 'like' and 'you know what I mean';
5   adverbial modifiers like 'just', 'really', 'actually' and 'fucking';
6   slang items and non-standard grammatical forms like 'gonna'.

Second, and even more surprisingly, Burton had a marked stammer, which he had learned to partially control by the use of what speech therapists call a 'step word', a word which the speaker learns to produce automatically to disguise the fact that s/he is experiencing difficulty with the articulation of other words. In the case of Burton the step word was 'like' and this too had not simply been reproduced in the 'remembered' records, but reproduced in the kinds of linguistic contexts in which Burton typically used it. Many of these discourse features are exemplified and highlighted in bold in extract 6.3 from one of Charlie's records:

Extract 6.3

I said,   'You **gonna** take something heavy, do **you know what I mean**, to make things easier in there.'
Bob said,   'No, **fuck off, like** that's too much, I'll **just** have a blade, that'll do.'
I said,   '**Yeah okay**.'
Bob said,   'I'm **just** a bit jittery **like** as its getting close **like**.'
I said,   '**Yeah, okay** but keep in touch.'
Bob said   '**Yeah,** sorry about that Charlie, there's no problems honest, I'll chase that **bloke** up and find out what's happening whether there's 2, 3 or 4 there.'
I said,   '**Okay** we may have to do it on two to get it done by Christmas.'
Bob said,   '**Yeah okay**.'
I said,   '**Alright,** see you later Bob.'
Bob said,   '**Yeah** later Charlie **mate**.'

In order to test the ability of a group of lay people to remember conversations, Burton and Coulthard had a short, three minute conversation about aspects of the case in the presence of ten 'subjects' who knew that their task was to produce immediately afterwards a verbatim record of what had been said. In order to give the 'subjects' at least the same advantage as 'Charlie' would have had, they were allowed to make notes, in any form they wished. One of the ten subjects was a trained shorthand typist and she was asked to take down contemporaneously as much as she could in shorthand and was then allowed to go back and make any alterations and additions she thought necessary.

The subjects in the experiment varied considerably in their accuracy rate. As one would expect none of them could match the shorthand secretary in terms of accuracy of wording and most had significant problems with the gist as well – they all omitted and/or mis-remembered crucial information. For example, extract 6.4 is from a verbatim transcription of the tape-recording of the conversation, followed by the secretary's shorthand version (extract 6.5) and then by the version produced by one of the subjects (extract 6.6). I have indicated what they omitted in ~~strikethrough~~ form contained inside square brackets in order to assist comparison:

Extract 6.4: Actual

M. where were the meetings
B. there was a meeting at Kings Cross
M. yep
B. and there was a meeting at Chesterfield
M. were these night meetings or day
B. no they was during the day

Extract 6.5: Secretary's version

M. Where were the meetings
B. There was a meeting at Kings Cross, [~~yep and there was~~] a meeting at Chesterfield
M. Were they night meetings
B. No [~~they was~~] during the day

Extract 6.6 Subject 1's version

M. where were the meetings
B. [~~there was a meeting at Kings Cross~~]
M. [~~yep~~]
B. [~~and there was a meeting at~~] Chesterfield
M. were these night meetings [~~or day~~]
B. [~~no they was during the day~~] mainly at night, yeah

As you can see Subject 1 misses out the Kings Cross meeting altogether and wrongly reports the Chesterfield one as being at night. These findings robustly confirmed that it is impossible to remember verbatim what was said, even immediately afterwards – even when, as noted above, the task for the subjects in the experiment was much less demanding than that facing Charlie, because they had much less to remember and consequently a much shorter time over which to remember it before, starting to write it down.

The linguistic evidence supporting the claim that some of the telephone records were too accurate to be a record of a remembered interaction was accepted unchallenged, but the appeal failed on other grounds.

Narrative analysis of a disputed statement

There are times when the linguist's knowledge of the rules for producing spoken narratives is relevant. It is not uncommon for an accused to claim that a monologue confession attributed to him was in fact the product of a question and answer session during which the police officer provided much of the information. The 2001 appeal of Iain Hay Gordon against his 1953 conviction for murder involved such a claim:

> The whole statement was his entirely, in thought and wording … To give just one instance of what is typical of the whole statement, when he said 'Would you offer to escort her home?' and I said 'Probably', that went down as 'I offered to escort her home'.
>
> (tape-recorded interview, 2001)

Gordon makes a similar claim about the statement that was taken on the previous day, 'all this statement was in reply to questioning'. It was certainly not unknown for police officers at times to do exactly what Gordon claimed happened on this occasion. Chief Inspector Hannam, in another murder case, that of Alfred Charles Whiteway in 1953, explained to the court how he had elicited a statement from the accused in this way:

> I would say 'Do you say on that Sunday you wore your shoes?' and he would say 'Yes' and it would go down as 'On that Sunday I wore my shoes'.
>
> (Court Transcript, p 156)

It had been put to Gordon that he probably did not remember much about the murder as he must have had some kind of a blackout at the time and Gordon said he was persuaded by this. If Gordon's claims are true, one would expect to find in his statement not only traces of the language used by the interviewing officers and their structuring of the content, but also an unusual number of expressions of uncertainty about the facts. In extract 6.7 Gordon apparently confesses to the murder and disposal of the murder weapon, with items indicating uncertainty highlighted in bold:

Extract 6.7

I am **a bit hazy** about what happened next but I **probably** pulled the body of Patricia through the bushes to hide it. I dragged her by her arms or hands, but I **cannot remember.**

Even before this happened I do **not think** I was capable of knowing what I was doing. I was confused at the time and **believe** I stabbed her once or twice with my service knife. I had been carrying this in my trouser pocket. I am **not quite sure** what kind of knife it was.

I **may** have caught her by the throat to stop her from shouting. I **may** have pushed her scarves against her mouth to stop her shouting.

It is all **very hazy** to me but **I think** I was disturbed **either** by seeing a light **or** hearing footsteps in the drive. I **must have** remained hidden and later walked out of the Glen at the Gate Lodge on to the main road.

As far as I know I crossed the main road and threw the knife into the sea.

As we can see the majority of the reported facts have an associated overt marker of the potential unreliability of the assertion. This is very odd for a single author narrative, but of course quite natural for a narrative which has been constructed piece by piece out of a sequence of questions to which the required answer is simply an indication of the truth, probability, possibility or falseness of the proposition – i.e. such answers would be versions of 'yes', 'probably', 'possibly', 'no' – or alternatively expressing an inability to give a firm opinion – 'I don't know', 'I can't remember'.

The Appeal Court judges accepted that these linguistic observations cast 'a substantial degree of doubt upon the correctness of the officers' averments (sic)'. As a consequence they felt that the confession could not be used as evidence and that without it the conviction, which had stood for 48 years, was 'unsafe'.

The challenges for non-native speakers

a) Language comprehension

There are many cases when defendants claim that their competence in the language in which they were arrested and/or interviewed was inadequate. The claims can range from whether, on being arrested, they understood the caution or Miranda warnings sufficiently well, to whether, on being interviewed, they should have been offered the services of an interpreter. Although applied linguists have a great deal of experience in assessing the linguistic performance of non-natives, most of their tests are predicated on the assumption that the testee is trying to do their best, whereas in many court cases it may be in the interest of the accused to under-perform. One solution is to use naturally occurring interaction, rather than samples specially elicited for assessment purposes.

In evidence presented in the trial of *R* v. *Javid Khan*, Cotterill (personal communication) used an analysis of 21 minutes of police station CCTV footage of Mr Khan being interviewed on the night of the offence in order to support her opinion that Mr Khan's level of English, 'both in receptive and productive terms … would cause him serious communicative difficulty'. She cites examples as in extract 6.8:

Extract 6.8

Officer.	And your occupation please?
Mr Khan.	Er (?) Market Rasen (place)
Officer.	How tall are you Javid?
Mr Khan.	Sorry?
Officer.	How tall are you?
Mr Khan.	Sorry?
Officer.	*(Gesturing)* How tall are you?

Mr Khan.	How tall, I don't know. Maybe er 5 something *(gesturing '5' with hand)*, 5 3, 5 4, I don't know
Officer.	Did you say you suffer from a weak heart?
	(Mr Khan looks at the two arresting officers for clarification)
Officers 2/3.	*(gesturing at heart)* Heart problem?
Officer.	Have you got a heart problem?
Mr Khan.	Yeah I said somebody [unintelligible]
Officer.	You haven't got a heart problem then?
Mr Khan.	No, no, I don't have a heart problem

She notes that, despite this practical evidence and despite Mr Khan explicitly confirming his communication difficulties:

| Officer. | Do you understand English properly? |
| Mr Khan. | *(Mr Khan shakes his head)* Not properly |

he was not offered the services of an interpreter at any point. All too often though, the linguist does not have access to such relevant data and has to argue from present measured competence to supposed earlier competence.

b) Language production

There are times when the defence wants to challenge a police record on the grounds that some of the language in it could not have been produced by their client. Evidence submitted by two linguists in the case of *Regina* v. *Lapointe and Sicotte* (see Canale *et al.* 1982) highlighted significant linguistic differences between the level of English produced by two French-speaking defendants in tape-recorded interviews and that attributed to them in typed versions of confession statements. However, as we have noted elsewhere, police officers are not trained transcribers and even trained transcribers make notable mistakes when recording in real time, so the weight given to such evidence can vary from court to court. In this particular case the court, while accepting the observations of the linguists, concluded that the changes were not deliberate attempts by the police to alter the content of what was said.

McMenamin (2002) reports the case of a contested will of a woman who died at the age of 85 in Alaska, having been born in Japan and grown up in Hawaii. Her will apparently left everything to a couple of neighbours and was supported by photocopies of five letters on the topic of the will. These letters had supposedly been dictated by the deceased to a friend called Kim and later discovered in the boot of a car. Kim was untraceable, as were the originals of the letters.

The 'Kim' letters had a series of typical creolized English features such as the deletion of articles, subjects, objects and some auxiliary and copula verbs, as well as the omission of plural and tense morphemes. However, by contrast, the known writings of the deceased, although they 'evidenced some features of Hawaiian Creole English' (McMenamin 2002: 132), were much closer to Standard English.

In addition some of the creolizations found in the letters did not occur at all in the known writings. More worryingly, all the creole features in the suspect letters were deletions of grammatical elements, whereas McMenamin notes that there is 'no variety of English known to be defined by a single process of variation like deletion' (McMenamin 2002: 132). To add further doubt, the known writings of the deceased did include other creole features that were not simply deletions, such as mismatch between verb and complementizer and mass nouns used as count nouns. The reported linguistic facts and the derived opinions convinced the judge, who found that:

> the ... "Kim" papers were prepared by the [neighbors] or at their direction ... [and that] the language usage ... is concocted and a fraud.
>
> (McMenamin 2002: 135–6)

c) Cross-cultural differences in rules of interaction

One problem in native–non-native interaction is that the native speaker will assume that the non-native when interacting is using the same rules as s/he is and therefore linguists may need to explain the basis of the consequent misinterpretations to the court. Eades (2002) reports some of the problems Aboriginal witnesses face in English speaking courts. First, silence following a question has a totally different significance for the two speech communities. An Aborginal will typically pause before answering a question in order to show s/he is giving proper weight and consideration to it, whereas for an English audience, silence, particularly following a question in court, raises doubts about the veracity of the answer.

Eades borrows the term 'gratuitous concurrence' from Liberman (1985) to label another intercultural communication problem, 'the tendency of Aboriginal people to say 'yes' in answer to a question ... regardless of whether the speaker agrees with the proposition and [even] at times [when] the speaker actually does not understand the question' (p.166). (Those who have struggled to communicate in a foreign language in which they have low competence, will recognize this strategy.)

Eades demonstrates how *gratuitous concurrence* functioned to greatly disadvantage three teenage Aboriginal witnesses in a crucial trial where police officers were accused of unlawfully depriving them of their liberty. Six police officers picked up three adolescents aged 12, 13 and 14 in a shopping mall after midnight, drove them 14 kms out of town to an industrial wasteland and then left them to find their own way back. The defence was that 'the boys voluntarily [gave] up their liberty, while the police took them for a ride' (2002: 162). Eades exemplifies (extract 6.9) how the boys were frequently asked multiple questions, with the answer being assumed to apply to all components.

Extract 6.9

[L = Lawyer; D = David]

L1 David – let me just try to summarize if I can – what you – what you've told us. (3.1) You told us yesterday that the <u>real</u> problem wasn't anything that happened getting into the car or <u>in</u> the car but the fact that you were left at Pinkenba – that right?

D1 (1.5) Mm.

L2 Mm – that's the truth, isn't it?

D2 Mm.

(4.3)

L3 You see – you weren't deprived of your liberty at all – uh in going out there – it was the fact that you were left there that you thought was wrong?

D3 (1.2) Yeah.

L4 Eh?

D4 Yeah.

(3.5)

L you got <u>in</u> the car (2.1) without being forced – you went out there without being forced – the problem began when you were left there?

D5 (1.5) Mm.

Fortunately, at this point the prosecution lawyer made one of his all too rare interruptions, which caused a surprising and highly significant change in the boy's responses:

[PL = Prosecuting Lawyer; Mag = Magistrate; L = Lawyer; D = David]

PL With respect Your Worship – there are <u>three</u> elements to that question and I ask my Friend to break them down.

Mag Yes – just break it up one by one Mr Humphrey.

L6 You got into the car without being forced David – didn't you?

D6 (1.5) No.

L7 You told us – you've told us a (laughs) number of times today you did.

D7 (1.3) They forced me.

This and similar examples cited by Eades provide a powerful tool for linguists to contest 'confession' interviews in which the interviewee only confesses by concurring. Her observations and explanation were subsequently supported by Gibbons (1996) who reports a case of a recorded confession interview in which an Aboriginal suspect had concurred with proposals of his guilt offered by the interviewing police officer. In this case, however, the suspect also gratuitously concurred with the final question in the interview, 'Has any threat, promise or inducement been held out to you to give the answers as recorded in this interview'. This concurring 'yes' negated the evidentiary value of all the previous concurrences!

Eades (1994) reports another case in which she contested the accuracy of a police record of a confession to murder by an Aboriginal on the grounds that it contained 'an alarming number of precise answers with quantifiable specification', for example:

Q. When did you do this?
A. Quarter past four
Q. How long has she been your woman?
A. Three weeks

(Eades 1994: 122)

She successfully argued that such replies were 'most uncharacteristic of Aboriginal English ways of being specific – these she noted are typically 'relational, using social, geographical or climatic comparisons, for example '"When did that happen?" "Not long before the sun went down"' (Eades 1994: 122). In other words, although these two exchanges may seem unremarkable to a native speaker of Australian English, the responses are abnormal for Aboriginal interaction. Further than this the expert cannot go; it is up to the court to decide whether it is more likely that the evident unnaturalness is a product of very inaccurate and unreliable note taking or of deliberate fabrication.

Different language communities also have different conventions for the form of responses to polar questions. For instance, whereas in standard English the typical response to what is labelled, for this very reason, a yes/no question, for example 'Was she bleeding?' would be 'Yes' with the optional addition of 'she was', for a Portuguese native speaker carrying over into English the Portuguese response rules, the natural response form would be 'she was bleeding', with no 'yes' at all. Eades (1994: 123) notes that there are also different conventions in Aboriginal English. In the same suspect interview referred to above, a third of the replies to yes/no questions were in the form 'Yes' + auxiliary phrase, whereas this form actually occurred in only 1 per cent of the responses in an authenticated interview, which again suggested at best mis-transcription by the recording officer.

d) Language testing for immigration

One of the newest areas in which forensic linguists have been asked to express opinions is determining the nationality of people claiming refugee status. There is currently perceived to be a major problem of people applying for political asylum and falsely claiming to be citizens of countries where the political situation makes such applications legitimate under the 1951 Geneva Convention. Several countries have chosen to make language testing part of the process, but linguists in many countries have questioned the reliability of the current procedures and the professional competence of many of the testers.

Most criticism has been levelled against the Swedish Immigration Authority which, at the time of writing, delegated the work to two private companies, Eqvator and Sprakab, which have also done work for the Australian and several European governments. Eades *et al.* (2003), focusing on analyses by Eqvator of Afghani applicants for asylum in Australia, concluded that the staff lacked the expertise necessary to construct an informed judgement as apparently their main qualification was an ability to speak the language, not any training in linguistics.

Thus, the central question raised earlier needs to be reformulated: If carried out by someone trained in linguistics, is 'linguistic' analysis a viable way of determining a person's nationality? Singler (2004) argues: 'in some cases at least and with reformulation of the notion "nationality" to "country of socialization," it is possible to carry out [reliable] "linguistic" analysis', a contention supported by Maryns (2004). However both express the caveat that this is only possible when there is sufficient linguistic knowledge of a sociolinguistic and dialectal nature and warn that for some populations such data do not exist. Singler (2004: 232) quotes Eades *et al.* criticizing Eqvator's work on Afghan claimants

> because the firm claimed to be able to distinguish whether speakers of Hazaragi came from Afghanistan or Pakistan when, as Eades *et al.* observe, 'The border between Afghanistan and Pakistan has had very little linguistic study' (p. 11). ... So long as the fundamental linguistic work has not been done, it is not possible to determine whether Hazaragi in Afghanistan can be reliably distinguished from Hazaragi in Pakistan or in Iran, where it is also spoken.

Thus this is an area where developing the linguistic methodology and resources is in its infancy.

Conclusion

We have tried in the space available to give an idea of the diversity of the problems tackled and the techniques used by forensic linguists. The field is expanding rapidly as more lawyers become aware of the potential of linguistic analysis and readers are urged to consult the latest volumes of *The International Journal of Speech, Language and the Law*, particularly the Case Reports section. Details of many other cases not referred to above can be found in the further reading.

Further reading

Cotterill (ed.) (2002), particularly chapters by Berk-Seligson, Coulthard, Dumas, Solan, Stygall and Tiersma; Gibbons (2003, chapter 9); Levi (1994b); Shuy (1998, particularly chapters 4, 5, 6, 8 and 9); Shuy (2002, particularly chapters 3, 7, 8 and 14).

Research tasks

1 Japan is one of the world's major markets for whisky and there are many local and imported brands. Several years ago the makers of the Scottish whisky *White Horse* sued the Japanese makers of a whisky labelled *Golden Horse* for infringement of trademark. What linguistic arguments would you give the lawyers representing *White Horse* and what response(s) could the *Golden Horse* lawyers use to defend their client?

2 Below is the text of the will of a wealthy semi-literate unmarried Californian
   real estate developer. There was a dispute between his long time partner,
   Ms Carolyn Davis, and his relatives over the interpretation of the text – the
   question is whether the will assigns the whole of his estate, or just $2 million
   plus the house, to Ms Davis. What linguistic evidence and arguments can
   you adduce to resolve the problem? When you have reached your own argued
   conclusion you may like to read Kaplan (1998).

side one
THis is my will
incase something
Happens if I am
disabeled that I can
not speake or am
unable to do my
ability to speke or
Parilized Carolyn Davis
shall Have the full
wrights as my wife

side two
in case I die
this is my will +
I leave her $2,000,00
2 million dollars AND
my Home as 51 Monte
MAR Dr SUALito CALIF
This will is made out
on THis DAY FEB 18 1995
unless superseded
By a future will AFRE
THIS DAY IT STANDS AS
A LEGAL will

3 Collect a set of warnings from 'over the counter' medicines and household
   cleaning products. How clear are they and how much inferencing is required
   of the reader? What changes would you propose to ensure that the average
   customer fully understands the warnings and what changes would you suggest
   to the manufacturer in order to make the warnings proof against claims for
   damages?

7 The work of the forensic phonetician and the document examiner

The work of the forensic phonetician

The forensic phonetician is concerned with all aspects of speech as evidence. This ranges from the creation of accurate transcriptions of what was said, through deriving information about a speaker's social and regional background, to expressing an opinion on whether the speaker in two or more separate tape-recordings is the same. In addition, they help to design and interpret voice line-ups, which allow victims and witnesses to express an opinion as to whether the voice of a suspect is that of the criminal.

Transcription

Many court cases involve the presentation of transcriptions of tape-recorded evidence. The tape-recording(s) concerned may be of people talking about future or past criminal activity or of them actually committing a crime, as in the case of bomb threats, obscene phone calls, ransom demands, hoax emergency calls or negotiating the buying or selling of drugs. Very few of the transcriptions presented in court have been made by someone with a qualification in phonetics, although occasionally a forensic phonetician is called in, typically when there is a dispute over a small number of specific items, which could be single words or even an isolated phoneme. Sometimes the transcription problem is not phonologically difficult, and the original mis-transcription has resulted from the original transcriber hearing what they expected rather than what was actually said. So, for example, in one case in which Coulthard was involved, an indistinct word, in a clandestine recording of a man later accused of manufacturing the designer drug Ecstasy, was mis-heard by a police transcriber as 'hallucinogenic':

> but if it's as you say it's hallucinogenic, it's in the Sigma catalogue

whereas, what he actually said was 'German'

> but if it's as you say it's German, it's in the Sigma catalogue.

In another case, a murder suspect, with a very strong West Indian accent, was transcribed as saying in a police interview that he 'got on a train' and then 'shot a man to kill'; in fact what he said was the completely innocuous and contextually much more plausible 'show[ed] a man ticket' (Peter French, personal communication). Such mis-transcription problems can often be rectified simply by careful listening using a high quality reproduction system and earphones, but at times instrumental/acoustic analysis is necessary.

French (in Baldwin and French 1990) reports a much more difficult case, which appeared to turn on the presence or absence of a single phoneme, the one that distinguishes *can* from *can't*. Most readers, if they tape record themselves reading these two words aloud, will notice not one but two phonemic differences between their pronunciations of the words – the absence/presence of a /t/ and a different vowel phoneme. Using an educated British accent, at least when the words are produced as citation forms, the vowel in 'can't' is also longer. However, in an ordinary speech context, as in the phrase 'I can't refuse', the /t/ often disappears and the vowel is shortened, so that the phonetic difference between the two words is very much reduced. It may seem surprising that a language allows such a significant morphemic distinction, that is the one between positive and negative, to be realized by such a small phonetic difference and even more surprising that, at least for some accents in some contexts, the distinction may not be marked by even an extra phoneme, but simply by a slight difference in the quality of vowel.

In French's case a doctor, who spoke English with a strong Greek accent, had been surreptitiously tape-recorded apparently saying, whilst prescribing tablets to a drug addict, 'you can inject those things'. He was prosecuted for irresponsibly suggesting that the patient could grind up the pills and then inject them. His defence was that he had actually said just the opposite, 'you can't inject those things'. An auditory examination of the tape-recording showed that there was certainly no hint of a /t/ at the end of the 'can' word and thus confirmed the phonetic accuracy of the police transcription. However, the question remained, was the transcription morphologically incorrect; that is was the doctor intending and actually saying his version of 'can't'?

Auditory analysis of a taped sample of the doctor's speech showed that there was standardly an absence of final /t/ in his production of 'can't'. In addition, his 'a' vowels, when produced in words which, it was possible to deduce from the context, were unambiguously intended as either 'can' or 'can't' were virtually indistinguishable, even to a trained phonetician. So, whichever the doctor's intended meaning on any particular occasion, it had to be determined by the untrained listener from the contextually and not auditorily. And there would therefore be occasions when there was genuine ambiguity. It was at this point that an acoustic analysis became necessary.

A brief digression on the acoustic analysis of speech

Acoustically, speech is a very complex and constantly changing combination of multiple and simultaneously produced noises and musical notes or *frequencies* ranging across much of the audible spectrum. These sounds are produced by restricting and sometimes momentarily stopping the stream of exhaled air as it passes from the lungs, through the vocal tract to exit through the mouth or nose.

At this point a brief consideration of the physiology of speech will help. As we breathe normally air passes freely to and from the lungs through the *glottis*, a gap between two small muscular folds in the *larynx*, which are popularly called the *vocal cords*. When we start to speak, the position of the vocal cords is altered to narrow the gap between them and the pressure of the escaping air now causes them to vibrate and in so doing to create sound.

Any vibrating object emits a sound, or note, whose perceived pitch is directly related to the *frequency* of the vibrations – thus anything, be it vocal cords, piano wires or guitar strings, vibrating 262 times or *cycles* a second will produce the sound we have learned, at least in the English speaking world, to call middle C. The frequency at which an object vibrates and therefore the perceived pitch of the sound it emits, is a function of both its physical composition and its length and thus an alteration in either or both will affect the vibration rate and therefore the perceived pitch. If one were to take a piano wire and cut it in half it would vibrate exactly twice as fast and produce a note exactly an *octave* higher; cut it in half again and it would vibrate four times as fast and produce a note two octaves higher.

However, whereas each note on the piano has its own wire, speakers have only one set of vocal cords and so variations in the pitch of the voice have to be achieved by tightening and slackening the muscles and thereby altering both the length and the thickness of the cords and thereby the frequency at which they vibrate. Whereas boys and girls have similarly pitched voices, the male vocal cords thicken and lengthen at puberty and thus adult male voices have on average a significantly lower pitch than female voices, although there is significant individual variation, which means that some female voices are naturally lower in pitch than some male voices. In addition, in normal speech the pitch of the voice can vary within a range of an octave to an octave and a half, so there is a great deal of individual variation for the forensic phonetician to focus on, both in terms of the average pitch of a voice over time and the degree of movement above and below that average.

What we call vowels are literally multi-note chords, that is combinations of several separate pitches, which are produced simultaneously by modifications of the vocal tract, which thereby allow separate sections to amplify multiples, or *harmonics*, of the underlying base frequency vibration of the vocal cord. These notes or pitches are called *formants* and most acoustic analysis focuses on the first, second and third, with occasional interest in the fourth. Each vowel has a unique chord combination and thus it is possible to synthesize vowels by generating the component frequencies or formants simultaneously. Rose (2002: 237) notes that 'formants in the higher frequency region (formants 3 and above) reflect individual characteristics more than those in the lower frequencies'. The third formant is a good indicator of a speaker's vocal tract length and therefore of general physical size while formants 4 and 5 give information about a speaker's voice quality. These would seem to provide highly important forensic information but, sadly, all too often in case work it is not possible to extract these formants due to the poor quality of the recordings.

Much acoustic analysis focuses on the underlying pitch of the voice and on vowel formants rather than on consonant phenomena, although nasal consonants are forensically important because the relative rigidity and complicated internal structure of the nasal cavity 'ensures a low within-speaker variation … and … relatively high between speaker variation' (Rose 2002: 135). The output of the analysis can be numerical, as for instance in the observation that, say, the average pitch of a given voice over time is 124cps, or it can be visual as in the *spectrogram* in Figure 7.1 (p 150), where one can see all the different component pitches on the vertical axis and how they change over time along the horizontal axis. *Intensity*, or perceived loudness, is represented by a darkness scale – the darker the print, the louder the sound. In arguing for the use of acoustic analysis, in forensic phonetic work, Nolan observes 'in principle … the ear may be inherently ill-equipped to pick up some differences between speakers, which show up clearly in an acoustic analysis' (1994: 341).

Reprise

In the case of the Greek doctor, acoustic analysis confirmed the phonetician's perception of a slight audible difference between the two /a/ vowels in the doctor's production of 'can' and 'can't'. Acoustically this perceived difference was seen to be the result of the vowel in words intended as 'can' having a lower first formant and a higher second formant than the vowel in 'can't' words. This analysis finally allowed the doctor's disputed word to be classified as a realization of 'can't' not 'can' and thus supported the meaning the doctor had claimed he was trying to convey.

For another fascinating and unusually complicated transcription problem, this time involving the detailed acoustic analysis of an answer-phone message, see the case report of Jessen *et al.* (2003).

Occasionally, the quality of the recording is so poor it has to be 'cleaned' before it can be properly transcribed. Braun (1994) reports work on the Rodney King video, dating from 1991, which 'showed several (white) Los Angeles policeman beating a (black) person called Rodney King' (p. 217). The problem with transcribing the audio track was that there was the noise of a helicopter partially obscuring what was being said. Braun was able to use standard noise reduction techniques to remove most of the helicopter noise and to reduce much of the other background noise. Only then could she begin to try to establish whether there was any audible evidence of 'chanting of the words "run nigger run" or any racial slur of any kind' (p. 218) that King claimed had occurred. Although not all utterances were intelligible, even after enhancement, a large number were and these included repeated commands like 'Hands behind your back' and 'Get down'. There was, however, no evidence of chanting or of the use of racial epithets or other racially loaded words.

Speaker profiling

There are times when the police have a recording of a criminal's voice but no suspect, and are thus anxious to glean any information at all that might enable them to narrow down the suspect group. For instance, the phonetician may be able to derive information about the regional and/or social accent of the speaker and whether the accent is authentic or assumed. We have already mentioned in the Introduction one of the earliest high profile cases, dating from 1979, that of the Yorkshire Ripper where the forensic phonetician was amazingly successful in placing the speaker regionally, but such cases are not uncommon. On April Fools' Day 2000 a Second World War German Enigma encoding and decoding machine was stolen from a museum in Bletchley Park, which had been the home and offices of the war-time English code-breakers, whose daily task it had been to try to break the Enigma code of the day. A series of written ransom demands were received and then a tape-recording of a man speaking with a 'foreign', perhaps South African, accent. Phonetic auditory analysis suggested the accent was a disguise, overlaid on top of a British English accent and eventually an antiques dealer from the English Midlands was arrested and admitted to being the author of the letters and the tape.

Speaker identification by professionals

The vast majority of the cases undertaken by forensic phoneticians are in fact speaker identification; these are cases where there is a recording of a voice committing a crime and one or more suspects and the phonetician is asked to express an opinion as to whether any of the suspect voices does or does not match that of the criminal.

A basic problem to overcome is that there will always be differences between any two speech samples, even when they come from the same speaker and are recorded on the same machine and on the same occasion. So, the task for the forensic phonetician

> involves being able to tell whether the inevitable differences between samples are more likely to be within-speaker differences or between-speaker differences.
>
> (Rose 2002: 10)

Discrimination becomes progressively easier the more features or *dimensions* or *parameters* are included in the comparison, but even so some features are more discriminatory than others. The ideal ones to choose:

1 show high between-speaker variability and low within-speaker variability;
2 are resistant to attempted disguise or mimicry;
3 have a high frequency of occurrence in the relevant materials;
4 are robust in transmission;
5 are relatively easy to extract and measure; and
6 are maximally independent of other parameters.

(List adapted from Rose 2002: 52)

There are two major traditions for analysing speech samples – the auditory and the acoustic – which were associated with Britain and the United States respectively, although the consensus now is very much that a mixture of the two methods should be used. Britain always had a strong academic tradition in descriptive phonetics, with a direct line running from Daniel Jones (the model for Professor Higgins, *Pygmalion/My Fair Lady*) to A.C. Gimson, whose *An Introduction to the Pronunciation of English* (1962) was the standard text for a whole generation of phoneticians. Learning to be a phonetician traditionally involved much ear training both to refine the hearing skills and to become proficient in the use of the phonetic alphabet devised by members of the International Phonetics Association (http://www.arts.gla.ac.uk/ipa/ipachart.html (accessed 5 September 2007)). With this alphabet phoneticians can produce accurate transcriptions of what they hear, which can then be reproduced unambiguously by other phoneticians. The main uses of these transcription skills were in collecting pronunciation data for dialect analysis, in transcribing, analysing and subsequently phonemicizing the sounds of 'new' languages and in assisting speech therapists to diagnose and correct the problems of people with speech defects.

In the early days of forensic phonetics in Britain, speaker identification was done by traditional phoneticians using traditional transcription methods and focusing upon the realizations of a selection of phonemes and sequences of phonemes which seemed to be distinctive for the particular voice(s) under consideration. So the analyst would concentrate particularly on anything s/he thought might be idiosyncratic, like a lisp or a non-standard 'r' sound, or 'overcorrections' revealing an earlier accent which had been superseded.

Segmental analysis would usually be supplemented by suprasegmental analysis, that is by an examination of intonation contours along with rhythm and fluency. As French (1994: 175) notes:

> these aspects of speech carry a degree of individual identifying potential, as quite wide divergences may be exhibited across speakers from similar regional and social backgrounds.

In addition, the forensic phonetician may note impressions of distinctive voice quality using some of the categories proposed by Laver (1980) in his *The Phonetic Description of Voice Quality*.

In the United States the dominant tradition was the 'voiceprint', a label deliberately formed with reference to 'fingerprint':

> closely analogous to fingerprint identification, which uses the unique features found in people's fingerprints, voiceprint identification uses the unique features found in their utterances.
>
> (Kersta 1962: 1253, as quoted in Rose 2002)

However, this method, introduced in the 1960s, never achieved the same level of reliability as finger-printing. Essentially it involves the visual matching of pairs of *spectrograms* showing the known and suspect speakers uttering the same word(s). The visualization displays pitch on the vertical dimension, so the higher the pitch the further up the print it occurs, and represents intensity by relative darkness, so the more intense the sound, the blacker the print, while momentary cessations of speaking are represented by whiteness. The attraction of the spectrogram is that it gives a 'picture' of the sounds spoken, but the fatal flaw of the voiceprinting method was that it involved checking the degree of similarity between two spectrograms by eye.

The major problem with this approach is that there is always significant within-speaker variation, for example, if a speaker uttered 'the train' 100 times in quick

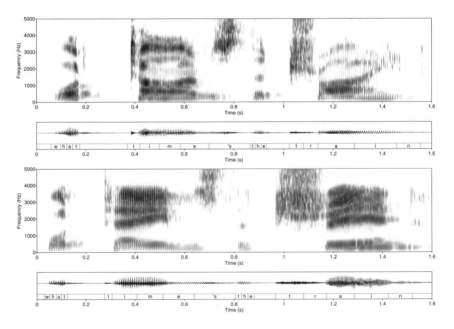

Figure 7.1 Comparison of spectrograms of two utterings of 'What time's the train'

succession no two utterings would be identical. You might like to spend a few moments trying to decide visually whether the two prints in Figure 7.1 of utterings of 'What time's the train?' are from the same or from different speakers. You will of course quickly realize that you do not know which bits to focus on, nor what weight to give to dis-similarities.

Both were in fact produced by the same speaker, but using different accents. However, neither of them is a disguise in the accepted sense, because both fall within the speaker's 'active natural repertoire, [that is] he may shift quite unconsciously between the two [accents] in response to perceived differences in the communicative situation' (French 1994: 172). Nevertheless, the two prints do look very different.

Critics of the voiceprint approach note that its practitioners failed to publish an explanation of the methodology (even when an auditory comparison was later added as an integral component of the analysis), and asserted that this was because there was no firm scientific basis to either of the components. The critics further observed that for the aural part of the comparison there was no evidence that the analysts were performing any better than an experienced layperson – they certainly did not have any professional training in descriptive or acoustic phonetics.

Despite this, Koenig (1986), after reviewing 2,000 FBI cases, stretching over a 15 year period, where voiceprints had been analysed, calculated an error rate of less than 1 per cent. Hollien, by contrast, claimed error rates of between 20 and 78 per cent in voiceprint analyses and reports that he has testified in court that voiceprint evidence is 'a fraud being perpetrated on the America public and the Courts' (1990b: 210). In 1985 a Californian court enquiry into voiceprint analysis concluded that 'there exists no foundation for its admissibility into evidence' (Rose 2002: 121). Despite this, voiceprint evidence is still admissible in some American States. Tiersma and Solan (2002: 231) note:

> as recently as 1999, the Alaska Supreme Court held that voiceprint evidence was admissible in a case involving a man accused (and later convicted) of making terrorist telephone calls.
>
> (*State v. Coon*)

The FBI, according to Nakasone and Beck (2001), uses voiceprints for investigative purposes, but does not permit the use of voiceprint evidence in court.

Given the obvious inadequacies of voiceprint analysis, some might argue for a purely auditory approach, but in fact, properly applied, an approach including instrumental analysis has much to recommend it. Indeed there is a growing consensus, supported by the majority of the members of the International Association for Forensic Phonetics and Acoustics, that forensic phoneticians should use a mixed method, with the detailed type of auditory analysis and a rigorous instrumental acoustic analysis reinforcing each other. This does not mean simply adding voiceprints to narrow phonetic transcriptions, but rather using spectrograms in a very different way, to focus not on the overall pattern, but on the acoustic make-up of (parts of) individual sounds and the transitions between them. In addition, one important feature which an acoustic analysis, though not an individual spectrogram, can reveal, is the average pitch of the voice, which when matched with information about the distribution of voice pitch across a particular population of speakers, can quickly indicate whether the voice being analysed is pitched unusually high or low and/or has an unusually wide or narrow pitch range.

French (1994: 177) exemplifies the use of spectrograms in a case involving a stammerer. He notes that there are two kinds of stammer, one called *prolongation*, typically co-occurring with fricatives, when the consonant is lengthened, and the other called *block*, typically associated with plosives, when the consonant is arrested. Spectrograms allow the length of individual sounds to be measured easily and so are ideal for such purposes. In French's case the suspect and the known sample not only shared the same two stammer phenomena, associated with two particular fricatives, /s/ and /ʃ/ and two particular plosives, /t/ and /d/, but also shared the same average stammer durations.

This mixed analysis method is not unknown in the United States; indeed an early application is reported in Labov (1988). The case involved a man from New York, but working in California, who was accused of making threats by phone to the airline PanAm. Labov's evidence was that whereas the suspect had a recognizable New York accent, the caller had a Bostonian accent, a difference which had apparently not been evident to the west coast lawyers. Labov presented both narrow phonetic transcriptions and a series of acoustic measurements to show that the criminal's accent was similar to that of a group of Bostonians and markedly different from the suspect's own New York accent. In the same case two other phoneticians were asked to evaluate some voiceprint evidence. The judge relied directly on the evidence of all three, which he praised for its 'clarity and objectivity', and acquitted the defendant (1988: 180, as reported in Levi 1994b).

Some people, worried about the possibility of human error in auditory analyses (see McClelland (1994) for a disturbing example of this), might want to argue that only the results from acoustic analysis should be used, but such results, unchecked by auditory analysis, can be misleading or even wrong. For example, acoustic output is very much dependent on physical features of the vocal tract and thus identical twins may differ only minimally in terms of acoustic output and may therefore be confused. However, Nolan and Oh (1996) report an investigation in which it was possible to distinguish auditorily between two identical twins. Auditory analysis showed that, while the majority of the speech sounds they produced were very similar, they systematically used a different phonetic realization for the /r/ phoneme.

Voice line-ups and Naïve Speaker Recognition

In 1933 the baby son of the American aviator Charles Lindbergh, famous as the first man to fly solo across the Atlantic, was kidnapped and later found murdered, but not before a ransom had been demanded and paid. Eventually the police arrested and charged a suspect. Lindbergh had talked to the kidnapper twice, once on the telephone, which in those days would not have provided a very good reproduction and once in person, briefly and at night, while handing over the ransom money. Some two years later when the case came to trial Lindbergh testified that he recognized the voice of the accused as being that of the man he had talked to. The defence set out to challenge his testimony and employed a psychologist to discover what was and what was not possible in terms of memory for voices. Seventy-five years on there is now a vast literature on how to evaluate the evidence of what the professionals call Naïve Speaker Recognition, ranging from the evaluation of individual abilities, through how memory decays over time, to the design of voice line-ups, which are the vocal equivalent of identity parades, to ensure that they are fair to both sides and likely to produce reliable results.

As a starting point Hollien *et al.* (1995) warn that the available evidence suggests that 'the witness who uses auditory perception for identification purposes does not do as well as an eyewitness' (p. 145). Broeders (1996) notes:

> there are indications that listeners may have considerable difficulty in recognising voices of familiar speakers (Ladefoged and Ladefoged 1980; Eisenberg 1995) and that voices are harder to learn than faces (Legge *et al.* 1984).

And then there are many other complex factors to be taken into account which affect performance, before one even considers how to evaluate a real witness's claim to have remembered and then successfully matched a criminal's voice with one in a voice line-up.

First, there are significant differences in recognition success depending on whether it is a familiar or an unfamiliar voice. Rose (2002: 98–9) reports experiments which show listeners being twice as successful in correctly recognizing familiar voices. Second, even with familiar voices, listeners make mistakes roughly one third of the time. Third, one cannot extrapolate from these scores for average success to the likelihood of a given witness being able to recognize a known voice, because there is massive individual variation; listener success in one experiment which was testing the ability to recognize 25 famous voices ranged 'all the way from totally correct (100) to chance (46)' (Rose 2002: 100). And then, as one would expect, delay has a growing effect on accuracy. McGehee (1937) reported 87 per cent correct identification after two days, falling to 13 per cent after five months. Also, voices heard only on the telephone are more difficult to recognize due to the degradation of the signal (Kunzel 1994). On the other hand, it appears that stress at the time the voice is heard can enhance memory (Atwood and Hollien 1986) and the longer the sample of speech presented to the witness the better the success rate. Thus, the general opinion seems to be that 'prosecutions based solely on a witness's identification of a suspect's voice ought not to proceed' (Bull and Clifford 1999 as quoted in Rose 2002: 100).

So, how should one design and administer a voice line-up? Nolan and Grabe (1996) describe in detail a sexual assault case for which they were invited by the police to help set up a voice line-up. As a first step the police provided a set of recordings, a tape of an interview with the suspect plus tapes of eight volunteers. The voices of the volunteers were examined by Nolan to ensure that none of them was markedly different from that of the suspect in terms of accent or voice quality; he noted that three of the *foils* (as the voices of non-suspects used for comparison purposes are known), were 'particularly close in terms of accent, voice quality and delivery' (p. 80). A major problem was selecting usable utterances from the suspect's taped interview; that is, utterances which were audible but in no way incriminating. Eventually they managed to extract six utterances, totalling some 35 seconds. Six samples of similar durations were then selected from the tapes of each of the foils.

Nolan then tested the degree of similarity between the suspect and each of the foils using a group of listeners, half of whom had some phonetic training. The listeners were asked to listen to pairs of utterances, in which the first speaker was always the same, and to rate the degree of difference between the two voices on a 9-point scale. Four of the foils were judged good matches, none went beyond point 6 on the scale and the mean was 4.5, which seemed to suggest that the listeners 'found the voices "similar" rather than "different"' (p. 85). However, just to be sure, the two foils with the highest distance rating were excluded, reducing the mean to 4.1.

A second test was conducted, this time with only female listeners, to check that there was no way in which any of the voices was somehow seen to fit with a female stereotype of how 'the voice of a person who might commit a crime would sound' (p. 85). Subjects were asked to rate all voices in terms of how likely the speaker was, *under some circumstances*, to:

1   risk his life to save a stranger;
2   commit a sexual assault on a woman;
3   nurse a terminally ill friend;
4   attempt suicide;
5   report a relative to the police for robbery with violence.

The raters felt it was unlikely that any of the speakers would commit a sexual assault and much more likely that all of them would nurse a friend and risk their life to save a stranger. The suspect was thought to be almost twice as likely to risk his life for a stranger as to commit a sexual assault, so it was clear there was nothing in his voice that conformed to a rapist stereotype.

At the time of the line-up the witness was told that she would hear composite 30-40 second samples of eight speakers and that the voice of her attacker might not even be there. She was instructed that, after each sample, she should say *yes*, *no* or *defer* and that she could hear any or all of the samples again. She listened, deferring judgement, to all eight and then to all of them again and then began to eliminate, until she chose the voice of the suspect. She afterwards said that she had recognized the voice on first hearing, but then listened repeatedly just to be absolutely sure.

In evaluating the woman's identification, Nolan and Grabe (1996: 89) note:

whilst a clear correlation between confidence and accuracy has failed to emerge in studies of visual identification, Clifford (1983: 212) writes 'in our voice studies we have consistently found positive and significant correlations between confidence and accuracy'. There is some justification then for taking into account the witness's lack of doubt in making her identification.

One of the questions which this very clear study raises is: on what criteria should the foils be selected and some of them later rejected? As Nolan and Grabe (1996: 92) note: 'the standard assumption has been that foils should be similar to the actual suspect', but they point out that an alternative, derived from suggestions for eyewitness line-ups by Wells (1993), would be to match foils to the witness's description of the voice of the criminal. If one matches foils to the suspect, the process depends in part on the skill of the phonetician to match the voices and the chosen rejection level for perceived differences, but this could result in an 'ideal' line-up consisting of a set of voices so close that identification would be virtually impossible. However, a problem with the alternative, that of attempting to match voice foils to the witness's description, is that lay witnesses find it much harder to describe voices than they do faces and 'exhibit a wide variety of subjective categories' (Künzel 1994: 48). He notes that, while

> in some cases witnesses' descriptions are so precise that the expert only needs to convert them into scientific terminology ... other subjects are unable to indicate any categories for their judgements.

Thus, what may be needed is some kind of voice identikit or voice profile questionnaire, which would use an agreed set of descriptors to elicit a characterization of the voice.

In another case report, Nolan (2003) includes as an Appendix a 29 item set of guidelines for voice line-ups, drawn up by a serving police officer for use in England and Wales and praised by the trial judge (pp. 288–91). As a result of his experience in this and the earlier case reported above, Nolan suggests an addition to the guidelines, a warning that the decision to commission a voice line-up should not be taken lightly as 'it is very difficult to achieve a voice parade whose fairness cannot be called into question for one reason or another' (2003: 187).

As an additional precaution, Broeders (1996) observes that, if there are serious doubts about the reliability of an earwitness, it is a useful procedure to have a first voice line-up from which the suspect is absent and only then, if the witness does not select one of the foils, present a line-up which includes the suspect. This, he suggests, 'will cause a positive identification to be assigned greater credence' (p. 7). Künzel (1994) reports a different kind of safeguard – in Germany the courts often appoint a forensic phonetician to evaluate the performance of voice witnesses.

Despite all these problems and reservations, Künzel (1994: 55) noted that '[Speaker Identification] by non-experts may attain a high degree of reliability under favourable circumstances'. And two years later, Nolan and Grabe (1996) drawing on earlier work by Broeders and Rietveld (1995), suggested that if, in an eight-member line-up, an earwitness makes a positive identification, the chances of the person selected actually being the culprit is 91.5 per cent. They conclude that 'a carefully carried out voice parade should, therefore, be capable of contributing usefully to the balance of evidence' (p. 77).

The work of the document analyst

There are two groups of experts on text analysis with whom we will be hardly concerned at all, despite their labels – graphologists and handwriting analysts. Graphologists are not, as the name at first implies, in some way equivalent to phonologists; that is, working on the written instead of the spoken substance of languages. Rather, the expertise they claim is the ability to link certain handwriting features to 'character' and thereby, for instance, to be able to comment on a person's suitability for a particular employment. However, as no one has managed to make their analyses replicable, we will not consider it further.

Handwriting analysts have much firmer scientific credentials. They focus on distinct letter forms, or *graphemes*, and on graphetic variation within each form. Just as there can be marked variation in pronunciation within the speech of a single speaker, so there can be marked variation within the letter forms of a single writer and handwriting analysts work on the assumption that, although there will be overlap between writers so that sometimes some individual symbols will be indistinguishable, taking the totality of the forms, each writer is unique. As Ellen (1989: 29) puts it:

> there is no practical possibility that one [writer] will resemble [any] other in every respect.

A significant proportion of the work is with disputed signatures, which for the analyst have the disadvantage of being very short, but with the twin advantages of being both well-rehearsed and frequently containing idiosyncratic letter forms. Davis (1986: 200) gives a nice illustrative example, see Figure 7.2 below, of a suspect signature set beside six authentic ones and notes that here the analyst would focus on such features as the relative size of capital and lower case letters, the overwriting of the 'o' in Naomi and the 'poor' line quality of the 'D' of Davis which is clearly not a smooth curve. Experience shows that:

> for copied signatures, a close approximation to the shape of the signature imitated will tend to correlate with a deterioration in the line quality, whereas if the copyist concentrates on good line quality – smooth curves, lack of tremor and a relatively rapid movement of the pen, then there will tend to be a perceptible divergence from the graphic shapes imitated.

> (p. 201)

Handwriting analysis suffers from the same problem of subjectivity that we have already seen with auditory phonetics, but so far it does not have a sophisticated

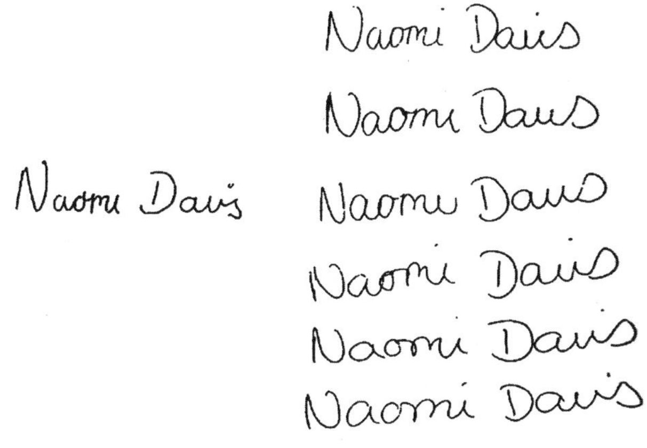

Naomi Davis

Naomi Davis

Naomi Davis   *Naomi Davis*

Naomi Davis

Naomi Davis

Naomi Davis

Figure 7.2 A comparison of one suspect and six authentic signatures

instrumental equivalent of acoustic phonetics to give objective support. However, as a first step toward an objective and replicable analytic system, Lafone-Walshe (2004) reports research into imitated signatures, which showed that imitations consistently differed from authentic signatures in terms of overall length and/or height. In other words, although good imitators could produce signatures that were indistinguishable on the basis of the individual letter forms, they were measurably different.

Even so, 20 years later, Davis's (1986: 198) observation is still true:

> the judgements of handwriting experts are largely based on experience and that experience has not, on the whole, been quantified and calculated; nor can it be wholly described in words.

For this reason, although the opinions of handwriting analysts are still standardly admitted as evidence in British courts, they are not accepted in American jurisdictions.

There is, however, one area of the document analyst's expertise that is not disputed, because the results are totally replicable, and this is ESDA analysis. Although this type analysis is not strictly linguistic, we chose to include it because of its high interest value and the fact that it frequently provides confirmatory evidence in cases where the forensic linguist is giving an opinion about authorship.

The acronym ESDA stands variously for 'Electro-Static Document Analyser' and 'Electro-Static Detection Apparatus'. It was developed by accident in 1978 by scientists at the London College of Printing working with the Metropolitan Police and trying to design a machine which would more effectively detect finger prints on paper, a notoriously difficult medium. They failed, but instead developed a machine which enables the operator to visualize the indentations made by hand-writing on a sheet of paper. This machine assumed great significance when it was discovered that it made it possible to read the indentations created by someone writing on other sheets which had been resting on top of the particular sheet being analysed, sheets which might no longer even exist. (For more details of the machine see Davis 1994.)

The forensic significance of the machine was first demonstrated in the case of Paul Dandy who was prosecuted for robbery in Birmingham in 1987. The main evidence against Dandy was two confessions allegedly made in interviews with the police – Dandy disputed the accuracy of those parts of the interview records where admissions were made. In the period when Dandy was interviewed, the police were working within a system which required them to record interviews with suspects in handwritten form, contemporaneously and verbatim. These handwritten interview records were later typed up, and normally it was these typed versions that were presented in court, although the originals had to be available for inspection.

For the production of the handwritten records there was a special first page and then the rest of the interview was recorded on continuation sheets, a pile of which was generally available in the interview room. Typically the recording officer would take a handful of sheets from the pile and start writing on the top sheet, placing it to one side when it was full and continuing on the next sheet and so on. In so doing, the officer, without realizing it, was creating multiple copies of each page that he wrote by creating indentations on the page(s) below – an officer using a ballpoint pen and pressing quite hard might make indentation copies on up to three subsequent pages.

In the Dandy case a disputed admission occurred as the fourth utterance on the eighth and final page of an interview. Davis (1994: 82–3) reports that it read as in extract 7.1:

Extract 7.1
[PO = Police officer; D = Dandy
PO. 'WILL YOU SIGN AN AUTHORITY FOR US TO LOOK
    AT YOUR BANK ACCOUNT?'
D. 'NO'
PO. 'I TAKE IT FROM YOUR EARLIER REPLY THAT YOU ARE ADMITTING
    BEEN (sic) INVOLVED IN THE ROBBERY AT THE M.E.B.?'
D. 'YOU'SE GOOD, THURSDAY, FRIDAY, SATURDAY, SUNDAY AND
    YOU'VE CAUGHT ME NOW YOU'VE GOT TO PROVE IT'.
PO. 'DO YOU WANT TO READ OVER THE NOTES SIGN AND CAPTION
    THEM'.
D. 'I'LL INITIAL THE MISTAKES, BUT I WON'T SIGN THEM'.
(end of interview)

A linguistic analysis shows that the third utterance is neither cohesive nor coherent – there is no 'earlier reply' that can be taken to be 'admitting been involved' in a robbery. Davis's ESDA analysis found the following indentations (Extract 7.2) on the final page of another handwritten interview record (square brackets indicate that the ESDA print was indistinct at that point and the word could not be deciphered with certainty).

Extract 7.2
PO. 'WILL YOU SIGN AN AUTHORITY FOR US TO LOOK AT YOUR BANK [ACCOUNT]?'
D.   'NO'
PO. 'DO YOU WANT TO READ OVER [THE] [NOTES SIGN] AND CAPTION THEM'.
D.   'I'LL INITIAL THE MISTAKES, BUT [I] WON'T SIGN THEM'.

The significant difference between this page and the one presented as evidence at trial is the absence of the incriminating two-part exchange, beginning 'I TAKE IT FROM YOUR EARLIER REPLY…'. Given the identical nature of the four shared utterances that can be clearly identified in the ESDA prints, this is indisputably an earlier record of the same part of the same interview, to which the incriminating sentences must have been added later. As Davis (1986: 82) notes:

> whether this was done without, or, as the officers involved were later to allege, with the consent of Paul Dandy, cannot be determined from this evidence alone. But the possibility of its having been done without his knowledge was strong enough to persuade the judge in his trial to dismiss the case against him.

This was the first positive support for the claims of many criminals in the Birmingham area that they had been 'verballed' by an elite police group known as The West Midlands Serious Crime Squad. Within hours of the dismissal of a second prosecution case, when the defence used the same ESDA evidence from the Dandy case to mount an attack on police credibility, the Chief Constable disbanded the Serious Crime Squad; 51 officers were suspended and lengthy periods of sick leave, early retirements and prosecutions followed. ESDA prints were also used in the successful Bridgewater Four appeal (see Chapter 9, pp. 191ff), when they confirmed Malone's assertion that he had been shown a confession by one of the other accused and in many other appeals which were based on claims that the police had fabricated verbal evidence.

Conclusion

Whereas the forensic linguist can make a lot of progress in many cases with a simple set of descriptive tools and little more than a pencil, the modern forensic phonetician is highly dependent on computerized acoustic analysis; indeed, their professional association – International Association for Forensic Phonetics – has recently added 'and Acoustics' to reflect this. What this means for you, the reader, is that while you can try your hand at some forensic linguistic problems, unless you have a good training in phonetics and acoustics and access to sophisticated software, forensic phonetics will be something you can only learn about by reading.

Handwriting analysis is more accessible, more a case of learning to discriminate, and while only those with access to specific equipment can create ESDA prints, the reading and interpreting of them is still an art rather than a science.

Further reading

Ellen (1997, chapters 2, 3, 5 and 6 for handwriting and chapter 9 for ESDA); French (1994); French, Harrison and Windsor Lewis (2007); Rose (2002) (chapters 2, 6, 5, 7 and 10, in that order).

Research tasks

1   As we have seen, the voices of identical twins can be virtually indistinguishable, but, at least on the telephone, it is also quite common to confuse children with their same sex parent. Tape record same-sex members of a family who you think have similar voices. Choose one as the 'criminal' and then design a voice line-up, using the other family members and adding extra voices, until you have six foils. Select three extracts, each seven to ten seconds long, from the recording of each of the seven speakers and then create a single tape consisting of the 21 extracts presented in random order and with a five-second break between each extract. Recruit a minimum of ten listeners. First, ask them to listen to a three-minute extract of the 'criminal' talking, with contributions by other speakers edited out. Then, after a delay of at least a day, ask your listeners to attempt to identify the 'criminal' voice in the 21 extracts you are going to play to them. Tell them the 'criminal's' voice may not appear at all, but equally it may appear once or more than once. Repeat the test, preferably after a gap of at least a day, and compare the results to see how (un)reliable your listeners are.

2   Tape record a professional mimic producing the voice of a famous politician or media person. Collect authentic samples of the famous person and of amateurs imitating the voice. Now set up a voice line-up as in Task 1. Are your subjects any more successful with the famous voice than they were with the unknown voice in Task 1? You may find it helpful to read the article by Schlichting and Sullivan (1997).

3   Take ten examples of your own signature, which were produced in a natural context over a period of at least a year. There will be variation. Following Lafone-Walshe's methodology, measure the total length of the signature and the heights of each of the spikes. Do this for all ten signatures and average the results. (You may find that it helps to magnify the signatures either on a photocopying machine or electronically on your computer.) Now select one signature, which is mathematically close to the average, and ask ten subjects to imitate it. How do the measurements of the imitations match up to those of the original?

8 Idiolect and uniqueness of encoding

JonBenét Ramsey Ransom Letter
Mr. Ramsey,
Listen carefully! We are a group of individuals that represent a small foreign faction. We respect your bussiness but not the country that it serves. At this time we have your daughter in our posession. She is safe and un harmed and if you want her to see 1997, you must Follow our instructions to the letter.
(Opening of letter as transcribed in McMenamin 2002: 185–6)

Introduction

The linguist approaches the problem of questioned authorship from the theoretical position that every native speaker has their own distinct and individual version of the language they speak and write, their own *idiolect*, and the assumption that this *idiolect* will manifest itself through distinctive and idiosyncratic choices in speech and writing. The term idiolect seems to have been used first by Bloch in 1948, although McMenamin (2002) traces the underlying concept back to the *Biographia Literaria* written in the early nineteenth century by the English poet Coleridge.

Every speaker has a very large active vocabulary built up over many years, which will differ from the vocabularies others have similarly built up – these differences will be manifested not only in terms of the actual items available, but also through preferences for selecting certain items rather than others. Thus, whereas in principle any speaker can use any word at any time, in fact they tend to make typical and individuating co-selections of preferred words. This implies that it should be possible to devise a method of *linguistic fingerprinting*, in other words that the linguistic 'impressions' created by a given speaker should be usable, just like a signature, to identify them. So far, however, practice is a long way behind theory and no one has even begun to speculate about how much and what kind of data would be needed to uniquely characterize an *idiolect*, nor how the data, once collected, would be analysed and stored. Indeed work on the very much simpler task of identifying the linguistic characteristics or 'fingerprints' of single *genres* is still in its infancy (Biber 1988, 1995; Stubbs 1996).

In reality, the concept of the linguistic fingerprint is an unhelpful, if not actually misleading metaphor, at least when used in the context of forensic investigations of authorship, because it leads one to imagine the creation of massive databanks consisting of representative linguistic samples, or summary linguistic analyses, of millions of idiolects, against which a given text could be matched and tested. In fact such an enterprise is, and for the foreseeable future will continue to be, impractical, if not impossible. The value of the physical fingerprint is that every sample is both identical and exhaustive; that is, it contains all the necessary information for identification of an individual, whereas, by contrast, any linguistic sample, even a very large one, provides only very partial information about its creator. This situation is compounded by the fact that many of the texts which the forensic linguist is asked to examine are very short indeed – most suicide notes, ransom demands and threatening letters, for example, are well under 200 words long and many consist of fewer than 100 words.

Nevertheless, the situation is not as bad as it might at first seem, because such texts usually contain information or clues, which massively restrict the number of possible authors. Thus, the task of the linguistic detective is never one of identifying an author from millions of candidates on the basis of the linguistic evidence alone, but rather of selecting (and, of course, *deselecting*) from a very small number of candidate authors, usually fewer than a dozen and in many cases only two (Coulthard 1992, 1994a, 1997; Eagleson 1994).

An early and persuasive example of the forensic significance of idiolectal co-selection was the Unabomber case. Between 1978 and 1995, an American, who referred to himself as FC, sent a series of bombs, on average once a year, through the post. At first there seemed to be no pattern, but over time the FBI noticed that the victims seemed to be people working for *U*niversities and *a*irlines and so named the unknown individual the *Una*bomber. In 1995 six national publications received a 35,000-word manuscript, entitled *Industrial Society and its Future*, from someone claiming to be the Unabomber, along with an offer to stop sending bombs if the manuscript were published. (For an accessible version of the events, from someone who, though not a linguist, was commissioned to write a report on the language of the manuscript, see Foster 2001.)

In August 1995, the *Washington Post* published the manuscript as a supplement and three months later a man contacted the FBI saying that the document sounded as if it had been written by his brother, whom he had not seen for some ten years. He cited in particular the use of the phrase 'cool-headed logician' as being his brother's terminology, or in our terms an idiolectal preference, which he had noticed and remembered. The FBI traced and arrested the brother, who was living in a wooden hut in Montana. They seized a series of documents, including a 300-word newspaper article on the same topic as the manifesto, which had been written a decade earlier, and analysed its language. The FBI claimed that there were major linguistic similarities between the 35,000 and the 300 word document – a series of lexical and grammatical words and fixed phrases – which, they argued, was evidence of common authorship.

The defence contracted a linguist, Robin Lakoff, who counter-argued that one could attach no significance to the fact that both documents shared these items, on the grounds that anyone can use any word at any time and that consequently shared vocabulary can have no diagnostic significance. Lakoff singled out 12 words and phrases for particular criticism, on the grounds that they were items that could be expected to occur in any text that, like these two, was arguing a case – *at any rate, clearly, gotten, in practice, moreover, more or less, on the other hand, presumably, propaganda, thereabouts,* and words derived from the roots *argu** and *propos**. In response, the FBI searched the internet, which in those days was a fraction of the size it is today, but even so they discovered some three million documents, which contained one or more of the 12 items. However, when they narrowed the search to only documents which included instances of all 12 items, they found a mere 69. On closer inspection, every single one proved to be an internet version of the 35,000-word manifesto. This was a massive rejection of the defence expert's view of text creation as purely open choice, as well as a powerful example of the idiolectal habit of co-selection and an illustration of the consequent forensic possibilities that idiolectal co-selection affords for authorship attribution.

Early interest in authorship attribution

The interest of linguists in questions of authorship is comparatively recent, but there has been a recorded interest in assigning authorship for over 2,000 years; for an excellent historical survey see Love (2002: 14–31). Davis (1996) reports humorously on an early unsuccessful attempt. He tells of how in Greece, in the fourth century BC, two philosophers, Heraklides and Dionysius, fell out and, in order to revenge himself, Dionysius wrote a tragedy, which he then presented as a recently re-discovered work, possibly written by Sophocles. Heraklides, who also had a reputation as a literary critic, was asked for his opinion on the authenticity of the work and, after studying it, pronounced that it had indeed been written by Sophocles. At this point Dionysius announced that he had actually written the play himself. However, Heraklides rejected the claim and stood by his initial judgement that the play was indeed written by Sophocles and produced stylistic evidence to support his attribution.

> Dionysius replied by asking, if it was genuine, how was it that the first letters of the [first eight] lines of the play were an acrostic that ... spelled P-A-N-K-A-L-O-S, ... the name of Dionysius' lover. Obviously, said Heraklides, it was a coincidence. At this point, Heraklides pointed out that first letters of the next consecutive lines of the play were another acrostic: they formed a couplet, which, loosely translated, went:

> Who says an old monkey's not caught in a snare?
> All it takes is the time to get him there.

> And … he invited his enemy to read the first letters of the next few lines … yet *another* acrostic: … 'Heraklides knows nothing whatsoever about literature'. When he read this, it is said, Heraklides blushed.
>
> (Davis 1996: 53–4)

In the next 2,000 years considerable effort was expended on attempts to resolve questions about the authorship of crucial religious texts, such as: the Gospels and some of the Pauline letters (Morton and McLeman 1964, 1980); significant literary texts, particularly some of Shakespeare's plays, for which there were other candidate authors (Merriam 2002); and of some important political texts, like the Confederate Papers (Mosteller and Wallace 1964) and pamphlets about the eighteenth-century British Regency crisis caused by the madness of King George (Clemit and Woolls 2001).

The first proposal to solve questions of authorship by accessing assumed individual linguistic regularities was made by de Morgan in 1851 in a letter replying to a biblical scholar, who had asked him to devise a way of deciding on the authenticity of a series of letters traditionally attributed to St Paul. De Morgan hypothesized that average word length, measured simply in terms of letters per word, would be writer-specific and virtually constant and would even survive translation (de Morgan 1882). The first person to actually test this hypothesis was Mendenhall (1887) who counted by hand the lengths of hundreds of thousands of words drawn not only from the Pauline letters, but also from works by Shakespeare and two of the major candidate authors for some of his plays, Marlowe and Bacon. While this measure discounted Bacon as a possible author, the word length scores for Marlowe's later plays correlated more closely with Shakespeare's histories, tragedies and Roman plays than did Shakespeare's own comedies: r = .9998 compared with .9986 ('r' is the correlation that is observed within a limited sample of $X_i Y_i$ pairs). Despite this apparent success, neither Mendenhall himself nor anyone else re-used or developed the method, although he had founded what came to be called *stylometrics*. (See Klarreich 2003 for more information about and examples of stylometry.)

As we shall see this was the first, but by no means the last time that a method for authorship attribution was applied to disputed texts without having been first tested for reliability on texts whose authorship was already known. However, it should also be mentioned that word length was one of only 11 authorship markers, out of some 180 tested, that survived Grant's (2005) rigorous reliability tests.

In 1938 Yule proposed *average sentence length* as a marker likely to discriminate well and Winter and Woolls (1996) report a study which combined this measure with one of *lexical richness* derived from work on the significance of vocabulary selection by Honoré (1979). Both of these markers were also among those approved by Grant. In the early 1990s Winter and Woolls were challenged by a literature colleague to distinguish between the individual styles of two late-Victorian authors who had jointly written a novel. Winter and Woolls were provided with neither the authors' names, nor the whole text of the novel in question, but simply 1,000 running words from the beginnings of the first five and the final six chapters (numbered 28–33). They were also supplied with the opening 2,500 words of a second novel, which, they were told, had been written unaided by one of the two authors.

The two features which Winter and Woolls chose as potentially significant, average sentence length and lexical richness, are interesting because, unlike word length, they are under the (usually sub-) conscious control of the writer. It has been suggested that one function of the sentence boundary is to act as an interaction point; that is, the reader allows the writer time to clarify a potentially contentious point, as I hope you are doing at this moment, until I mark, by using a full stop, that some kind of an end has been reached and then you react, deciding whether to accept or reject what I have written or to withhold evaluation until I have said more. It is a writer's decision how much to pack into a single sentence. It is similarly a writer's decision whether to have a long followed by a short sentence, as I have just done, because, obviously, I could equally well have chosen to make the short sentence a linked part of the previous, already over-long one. Thus sentence length is a reasonable candidate for a marker of stylistic difference.

A second feature that is under the writer's direct control is pace – just as some speakers articulate faster than others, so some writers cover material faster, and/or in a more varied way, than others. New content necessarily requires new vocabulary and thus the more rapidly a writer moves from topic to topic the more new vocabulary will be introduced. This phenomenon can be exaggerated by *elegant variation*, that is the decision to relexicalize while talking about the same topic and to use context-specific synonyms, for instance by replacing 'system' with 'category' and then with 'division' (see Johns 1994). What this means for the statistics of style is that writers can vary quite widely in terms of the number of new vocabulary items they introduce over similarly sized stretches of text.

Honoré (1979) is an early study of differences in vocabulary choice where he postulated that the frequency of *hapax legomena* (that is, words which the writer chooses only once), would be a significant measure of the *richness* of the vocabulary of a text. He produced a formula to measure this 'richness' – $100 \times \log N/(1 - V_1/V)$ – where N is the total length of the text in running words (tokens), V_1 is the total of hapaxes and V is the total vocabulary in terms of types. What Honoré did not realize was that he was conflating the measurement of what linguists call *open* and *closed* set (or *lexical* and *grammatical*) items. The problem with doing this is that the language has a comparatively small number of grammatical words which are therefore used very frequently – for instance the four most frequent grammatical items, *the*, *of*, *and* and *a*, make up on average 14 per cent of written texts – and for this reason the larger the text the smaller will be the *proportion* of grammatical words which are used only once. So, in order to allow texts of different sizes to be compared more reliably, Winter and Woolls resolved to measure only lexical richness (and not the richness of the whole vocabulary), and therefore substituted L(exical)V_1 for V_1 in Honoré's formula.

The results for the individual 1,000 word extracts are presented in Table 8.1. Both the sentence length and the lexical richness scores group together the first three odd numbered chapters, 1, 3 and 5, and distinguish them from the even

Table 8.1 Scores for average sentence length and lexical richness

	Av. sentence length	Lex. richness
Ch 1	33.3	875
Ch 3	51.4	913
Ch 5	43.2	810
Ch 33	30.1	928
Ch 2	23.6	765
Ch 4	12.5	624
Ch 32	12.1	709
Ch 28	13.9	832
Ch 29	19.6	785
Ch 30	19.4	884
Ch 31	15.9	822
Ctrl 1	23.9	703
Ctrl 2	14.7	735
Ctrl 3	17.0	693

numbered chapters 2 and 4. This suggests that a stylistic difference between the two authors was being successfully measured. When the results for the final six chapters were examined, the penultimate chapter, 32, was found to have scores comparable with those of chapters 2 and 4, while the scores for chapter 33 seemed to fit with those for chapters 1, 3 and 5. The scores for the remaining four chapters, 28–31, fell in between and this led Winter and Woolls to suggest that the two authors may have collaborated on writing them. Scores for the three consecutive 835 word samples, into which they had subdivided the 2,500 words from the other, single-author, novel, were comparable with those for chapters 2, 4 and 32, and therefore it was suggested they shared the same author (for more details of the analysis see Woolls and Coulthard 1998: 37–41).

Once the analysis had been completed, the jointly authored book was revealed to be *Adrian Rome* and the two authors Arthur Moore and Edward Dowson, while Dowson was also the sole author of the control text *Souvenirs of an Egoist*. An examination of letters written by the two authors during the period when they were engaged in writing the book, confirmed that Dowson had indeed written chapters 2 and 4, and that Moore had both started and completed the novel. The authors had intended to write alternate chapters at the rate of one a week. However, because of the dilatoriness of Dowson, the project took some two years and towards the end the authors met and worked together on some of the later chapters.

Coulthard (2002) reports using this methodology to compare the style of six 1,000-word extracts, two from each of three chapters in Sarangi and Coulthard (2000). The scores on these same two measures successfully linked the pairs of extracts and separated them from the members of the other two pairs. Clemit and Woolls (2001) report a study which investigated the authorship of two eighteenth-century pamphlets concerned with the Regency crisis. This study used not only a measurement of lexical richness, but also considered *hapax dislegomena*; that is, words occurring twice in the text, along with the proportion of core vocabulary.

The linguistic analysis assigned the texts to William Godwin, who seemed, from biographical and bibliographical evidence, to be the most probable author.

Cusum

Morton and Michaelson (1990) describe the first purely statistical approach to authorship to be used in court. The method revives the claim made by de Morgan that there are features of individual style, or more accurately 'habits', which are invariable across time, genre and even the spoken/written boundary. The habits Morton and Michaelson chose to measure are counter-intuitive to linguists who can see no reason why they should work, but then again it is difficult to explain why average word length measured in terms of letters should be significant either. Essentially, Morton (1991) used the sentence, rather than the text, as his basic unit of measurement and then calculated the frequency of occurrence, within each sentence, of variables like number of nouns, words beginning with a vowel, words consisting of three or four letters, or, most commonly, words consisting of two or three letters (2/3lw). Each of these measurements was matched against sentence length as calculated in terms of orthographic words. A novelty of the method was that the results were not expressed, as one might have expected, in terms of the percentage of words of a given category per sentence. Rather, a calculation was made separately, both for the sentence and for the variable under consideration, of the CUMulative SUM of the deviation of both from the average for the whole text. For this reason the method itself was labelled CUSUM. Graphs were then made from the resulting scores and one superimposed on top of the other.

To exemplify the method, let us imagine a text which has an average of 12 words per sentence and an average of five two- and three-letter words per sentence. The first three sentences are 20, 12 and 6 words long and contain respectively 7, 5 and 3 two- and three-letter words. The cumulative sums are calculated as follows: sentence 1 is 8 words longer than the average length, so the cumulative sum starts at 8 (actual words 20, minus average words 12, equals 8); sentence 2 is of average length, so the cumulative sum remains at 8, while the third sentence is a full 6 words below the average length, so the cumulative sum drops by 6 to 2. One then calculates the cumulative sum for the two- and three-letter words, for which the average for the text is 5, in exactly the same way. See Table 8.2.

Each of the individual Cusum scores is then plotted onto a graph and finally the two graphs are matched together. The assumption is that as habits are constant, if one is examining the same author, the graphs for the two measurements will shadow each other, but if there is a divergence this indicates that another author has contributed to the text. Morton used this method in criminal cases where it

Table 8.2 Calculating cusum scores

Sentence	Total words	Cusum words	23lw	Cusum 23lw
1	20	+8	7	+2
2	12	+8	5	+2
3	6	+2	3	0

was claimed that texts had multiple authorship, as for instance when police officers were said to have inserted text into otherwise genuine documents. Morton's claim was that the sentence and habit graphs would begin to diverge at the point where the insertion began and would resynchronize at the end of the insertion. In Figure 8.1, we can see how such graphs would look – here the two measurements begin to diverge around sentence 17 and start to converge again around sentence 23.

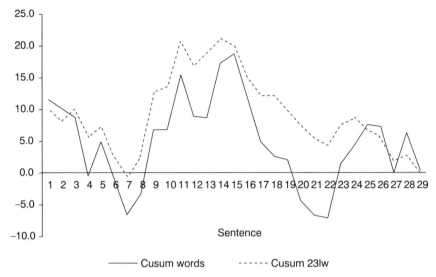

Figure 8.1 Cusum Graph – based on Grant (2005)

The fact that this method, which seemed to have no linguistic basis yet nevertheless appeared to work, was very disturbing for linguists, particularly as Morton would not or could not offer an explanation. Indeed, Morton's collaborator, Farringdon (1996), made an explicit comparison with fingerprint analysis, which, she pointed out, had been used for over half a century before the scientific basis could be explained and asked for the same kind of tolerance from the scientific and legal community for CUSUM.

Nevertheless, academic psychologists set out to test the method, with devastating results. Sanford *et al.* (1994) noted that the central assumption, that habits are invariable, is actually wrong; they found that 'variability within individuals … is as great as … variability between individuals', and concluded that the 'technique is based on assumptions which are at best of limited reliability and are most likely to be completely false' (pp. 164–5). Morton (1995: 231) totally rejected their observations, saying 'it is not my technique which they are examining', on the grounds that they had not applied the method correctly and had not produced proper cusum graphs.

Shortly afterwards, Canter and Chester (1997) set out to test the ability of CUSUM to reliably detect whether a text had a single or multiple authors.

They chose 21 texts, three each from seven authors, and used each text in three versions: first, in its original form; second, with eight sentences inserted from another text written by the same author; and third, with eight sentences inserted from a different author. The research question was how many texts would the CUSUM analysis correctly assign to the single and how many to the double author categories. The first results looked promising as all of the unaltered texts were classified as written by a single author; unfortunately so were all of the multiple author texts. Indeed, only three of the 63 texts were classified as having been written by multiple authors and all three of them belonged to the group of single author mixed texts. In the same year Hardcastle, a Home Office trained document examiner, concluded an evaluation of CUSUM with these damning words:

> The application … falls below the standards required of a forensic technique. It is clear that forensic scientists seeking a linguistic tool for the determination of authorship must turn their attention to other methods.
> (Hardcastle 1997: 138, as quoted in Grant 2005: 40)

Morton first presented CUSUM evidence successfully in the Court of Appeal in 1991 and three more times in the next 15 months, but success was short-lived, as there was an adverse court ruling in 1993, in *The Queen* v. *Peter Mitchell*. In 1994 Robertson *et al.* (1994), surveying the history of CUSUM in the courts, concluded that it 'appears only to have succeeded in obtaining acquittals… where the prosecution was unprepared to deal with it' (quoted in Grant 2005: 25). Even so, although Morton himself has not given evidence since 1993, some of his collaborators are still doing so, though not in the United Kingdom.

Specific analyses

The methods discussed so far utilize markers which permeate all sections of the text. Some methods focus only on a small number of items and look for differential use. Mosteller and Wallace (1964) report an analysis of the *Federalist Papers*, 85 essays that were published anonymously in 1787–8 and designed to persuade New Yorkers to adopt the new American Constitution. The papers are now known to have been written by three authors, Alexander Hamilton, James Madison, and John Jay, but both Hamilton and Madison claimed authorship of a set of 12 of them. In an attempt to resolve the dispute, Mosteller and Wallace assumed that there would be what we would now call idiolectal differences in preferences for the selection of a small set of lexical items. First they analysed a collection of texts known to have been written by Hamilton and Madison and selected items for which there were significant inter-author differences in usage. They found, for instance, that Hamilton used 'upon' some ten times more frequently than Madison, who in turn used 'also' twice as often as Hamilton. Armed with 30 such distinguishing preferences, Mosteller and Wallace considered each disputed paper. They ultimately assigned all 12 of them to Madison, a conclusion that coincides with the prevailing view reached by historians on the basis of other evidence. Since then, the *Federalist Papers* have been a favourite testing ground for researchers trying out new stylometric methods.

Matthews and Merriam (1993) and Merriam and Matthews (1994) report training a neural network to distinguish successfully between the plays generally agreed to have been written by Shakespeare and those by Marlowe. A neural network is a computer program modelled on the human brain which 'learns' from its mistakes. Matthews and Merriam trained the computer to distinguish between the two authors using ten function words plus a set of so called 'proportionate pairs', that is pairs of words which can be regarded as being in complementary distribution – where an author can choose one or other, but not both at the same time, for example 'all/any', 'on/upon' and 'in/into'. When the trained network was applied to the whole set of Shakespeare plays, *Henry VI, Part 3* was the only text attributed to Marlowe. As Klarreich (2003, vol. 164, p. 392) notes, 'this result lent support to the controversial view of some scholars that Shakespeare adapted this play from an earlier work by Marlowe'.

Kredens (2000) provides further evidence of the potential discriminating power of differential usage. In an examination of transcripts of press interviews with two British rock musicians, Robert Smith and Steven Morrissey, he found significantly different usage in three out of five discourse markers studied (ns = non-significant):

Table 8.3 Differential use of discourse markers

Marker	Smith	Morrissey	Sig. level
Like	14	0	.001
I mean	16	4	.009
Kind of/sort of	9	0	.009
You know	17	10	ns
Actually	9	7	ns

Mistakes and errors

As we noted earlier, all authorship studies work with some theory of idiolect; that is, the notion that all speakers/writers are unique in terms of their language resources and therefore in the individual linguistic selections they make. The problems for the forensic linguist are first, to know where to look for the distinguishing markers of the idiolects under investigation and second, how to evaluate and then present the findings. The investigations are thus essentially concerned with variation; both systematic intra-speaker variation and also the ways in which the idiolect of one speaker/writer varies systematically from that of another, while still sharing massive amounts of the language system. To give a simple example, one of the distinctive features of this author's email messages, when sent from an account which does not have a spell-checker, is the idiosyncratic spelling of 'the' and '-ing' as 'teh' and '-ign' respectively. Having learned to type comparatively late in life and imperfectly, he cannot now correct the low-level finger sequences that produce these mistakes. Even so, the majority of these items reach the addressee correctly spelled, because the texts are checked, but as eye-checking is imperfect, every so often he misses one.

At this point we need to introduce two new concepts – *mistake* and *error* – proposed by Corder (1973) to help categorize the problems of language learners. Both labels categorize deviations from the standard language, in terms of spelling, pronunciation, grammatical choice, lexical selection etc. However, *mistakes* are instances, like 'teh' and 'ign' above, where the producer knows s/he has deviated and will, if possible, correct the deviation and they are thus irregular in occurrence; by contrast, *errors* occur when the producer has acquired a different rule from that of the standard system, for instance the flower name 'anenome', which this author only discovered as an adult to actually be 'anemone'. Both mistakes and errors can be useful authorship markers.

Unfortunately, as McMenamin (2002) points out, 'unique markers are extremely rare, so authorship [attribution] requires the identification of an aggregate of markers, each of which may be found in other writers' (p. 172). Later he gives an exceedingly helpful list of all the 300 style markers which he has found useful in some 80 authorship cases. They are classified under the following headings: Text Format, Numbers and Symbols, Abbreviations, Punctuation, Capitalization, Spelling, Word Formation, Syntax, Discourse, Errors and Correction, and High Frequency Words and Phrases (McMenamin 2002: 216–31).

McMenamin points out that there are two major authorship questions that the analyst may be asked to answer. The first, a task which he labels 'looking for *consistency*', is concerned with whether a single text or a collection of texts have one author or several. If it is a collection of texts that is being investigated, it may be anything from a small set of short anonymous letters to a large collection of full-length plays, with the name Shakespeare on them. A second question is whether one or more of a known set of suspect authors might have produced one or more of the texts whose authorship is unknown – this McMenamin labels 'looking for *resemblance*'. Often, as part of the same investigation, the task may require first looking for consistency between the suspect texts to discover whether one needs to look for one or several authors, before going on to examine the resemblance between the suspect text(s) and those produced by the candidate author(s). In either case, McMenamin (2002) suggests, there are two approaches to providing the answer: qualitative and quantitative.

> The work is qualitative when features of writing are identified and then described as being characteristic of an author. The work is quantitative when certain indicators are identified and then measured in some way e.g. their relative frequency of occurrence in a given set of writings.
>
> (p. 76)

Consistency

McMenamin (2002: 77) exemplifies the qualitative approach with a case in which the questioned author consistently spelled the name Mary Ann as two words, as did his Suspect 1, whereas Suspect 2 consistently wrote the name as a single word. For the quantitative approach he uses a case in which the questioned and suspect authors both wrote a Californian zip code as Ca. 91001 and the task was to assess the rarity and therefore the significance of this format, by discovering how often these independent choices were co-selected in a corpus of addresses written by other authors. The results showed that the version Ca. – as opposed to alternatives like CA, CA., Ca, ca and ca. – occurred in 11 per cent of the 686 addresses examined, while the choice of two spaces between the letters and the numbers, as opposed to zero or one space or no numbers at all, occurred in 9 per cent of addresses. He then calculated that the two independent choices – 'Ca' and 'two spaces following the letters' – were co-selected very rarely, in fact in only 1 per cent of all addresses.

Resemblance

In an ideal forensic world there would be a substantial amount of known text to work with, either a long single text or a series of shorter texts which had already been shown to be consistent, and in addition a large collection of relevant comparable pre-crime texts produced by the suspect(s). However, the forensic world is rarely ideal and the texts are often unhelpfully short. McMenamin (2002: 181–205) exemplifies a resemblance analysis with a very detailed, 25-page treatment of the linguistic evidence in the famous 1996 JonBenét Ramsey murder case.

The facts of the case are as follows. Six-year-old JonBenét disappeared and was later found dead in the basement of the family home, but only after a three page, 370 word, ransom note had been discovered in the house. Both her parents became murder suspects and McMenamin was asked to compare the ransom note with a set of their writings. An analysis of the ransom note revealed a series of idiosyncratic spellings, word divisions and ways of writing sums of money – for example, *bussiness, posession; un harmed, out smart*; S|| (this indicates that $ was written as an S with two vertical lines) *118,000.00,* S|| *100* – which McMenamin felt were collectively likely to be distinctive. As the samples of comparable text from the suspects was limited to a few 'personal notes, calendar entries and letters', McMenamin decided to elicit 'rich' data by first dictating the text of the ransom letter to the suspects and then at a later date getting them to copy their own version of the dictated letter, hoping in this way to circumvent any possible attempts at disguise. Looking at these orthographic differences *qualitatively*, he found 15 stylistic differences between the ransom note and the father's versions and 18 between the note and the mother's versions, and he noted that these differences were consistent with their usage in their pre-crime writings.

In order to approach the question *quantitatively*, which he conceptualized as:

> how many writers in a representative population have the profile of joint occurrence of all the style variables identified in the questioned letter

(2002: 195)

he compared the style features of the ransom note with a corpus of 338 typed and handwritten texts from the American Writing Project. He isolated six variables for analysis because they occurred frequently in the comparison corpus and were ones on which Mrs Ramsey, who still remained a suspect, differed from the ransom note and calculated that the likelihood of all six co-occurring in the same text by chance was less than one in 10,000. Thus, he argued, both qualitative and quantitative measures supported the opinion that neither Mr nor Mrs Ramsey had written the ransom note. Eagleson (1994) reports a similar kind of analysis of a letter supposedly written by a wife who had disappeared and was presumed dead. Eagleson concluded that the husband had written the letter. The husband was charged with murder and eventually convicted of manslaughter; he later admitted to having written the letter.

A case report

It is not unusual for the expert to use more than one approach. Here is such a case, which also illustrates two more approaches to those texts where there is a doubt about internal consistency, in other words where it is possible that there was multiple authorship.

In November 1952 two teenagers, Derek Bentley aged 19 and Chris Craig aged 16, were seen climbing up onto the roof of a London warehouse. The police were called and surrounded the building and three unarmed officers climbed up onto the roof to arrest the boys. Bentley immediately surrendered; Craig started shooting, wounding one policeman and killing a second. Bentley was jointly charged with murder. The trial, which lasted only two days, took place five weeks later and both were found guilty, even though Bentley had been under arrest for some considerable time when the officer was killed. Craig, because he was legally a minor, was sentenced to life imprisonment; Bentley was sentenced to death and executed shortly afterwards. Bentley's family fought for a generation to overturn the guilty verdict and were eventually successful 46 years later, in the summer of 1998. The evidence which was the basis for both Bentley's conviction and the successful appeal was in large part linguistic.

In the original trial the problem for the prosecution, in making the case against Bentley, was to demonstrate that he could indeed be guilty of murder despite being under arrest when the murder was committed. At this point it would be useful to read the statement which, it was claimed, Bentley dictated shortly after his arrest. It is presented below as Extract 8.1; the only changes we have introduced, to facilitate commentary are: to number the sentences for ease of reference, to highlight negative clauses with bold and to put occurrences of 'then' in italic.

Bentley's barrister spelled out for the jury the two necessary pre-conditions for them to convict: they must be 'satisfied and sure'

   i) that [Bentley] knew Craig had a gun and
   ii) that he instigated or incited Craig to use it.

(Trow 1992: 179)

The evidence adduced by the prosecution to satisfy the jury on both points was linguistic. For point i) it was observed that in his statement, which purported to give his unaided account of the night's events, Bentley had said 'I did not know he was going to use the gun' (sentence 23). In his summing up, the judge who, because of the importance of the case was the Lord Chief Justice, made great play with this sentence, telling the jury that its positioning in the narrative of events, before the time when there was a single policeman on the roof, combined with the choice of '*the* gun' (as opposed to 'a gun'), must imply that Bentley knew that Craig had a gun well before it was used. In other words 'the gun', given its position in the statement, must be taken to mean 'the gun I already knew at this point in the narrative that Craig had'. In addition, his Lordship suggested, this sentence also showed Bentley to be an unreliable witness, because he contradicted himself later, in sentence 41, by saying 'I did not know Chris had [a gun] until he shot'.

The evidence used to support point ii), that Bentley had instigated Craig to shoot, was that the police officers in their statements and in their evidence given in court, asserted that Bentley had uttered the words 'Let him have it, Chris' immediately before Craig had shot and killed the policeman. As the judge emphasized, the strength of the linguistic evidence depended essentially on the credibility of the police officers who had recorded it and sworn to its accuracy. When the case came to appeal in 1998, one of the defence strategies was to challenge the reliability of the statement. If they could throw doubt on the veracity of the police, they could mitigate the incriminating force of both the statement and the phrase 'Let him have it' which Bentley, supported by Craig, had denied uttering, a claim that was reinforced much later by a fourth policeman, who was never called to give evidence at the original trial.

Extract 8.1 Derek Bentley's statement

> (1) I have known Craig since I went to school. (2) We were stopped by our parents going out together, but we still continued going out with each other – I mean **we have not gone out** together until tonight. (3) I was watching television tonight (2 November 1952) and between 8 p.m. and 9 p.m. Craig called for me. (4) My mother answered the door and I heard her say that I was out. (5) I had been out earlier to the pictures and got home just after 7 p.m. (6) A little later Norman Parsley and Frank Fasey called. (7) **I did not answer the door or speak to them.** (8) My mother told me that they had called and I *then* ran out after them. (9) I walked up the road with them to the paper shop where I saw Craig standing. (10) We all talked together and *then* Norman Parsley and Frank Fazey left. (11) Chris Craig and I *then* caught a bus to Croydon. (12) We got off at West Croydon and *then* walked down the road where the toilets are – I think it is Tamworth Road.
>
> (13) When we came to the place where you found me, Chris looked in the window. (14) There was a little iron gate at the side. (15) Chris *then* jumped over and I followed. (16) Chris *then* climbed up the drainpipe to the roof and I

followed. (17) Up to *then* **Chris had not said anything.** (18) We both got out on to the flat roof at the top. (19) *Then* someone in a garden on the opposite side shone a torch up towards us. (20) Chris said: 'It's a copper, hide behind here.' (21) We hid behind a shelter arrangement on the roof. (22) We were there waiting for about ten minutes. (23) **I did not know** he was going to use the gun. (24) A plain clothes man climbed up the drainpipe and on to the roof. (25) The man said: 'I am a police officer – the place is surrounded.' (26) He caught hold of me and as we walked away Chris fired. (27) **There was nobody else** there at the time. (28) The policeman and I *then* went round a corner by a door. (29) A little later the door opened and a policeman in uniform came out. (30) Chris fired again *then* and this policeman fell down. (31) I could see that he was hurt as a lot of blood came from his forehead just above his nose. (32) The policeman dragged him round the corner behind the brickwork entrance to the door. (33) I remember I shouted something but I forgot what it was. (34) **I could not see** Chris when I shouted to him – he was behind a wall. (35) I heard some more policemen behind the door and the policeman with me said: **'I don't think** he has many more bullets left.' (36) Chris shouted 'Oh yes I have' and he fired again. (37) I think I heard him fire three times altogether. (38) The policeman *then* pushed me down the stairs and **I did not see** any more. (39) I knew we were going to break into the place. (40) **I did not know** what we were going to get – just anything that was going. (41) **I did not have** a gun and **I did not know** Chris had one until he shot. (42) I now know that the policeman in uniform that was shot is dead. (43) I should have mentioned that after the plain clothes policeman got up the drainpipe and arrested me, another policeman in uniform followed and I heard someone call him 'Mac'. (44) He was with us when the other policeman was killed.

a) Single or multiple narrators

At the time of Bentley's arrest the police were allowed to collect verbal evidence from those accused of a crime in two ways: by interview, when they were supposed to record contemporaneously, verbatim and in longhand, both their own questions and the replies they elicited; and by statement, when the accused was invited to write down, or, if s/he so preferred, to dictate to a police officer, their version of events. During statement-taking the police officers were supposed not to ask substantive questions.

At the trial three police officers swore on oath that Bentley's statement was the product of unaided monologue dictation, whereas Bentley asserted that it was, in part at least, the product of dialogue, and that police questions and his replies to them had been conflated and reported as monologue. There is no doubt that this procedure was at that time sometimes used for producing statements. As mention on p 136 senior police officer, involved in another murder case a year later, explained to the Court how he had himself elicited a statement from another accused in exactly this way:

I would say 'Do you say on that Sunday you wore your shoes?' and he would say 'Yes' and it would go down as 'On that Sunday I wore my shoes'.

(Hannam 1953: 156)

There are many linguistic features which suggest that Bentley's statement is not, as claimed by the police, a verbatim record (see Coulthard 1993 for a detailed discussion). Here we focus only on evidence that the statement was indeed, at least in part, produced by dialogue being converted into monologue. First, the final four sentences of the statement:

(39) I knew we were going to break into the place. (40) I did not know what we were going to get - just anything that was going. (41) I did not have a gun and I did not know Chris had one until he shot. (42) I now know that the policeman in uniform that was shot is dead,

constitute some kind of meta-narrative whose presence and form are most easily explained as the result of a series of clarificatory questions about Bentley's knowledge at particular points in the narrative. In searching for evidence of multiple voices elsewhere in the statement we must realize that there will always be some transformations of Q–A which will be indistinguishable from authentic dictated monologue. In the Hannam example quoted above, had we not been told that 'On that Sunday I wore my shoes' was a reduction from a Q–A, we would have had some difficulty in deducing it, although the pre-posed adverbial 'On that Sunday' is certainly a little odd.

We can begin our search for clues with the initial observation that narratives, particularly narratives of murder, are essentially accounts of what happened and to a lesser extent what was known or perceived by the narrator and thus reports of what did *not* happen or was *not* known are rare and special. There is, after all, an infinite number of things that did not happen and thus the teller needs to have some special justification for reporting any of them to the listener, in other words there must be some evident or stated reason for them being newsworthy. (See Pagano (1994) for a discussion of the function of negative clauses in texts.)

We can see typical examples of 'normal' usage of negative reports in the sentences below which are taken from a crucial confession statement in another famous case, that of the Bridgewater Four, which is discussed in detail in Chapter 9.

i)   Micky dumped the property but **I didn't know where**.
ii) Micky Hickey drove the van away, **I don't know where he went** to
iii) **We didn't all go together**, me and Vinny walked down first.

(Molloy's statement)

In examples, i) and ii) the second negative clause functions as a *denial* of an inference which the listener could otherwise have reasonably derived from the first clause. Example iii) is similar, but this time it is a denial of an inference which the narrator guesses the listener might have made, as there is no textual basis for the inference. In other words such negatives are an integral part of the ongoing narrative. We find examples of negatives being used in a similar way in Bentley's statement:

(6) A little later Norman Parsley and Frank Fasey called.
(7) **I did not answer the door or speak to them**

When Bentley reported that his friends had called, the listener would reasonably expect him to have at least talked to them and therefore again there is a quite natural denial of a reasonable expectation. Similarly

(38) The policeman then pushed me down the stairs and **I did not see** any more

where the negative explains the end of the narrative of events; in other words 'not seeing anything more' has a clear narrative relevance.

However, there are some negatives in Bentley's statement which have no such narrative justification, like sentence (17) below:

(16) Chris then climbed up the drainpipe to the roof and I followed.
(17) Up to then **Chris had not said anything**.
(18) We both got out on to the flat roof at the top.

Chris is not reported as beginning to talk once they have got out onto the roof, nor is his silence contrasted with anyone else's talking, nor is it made significant in any other way later in the narrative. A similarly unwarranted example is:

(26) He caught hold of me and as we walked away Chris fired.
(27) **There was nobody else** there at the time.
(28) The policeman and I then went round a corner by a door.

None of the possible inferences from this denial seem to make narrative sense here – that is, that as a result of there being no one else there (i) it must be the policeman that Craig was firing at, or (ii) that it must be Craig who was doing the firing, or (iii) that immediately afterwards there would be more people on the roof. So, the most reasonable explanation for the negatives in these two examples is that, at this point in the statement-taking process, a policeman asked a clarificatory question to which the answer was negative and the whole sequence was then recorded as a negative statement. The fact that some of Bentley's statement may have been elicited in this way becomes particularly important in relation to sentence (23):

(23) **I did not know** he was going to use the gun

which is the one singled out by the judge as incriminating. This sentence too would only make narrative sense if it were linked backwards or forwards to the use of a gun – in other words if it was placed immediately preceding or following the report of a shot. However, the actual context is:

> (22) We were there waiting for about ten minutes.
> (23) **I did not know** he was going to use the gun.
> (24) A plain clothes man climbed up the drainpipe and on to the roof.

If it is accepted that there were question/answer sequences underlying Bentley's statement, it follows that the logic and the sequencing of the information were not under his direct control. Thus, the placing of the reporting of at least some of the crucial events must depend on decisions made by the police questioner to ask his questions at those points, rather than on Bentley's reconstruction of the narrative sequence. And so, crucially, that inference drawn by the judge in his summing up was unjustified. If sentence (23) is the product of a response to a police question, with its placing determined by the interrogating officer, there is no longer any conflict with Bentley's later denial: 'I did not know Chris had one [a gun] until he shot'. Neither is there any significance to be attached to Bentley saying '*the* gun'. All interaction uses language loosely and co-operatively and so, if the policeman had asked Bentley about '*the* gun', Bentley would have assumed they both knew which gun they were talking about. In that context the sensible interpretation would be 'the gun that had been used earlier that evening' and not 'the gun that was going to be used later in the evening' in the sequence of events that made up Bentley's own narrative.

By a remarkable coincidence a parallel sequence occurred during the trial itself. Bentley's barrister, whilst eliciting a narrative of the evening's events from him, produced the set of questions in Extract 8.2:

Extract 8.2
Q. Well, after some difficulty did you then get on the roof and find Craig
A. Yes sir, I went on Craig's drainpipe and got up
Q. Up to that time did you know that Craig had a loaded revolver
A. No Sir
Q. When you got on to the roof what happened then
A. Some lights in the garden; someone shone a light in the garden
(Trial Transcript p. 97)

If this set of utterances were turned into a monologue narrative, the 'knowledge' about the loaded gun would similarly be reported well in advance of its use.

b) A corpus assisted analysis of register

One of the marked features of Derek Bentley's confession is the frequent use of the word 'then' in its temporal meaning – 11 occurrences in 588 words. This may not, at first, seem at all remarkable, given that Bentley is reporting a series of sequential events and that one of the obvious requirements of a witness statement is accuracy about time. However, a cursory glance at a series of other witness statements showed that Bentley's usage of 'then' was at the very least atypical, and thus a potential intrusion of a specific feature of police register, deriving from a professional concern with the accurate recording of temporal sequence.

Two small corpora were used to test this hypothesis: the first composed of three ordinary witness statements, one from a woman involved in the Bentley case itself and two from men involved in another unrelated case, totalling some 930 words of text; the second composed of three statements by police officers, two of whom were involved in the Bentley case, the third in another unrelated case, totalling some 2,270 words. The comparative results were startling: whereas in the ordinary witness statements there is only one occurrence of 'then', it occurs 29 times in the police officers' statements, that is an average of once every 78 words. Thus, Bentley's usage of temporal 'then', once every 53 words, groups his statement firmly with those produced by the police officers. In this case it was possible to check the findings from the 'ordinary witness' data against a reference corpus, the Corpus of Spoken English – a subset of the much larger COBUILD Bank of English – which, at that time, consisted of some 1.5 million running words collected from many different types of naturally occurring speech. 'Then' in all its meanings proved to occur a mere 3,164 times, that is only once every 500 words, which supported the representativeness of the witness data and the claimed specialness of the data from the police and Bentley (cf. Fox 1993).

What was perhaps even more striking about the Bentley statement was the frequent post-positioning of the 'then's, as can be seen in the two sample sentences below, selected from a total of seven:

(15) Chris **then** jumped over and I followed.
(16) Chris **then** climbed up the drainpipe to the roof and I followed.

The opening phrases have an odd feel, because not only do ordinary speakers use 'then' much less frequently than policemen, they also use it in a structurally different way. For instance, in the COBUILD spoken data 'then I' occurred ten times more frequently than 'I then'; indeed the structure 'I then' occurred a mere nine times, in other words only once every 165,000 words. By contrast the phrase occurs three times in Bentley's short statement, once every 194 words, a frequency almost 1,000 times greater. In addition, while the 'I then' structure, as one might predict from the corpus data, did not occur at all in any of the three witness statements, there were nine occurrences in one single 980 word police statement, as many as in the entire 1.5 million word spoken corpus. Taken together, the average occurrence in the three police statements is once every 119 words. Thus, the structure 'I then' does appear to be a feature of a police (written) register.

More generally, it is in fact the structure Subject (+Verb) followed by 'then' which is typical of police register; it occurs 26 times in the statements of the three officers and seven times in Bentley's own statement. Interestingly, Svartvik (1968:

29–32) had made the same discovery, but had not actually stated it explicitly, because the analytical category he had used was 'clauses with mobile relator', with a gloss to the effect that 'such clauses include *then* and *also*'. What he did not emphasize, obviously because he did not have access to other corpora and therefore did not realize its significance, was that in *each and every one* of the 23 examples in his corpus the 'mobile relator' was in fact realized by 'then'.

When we turn to look at yet another corpus, the shorthand verbatim record of the oral evidence given in court during the trial of Bentley and Craig, and choose one of the police officers at random, we find him using the structure twice in successive sentences, 'shot him *then* between the eyes' and 'he was *then* charged'. In Bentley's oral evidence there are also two occurrences of 'then', but this time the 'then's occur in the normal preposed position: 'and *then* the other people moved off', 'and *then* we came back up'. Even Mr Cassels, one of the defence barristers, who might conceivably have been influenced by police reporting style, says '*Then* you'. Such examples, embedded in Bentley's statement, of the language of the police officers who had recorded it, added support to the claim that it was a jointly authored document and so both removed the incriminating force of the phrase 'I didn't know he was going to use the gun' and undermined the credibility of the police officers on whose word depended the evidential value of the remembered utterance 'Let him have it Chris'.

In August 1998, 46 years after the event, the Lord Chief Justice, sitting with two senior colleagues, criticized his predecessor's summing-up and allowed the appeal against conviction.

Conclusion

Ever since written texts existed, people have been interested in who composed them. Now, as our linguistic toolkit becomes ever more refined, we are getting better and better at attributing authorship and detecting multiple hands, or rather mouths and brains, in apparently single-author documents. For those in the field of education the major application of such work is in the detection of plagiarism, to which we will turn in the next chapter.

Further reading

Coulthard (1994a, b); Love (2002); McMenamin (2002, chapters 10, 3, 4, 9, 7 and 8 in that order).

Research tasks

1. The case of Paul Malone

After the fourth of a series of lunchtime robberies at local branches of the HBOS bank, Paul Malone was arrested on suspicion and, after being interrogated for two days, agreed to go out in a car with three police officers, so that he could show them where he was and what he was doing at the time of the most recent robbery. A police officer made handwritten contemporaneous notes on a piece of lined paper, secured to a clip-board supported on his knee. On returning to the police station Malone was invited to sign these notes as an accurate record of the car journey; which he did. Afterwards, he claimed that incriminating additions had been made; he said that the original document was written almost entirely on alternate lines, then afterwards all the blank lines were filled in with more text. It was certainly true that one could remove the disputed half of the text and that what remained still made sense and also that all of the incriminating items occurred in the disputed lines. Below is a transcribed version of the complete handwritten record with all undisputed text in bold.

A basic linguistic tenet is that language varies according to the context in which it is produced; Malone claimed that part of the text was an authentic record of what was said in the car and the other part was created afterwards in the police station. What linguistic differences can you find between the contested and the uncontested sections to support Malone's claim? You could focus on the following:

1   average word length;
2   lexical richness – in such a short text it is fairly easy to calculate by hand the proportion of hapaxes;
3   lexical density – which can be calculated simply by comparing the proportions of lexical and grammatical words in the two portions of the text;
4   grammatical structure – is there a noticeable spoken/written difference?

Inserting items coherently into a pre-existing text is not an easy task and one might expect the police officers to make mistakes, if that is indeed how the text was created. Can you find any instances where items, which Malone claimed were inserted, do not fit, cohesively or coherently, into the developing narrative? Concentrate particularly on the second page starting at line 2.1.

Disputed record of a car journey

1.1   **5 pm - O/S P. Station**
1.2   I/think/ **came past here yesterday** I then
1.3   **turned left. Up there (towards Suttonway).**
1.4   but I'll know for sure after
1.5   **5 06 pm At Mercury towards Stanlow** (not
1.6   **Little Sutton)** as I first said
1.7   this morning
1.8   **Left on A5302, Chester Rd**, Whitby
1.9   and went towards town centre
1.10 **Through T/L (Overpool Rd)**
1.11 and carried straight on
1.12 **Stopped near Offleys** + looked at

1.13	some of the cars down left side and some of the
1.14	**Cars down right hand side,** I got back
1.15	into car then.
1.16	**(Pointed out Patsy Ang.)** that's where
1.17	I get my dinner.
1.18	**Pointed out Halifax,** I might have
1.19	looked in the window there.
1.20	**Stopped on Sportsman car park** and
1.21	that's where I walked back.
1.22	**Went to Manny Cooks – no bet –**
1.23	I know Manny very well but I
1.24	**didn't speak to any staff.** Manny
1.25	wasn't in.
1.26	**Chippy further up – a bloke. –**
1.27	might have seen me in there he was a
1.28	**Chineese maybe** – half caste bloke or Iti
1.29	I can't say.
1.30	**Back to car.** – started driving off
1.31	that's when the woman saw me I suppose
1.32	**Left back to P.S.** + left into
1.33	Sutton way.
1.34	**Turn Flatt lane –U-turn.**
2.1	**Back to lights** + turn right and back
2.2	past the Estate agent.
2.3	**Back to Strawberry Roundabout,**
2.4	no deviation
2.5	**Turn right towards Mercury**
2.6	or the Ladbroke's I know it as.
2.7	**Turn right towards Little Sutton (A41)**
2.8	I was looking at houses there.
2.9	**Turn left at Lights Ledsham Rd.,**
2.10	where I was going to park and hide but
2.11	**PC in car on public car pk. (– of H Jones)**
2.12	saw me and I thought he was going to follow.
2.13	**Turn at Black Lion Lane** and I saw
2.14	PC was making some notes up
2.15	**Back to lights** but turned round
2.16	– went down the road a bit and came back
2.17	**to Travellers Rest car park** where I
2.18	parked the car up
2.19	**Into Henry Jones Betting Office** where I
2.20	spent some of the money. I won £200 and
2.21	**stayed to 5 pm or after 5 pm.**

2. Text messages are now used as evidence in criminal trials. Individual texting styles can be markedly different. The following message comes from a real case that will be discussed in Chapter 10:

> Hiya Stuart what are you up to. I'm in so much trouble at home at the moment. Everyone hates me even you. What the hell have I done now? Why wont you just tell me. Text back please. Love Danielle. Three kisses

First, collect ten authentic text messages from a friend; analyse them and then describe the linguistic rules the texter is subconsciously following. Now try to text the above message in your friend's style. Now ask your friend and nine other people, six from your own generation and three from a different generation, to text the message to you in their usual style. Analyse all 11 messages.

1 Can you distinguish between the styles of the two generations?
2 Can you group individuals according to their texting style, in particular the extremeness or idiosyncrasy of their abbreviations?
3 Which of the 11 versions of 'Hiya Stuart…' could not have been produced by your friend and why?
4 How close was your text message to your friend's? Were any of the differences the result of poor analysis on your part?

9   On textual borrowing

> The barge she sat in, like a burnished throne,
> Burned on the water
> (*Antony and Cleopatra*, II ii 199–200)

> The chair she sat in, like a burnished throne,
> Glowed on the marble
> (T. S. Eliot, *The Waste Land*, I, 77–8)

Introduction

For differing reasons the literary critic, the copyright lawyer and the teacher as well, of course, as the forensic linguist, are all interested in texts which apparently borrow from other texts – particularly when the borrowing is not acknowledged. With the T.S. Eliot example above it is assumed that the reader will recognize the reference to Shakespeare, but Eliot's readers were not always willing to accept that his borrowings were deliberate intertextual references, rather than the theft of a 'well-rounded' phrase. Indeed, Eliot had to defend himself in an interview in August 1961:

> In one of my early poems ['Cousin Nancy'] I used, without quotation marks, the line 'the army of unalterable law …' from a poem by George Meredith, and this critic accused me of having deliberately plagiarized, pinched, pilfered that line. Whereas, of course, the whole point was that the reader should recognize where it came from and contrast it with the spirit and meaning of my own poem.
>
> (quoted in Ricks 1998: 23–4)

The literary artist may be able to make the defence that any competent reader will recognize a borrowing and therefore that s/he does not need to explicitly acknowledge it, but this does raise important questions about *definition* and differing *disciplinary conventions*. First, there is the question of definition – whether plagiarism is defined as the simple textual phenomenon of unacknowledged borrowing, in which case Eliot was guilty, or the product of an authorial intention to deceive, in which case Eliot can claim (truthfully or not we cannot tell) to be not guilty. But the situation is much more complicated if categorization of any borrowing as plagiarism is the result of each reader's personal assessment, which will of necessity depend upon that reader first recognizing the unmarked borrowing and then categorizing it as either a deliberate intertextual reference or as barefaced theft. From this point of view Eliot might be found guilty by some readers and innocent by others. The conventions of individual disciplines cross-cut the problem, because some frown on plagiarism more than others – journalists apparently feel able to borrow large chunks of text with no attribution at all, whereas academics are ever more anxious to have every source acknowledged.

Normally, of course, even in the literary field, an accusation rests on much more than a single phrase and anyone who has read *The Waste Land* will know that Eliot is a habitual borrower, but then many of us only know that because the poem has the traditional academic apparatus of source attribution provided by the author himself in appended notes. To paraphrase, or recontextualize, into more familiar linguistic terms, what Eliot was doing in creating intertextual references was setting up a Matching Relation (see Hoey 1983, 2000) between (sections of) the two texts and so was using the quotation quite deliberately as the *constant*, in order to trigger the reader's search for the *variable*. This is what we see in the specific *Waste Land* example above, where readers are expected to bring all the associations they have built up about Shakespeare's Cleopatra and compare and contrast them with the high class prostitute who Eliot is actually describing. Seen in these terms plagiarism occurs when a writer sets out to conceal the matching relation that their text would otherwise create with the source(s) and instead to claim the whole text as his/her own.

The history of plagiarism

Plagiarism as we know it is very much the product of two major sociolinguistic changes in the past 600 years: the move from an oral to a written culture and the wider availability of written texts following the invention of the printing press in the 1440s. When literature was oral, it existed only in performance and although much was remembered, there is no doubt that each performance of *Beowulf* was unique, with the performer altering the sequence of some half lines, omitting others and creating yet others as he recited. No one knows who composed *Beowulf* or *The Odyssey*, nor even whether they ever had a single author, nor how many mouths they passed through and how many alterations they underwent, before they were committed to paper. For the few who could read, the majority of classic texts were accessed in translation, often in translations of translations, so no special status was given to the 'wording', while the ideas the texts contained were seen to belong to the community rather than to any individual author.

With the arrival of printing not a lot changed at first – Shakespeare did not acknowledge his sources, though he borrowed massively for his plots, but neither did anyone accuse him of plagiarism. However, the introduction of a speculator – the publisher – between the text producer and the text consumer did cause things to change. Publishers realized that they needed to defend 'their' texts in order to protect their investment – the authors themselves earned very little from sales. The Licensing Act of 1662 established a register of licensed books, along with the requirement to deposit a copy of the book to be licensed. The purpose was mainly political, even though the system was administered by the Stationers' Company, which was a collection of independent publishers given the power to seize any books which might contain writings attacking the Government or the Church. The original Licensing Act was repealed fairly quickly, but the Stationers' Company had realized its value and managed to have another law passed that established for its members the right of ownership of the content of the books they had published. It was only in 1710, however, with the Statute of Queen Anne, that the rights of the authors themselves were recognized and then only with a 14-year copyright. For further information see http://www.intellectual-property. gov.uk/std/resources/copyright/history.htm.

Universities and plagiarism

Nowadays it is not only publishers who are concerned with ownership; the academic community too is a rigorous defender of the intellectual property rights of its members. In the opinion of the editors of the highly regarded science journal *Nature*,

> Plagiarism is the most serious of the known crimes against scholarship … it amounts to the literal theft of another's words, thereby depriving the victim not merely of the credit for … the stolen words, but of whatever thought and imagination they embody.
>
> (Maddox 1991: 13)

Universities see it as one of their functions to instil the values and procedures of the academic community into initiates. Most set out to teach their new students explicitly about plagiarism and how to avoid it and then impose penalties on those offenders who are caught, even if they are senior academics. In July 2001 the Vice Chancellor of Monash University was forced to resign when examples of frequent plagiarism were discovered in his earlier academic work (ABC News 20 February 2007).

Typically, universities provide written guidance on plagiarism for their students and growingly this is available on their websites, although such documents are usually unattributed. Indeed, Pennycook (1996: 213) reports that some of Stanford University's documents about plagiarism were reproduced without attribution by the University of Oregon and notes ironically that there appears to be 'one set of standards for the guardians of truth and knowledge and another for those seeking entry'.

At its simplest, plagiarism, or more accurately the type of plagiarism linguists are competent to deal with, is the theft, or unacknowledged use, of text created by another. As the University of Birmingham's website used to express it:

> Plagiarism is a form of cheating in which the student tries to pass off someone else's work as his or her own. … Typically, substantial passages are 'lifted' verbatim from a particular source without proper attribution having been made.

There are two problems with the definition of plagiarism given here. First, it claims that plagiarism typically takes the form of substantial verbatim borrowings, whereas the vast majority of cases are actually texts which have been edited, even if only superficially. Second, the university seems to be committing itself to an 'intentionalist' definition – 'tries to pass off' – but this is very hard to apply in practice. However, the university can sidestep this problem by handing over the responsibility for ensuring the absence of plagiarism to the individual student. All students are required to sign a contract which in effect says that all the university needs is textual proof, because any student who (has signed to say that s/he) knows the rules, must be assumed to have intentionally broken them (see *Avoiding Plagiarism: A learning agreement* at http://www.studserv.bham.ac.uk/sca/exam/plag3.htm).

With growing frequency linguists are being asked to help academic colleagues in the detection or confirmation of student plagiarism. Any linguistically based investigation of plagiarism is based consciously or unconsciously on the notion of *idiolect*. In other words, it is expected that any two writers writing on the same topic, even if intending to express very similar meanings, will choose an overlapping, but by no means identical, set of lexico-grammatical items to do so. Indeed, and more importantly for some cases I will treat below, linguists from all persuasions subscribe to some version of the 'uniqueness of utterance' principle (Chomsky 1965; Halliday 1975) and so would expect that the same person speaking/writing on the same topic on different occasions would make a different set of lexico-grammatical choices. It follows from this that, in any comparison of two texts, the more similar the set of items chosen, the greater the likelihood that one of the texts was derived, at least in part, from the other (or, of course, that both were derived from a third text), rather than composed independently.

Extract 9.1

> A. It is essential for all teachers to understand the history of Britain as a multi-racial, multi-cultural nation. Teachers, like anyone else, can be influenced by age-old myths and beliefs. However, it is only by having an understanding of the past that we can begin to comprehend the present.

> B. In order for **teachers** to competently acknowledge the ethnic minority, **it is essential to understand the history of Britain as a multi-racial, multi-cultural nation. Teachers** are prone to believe popular **myths and beliefs; however, it is only by understanding** and appreciating **past** theories **that we can begin to** anticipate **the present.**

In most cases involving students there is little doubt about textual guilt, as the above openings of two essay answers to the question 'Discuss the kind of policy a primary school should have towards bilingualism and multilingualism' (Johnson 1997: 214) demonstrate – all items which student B 'shares' with student A are highlighted in bold.

Even these short extracts provide enough evidence to question the originality of at least one of the essays, or both, of course, if a third text later proves to be the common source. When this level of sharing is also instanced in other parts of the same texts there is no room for doubt or dispute. The case of essay C, however, (Extract 9.2) is not as clear-cut (items which C shares with one or both of essays A and B are highlighted).

Extract 9.2

> C. It is very important for us as educators to realize that **Britain as a nation** has become both **multi-racial** and **multi-cultural.** Clearly it is vital for **teachers** and associate teachers to ensure that **popular myths and** stereotypes held by the wider community do not **influence** their teaching. By examining British history this will assist our **understanding** and in that way be better equipped to deal with **the present** and the future.

Even though there is still quite a lot of shared lexical material here, it is evident that the largest identical sequence is only four running words long. Even so, one would still want to categorize this degree of lexical overlap, if instanced in other parts of the text, as unacknowledged, though more sophisticated borrowing and therefore as plagiarism, even if it does not fit easily within the Birmingham observation that 'Typically, *substantial* passages are "lifted"'. We will not discuss here the important question of whether a significant proportion of those student essays which technically fall within the textual definition of plagiarism, are really deliberate attempts to deceive. An alternative explanation is that they are the product of a writing process that is coming to be known as 'patchwriting', that is they are genuine, though flawed, attempts by students, who have somehow failed to acquire the academic rules for acknowledging textual borrowing, to incorporate the work of others into their own texts (see Pecorari 2002; Howard 1999a; Coulthard 2005).

Johnson's (1997) innovative solution to the detection of this form of student plagiarism or *collusion*, was to move away from a reliance on strings or sequences of words as diagnostic and concentrate simply on shared vocabulary. She decided to disregard grammatical words altogether, as they are small in number and more likely to be shared anyway, and to focus on the percentage of shared individual lexical *tokens* and *types* as a better measure of derivativeness. A *token* count sums all occurrences of each lexical *type*, so in the invented sentence 'The pretty girl gave the pretty ball to the other girl' there are four lexical types – *pretty, girl, gave, ball* – but six lexical tokens with *pretty* and *girl* occurring twice.

Johnson took the first 500 words of the three non-suspect essays and calculated the amount of shared lexical vocabulary. One would expect a degree of overlap in vocabulary choice between the essays as they were all writing on the same topic. In fact, the Control group was found to share only 13 lexical types, of which seven – *language, languages, school, children, multilingual, bilingual* and *policy* – were almost predictable, given the topic. As these words are central to the topic of the essay, they are not only shared but also repeated frequently and thus this set of 13 shared types made up some 20 per cent of the total lexical tokens used in the three extracts. With these figures as a base line for comparison Johnson returned to the suspect essays and found that they shared 72 lexical types, which accounted for some 60 per cent of all the lexical tokens.

It is possible to approach these texts from a different perspective and to examine how much lexical uniqueness there is. Whereas for the control group the vocabulary unique to each essay constituted between 54 and 61 per cent of the lexical tokens, two of the suspect essays had only 16 per cent unique lexis and the third, which had appeared to the examiner to be less derivative, had 39 per cent. Intensive testing has shown that such measures of lexical overlap successfully separate those essays which share common vocabulary simply because they are on the same topic, from those which share much more vocabulary because one or more of them is derivative (see Woolls and Coulthard 1998; Woolls 2003).

The problem for the human reader in trying to detect such collusion becomes evident when one discovers that none of the three colluding essays was unusual when compared with any of the control essays – in other words had the three 'guilty' essays been marked by different professors none would have been suspect. So, what is needed is an automated checking procedure to enable rapid and reliable comparison of every essay with every other one and this quickly becomes a large task, even with a comparatively small group of essays – comparing 30 essays each with every other one necessitates 435 comparisons. However, this can be done rapidly using *Copycatch Gold* (Woolls 2002) which has computerized Johnson's original insights – it calculates the amount of shared lexis and allows the individual user to decide, depending on subject areas and essay length, what percentage of overlap will trigger further investigation.

Unacknowledged use of published text

More frequent than collusion are cases of a single individual making unacknowledged use of already published text. In the past students typically borrowed from books or journal articles and had at least to write out or type the borrowed text. Now the process is much easier – the student-plagiarist can (re-)search the web, find a useful piece of text and paste it, apparently seamlessly, at least to the eye if not to the mind of the beholder, into his or her own text. However, although the text is physically seamless, the joins are usually evident to a skilled and careful reader, because of the clash of styles between the student's work and the 'borrowed' text(s). A clear example of a style clash is the opening of a story written by a 12-year-old girl (Extract 9.3, all the spelling is as in the original).

Extract 9.3 – The Soldiers

> Down in the country side an old couple husband and wife Brooklyn and
> Susan. When in one afternoon they were having tea they heard a drumming
> sound that was coming from down the lane. Brooklyn asks,
> **'What is that glorious sound which so thrills the ear?'** when Susan replied
> in her o sweat voice
> 'Only the scarlet soldiers, dear,'
> The soldiers are coming, The soldiers are coming. Brooklyn is confused he
> doesn't no what is happening.
> Mr and Mrs Waters were still having their afternoon tea when suddenly a
> bright light was shinning trough the window.
> **'What is that bright light I see flashing so clear over the distance so
> brightly?'** said Brooklyn sounding so amazed but Susan soon reassured him.

The first paragraph is unremarkable, but the second shifts dramatically, *'What
is that glorious sound which so thrills the ear?'*. The story then moves back to the
opening style, before shifting again to *'What is that bright light I see flashing so clear
over the distance so brightly?'*. It is hard to believe that an author so young could
write in both styles. When one meets a style clash like this in any student's work
and does not recognize the source, the first response is ever more likely to be
to search the internet. Many people do this laboriously by trying, as the police
sometimes do in analogous circumstances, to re-create the crime, that is, in the
case of plagiarism, by searching the kinds of topics that the student him/herself
had probably searched. However, what the theory of idiolect and the practice of
working with *Copycatch* have taught us is the importance to be attached to the
distinctiveness and individuality of lexical selection and co-selection.

If proof were needed of the distinctiveness and diagnostic power of words used
once-only – *hapaxes* as they are technically labelled – it comes from successful
internet searches in cases of suspected plagiarism. Experience confirms that
the most economical method to use when checking the internet for suspected
plagiarized text is to search using three pairs of collocates whose individual items
occur only once in the text in question. In the case of *The Soldiers*, if one takes as
search terms three pairs of collocated *hapaxes* 'thrills – ear', 'flashing – clear' and
'distance – brightly' one can see the diagnostic power of idiolectal co-selection.
The single pairing 'flashing – clear' yields over 500,000 hits on Google, but the
three pairings combined yield a mere 360 hits, of which the first 13, when we
searched, were all from W.H. Auden's poem 'O What is that sound'. When we
added a seventh word 'so' and searched for the phrase 'flashing so clear' all of the
hits returned were from Auden's poem (Extract 9.4).

Extract 9.4

> O **what is that** [glorious] **sound which so thrills the ear**
>   Down in the valley drumming, drumming?
> **Only the scarlet soldiers, dear,**
>   **The soldiers** [are] **coming**.

O **what is that** [bright] **light I see flashing so clear**
  Over the distance [so] brightly, **brightly**?
Only the sun on their weapons, dear,
  As they step lightly.

In incorporating five lines from the poem into her prose story, the girl had simply omitted the 'O's and added the adjectives 'glorious' and 'bright', the copula 'are' and the adverbial 'so'.

As an alternative to searching for themselves, British University staff now have access, through a national centre based in the University of Northumbria, to a Plagiarism Detection Service which employs the American company Turnitin, www.turnitin.org, to search for sources in cases of suspected plagiarism – the essay is returned with coloured highlighting of the plagiarized sections. This system is most successful with crude large-scale plagiarism, that is verbatim reproduction of sequences of sentences; the more the student has resorted to a patchwriting technique, the less successful it is.

Plagiarism is, of course, by no means confined to the student body. Figure 9.1 is a side-by-side comparison, created with the *Copycatch Gold* program, of extracts from two texts: one the infamous 'dodgy dossier' which the British government presented to the United Nations in February 2003, shortly before the beginning of the Iraq War, claiming it as an intelligence-based analysis of Iraqi power structures; and the other, an unclassified academic article, published shortly before, from which the 'dodgy dossier' had been substantially plagiarized. It is clear that, in the extracts we have chosen, the only contribution from British intelligence was to 'correct' the spelling of some words from American to British English (see Figure 9.1).

Do people repeat themselves?

Whereas (occasional) identical strings in two texts which are supposed to have different authors can be indicative of unacknowledged borrowing or plagiarism, it is harder to argue the case when the second text is (supposedly) produced by the same author on a different occasion without recourse to the first. The example I want to use is from a famous English murder case, dating from 1978, where one piece of strongly contested evidence was a record of a police interview with a suspect.

In this case, four men were accused, and subsequently convicted, solely on the basis of the confession of one of them, Patrick Molloy, of the murder of a 13-year-old newspaper delivery boy, Carl Bridgewater. There was no corroborating forensic evidence and Molloy later retracted his confession, but to no avail. He admitted that he did actually say (most of) the words recorded as his confession, but insisted that he was being told what to say, as he was dictating the confession, by a policeman who was standing behind him. He also claimed that he had only made the confession after being physically and verbally abused for some considerable

Iraq: Its Infrastructure Of Concealment, Deception And Intimidation UK Government release February 2003	Iraq's Security And Intelligence Network: A Guide And Analysis By Ibrahim al-Marashi *Middle East Review of International Affairs*, Vol 6, iii, September 2002
Under the Political Bureau, the Operations Office implements operations against these "enemies," including arrests, interrogations and executions.	Under the Political Bureau, the Operations Office implements operations against these "enemies," including arrests, interrogations and executions.
Another division is the Public Opinion Office, responsible for collecting and disseminating **rumours** on behalf of the state.	Another division is the Public Opinion Office, responsible for collecting and disseminating **rumors** on behalf of the state
The operations of Special Security are numerous, particularly in suppressing domestic opposition to the regime.	The operations of Special Security are numerous, particularly in suppressing domestic opposition to the regime.
After its creation in 1984, Special Security thwarted a plot of disgruntled army officers, who objected to Saddam's management of the Iran-Iraq War.	After its creation in 1984, Special Security thwarted a plot of disgruntled army officers, who objected to Saddam's management of the Iran-Iraq War
It **pre-empted** other coups such as the January 1990 attempt by members of the Jubur tribe to assassinate him.	It **preempted** other coups such as the January 1990 attempt by members of the Jubur tribe to assassinate him
It played an active role in crushing the March 1991 Shi'a rebellion in the south of Iraq.	It played an active role in crushing the March 1991 Shi'a rebellion in the south of Iraq.
Along with General Intelligence, Special Security agents infiltrated the Kurdish enclave in the north of Iraq in August 1996, to hunt down operatives of the Iraqi opposition.	Along with General Intelligence, Special Security agents infiltrated the Kurdish enclave in the north of Iraq in August 1996, to hunt down operatives of the Iraqi opposition.
It serves as the central **co-ordinating** body between Military-Industrial Commission, Military Intelligence, General Intelligence, and the military in the covert procurement of the necessary components for Iraq's weapons of mass destruction.	It serves as the central **coordinating** body between Military-Industrial Commission, Military Intelligence, General Intelligence, and the military in the covert procurement of the necessary components for Iraq's weapons of mass destruction
During the 1991 Gulf War, it was put in charge of concealing SCUD missiles and afterwards in moving and hiding documents from UNSCOM inspections, relating to Iraq's weapons **programmes**.	During the 1991 Gulf War it was put in charge of concealing SCUD missiles(32) and afterwards in moving and hiding documents from UNSCOM inspections, relating to Iraq's weapons **programs**.

Figure 9.1 Comparison of extracts from British secret service document on Iraq and an academic article (We are endebted to David Woolls for this comparison, which was created with the Copycheck program.)

time, and after being shown a confession dictated by one of the other accused, which incriminated him in the murder.

The police denied the existence of the other confession, and to reinforce the credibility of Molloy's confession, produced a contemporaneous handwritten record of an interview which they claimed had taken place immediately beforehand and which contained substantially the same information expressed in words very similar to those of the confession. Molloy denied that this interview had ever taken place – in his version of events he was being subjected to abuse at the time recorded for the interview – and counter-claimed that the interview record had been made up later on the basis of the, by then pre-existing, confession. As is evident from a cursory glance at the two extracts (9.5 and 9.6) which are taken, respectively, from the statement which Molloy admitted making and the interview record which he claimed was falsified, the similarities are enormous; I have highlighted them in bold.

Extract 9.5 – Extract from Molloy's statement

(17) **I had been drinking and cannot remember the exact time I was there but whilst I was upstairs I heard someone downstairs say be careful someone is coming.** (18) **I hid for a while and** after a while **I heard a bang** come from downstairs. (19) I knew that it was a gun being fired. (20) I went downstairs and **the three of them were still in the room.** (21) **They all looked shocked and were shouting at each other.** (22) **I heard Jimmy say, 'It went off by accident'.** (23) I looked and **on the settee** I saw the **body of the boy.** (24) **He had been shot in the head.** (25) **I was appalled and felt sick.**

Extract 9.6 – Extract from disputed interview with Molloy

P.   How long were you in there Pat?

(18)   **I had been drinking and cannot remember the exact time that I was there, but whilst I was upstairs I heard someone downstairs say 'be careful someone is coming'.**

P.   Did you hide?

(19)   Yes **I hid for a while and** then **I heard** the **bang** I have told you about.

P.   Carry on Pat?

(19a)   I ran out.

P.   What were the others doing?

(20)   **The three of them were still in the room.**

P.   What were they doing?

(21)   **They all looked shocked and were shouting at each other.**

P.   Who said what?

(22)   **I heard Jimmy say 'it went off by accident'.**

P.   Pat, I know this is upsetting but you appreciate that we must get to the bottom of this. Did you see the **boy's body?**

(Molloy hesitated, looked at me intently, and after a pause said,)
(23) Yes sir, he was **on the settee**.
P. Did you see any injury to him?
(Molloy stared at me again and said)
(24) Yes sir, **he had been shot in the head**.
P. What happened then?
(25) **I was appalled and felt sick**.

Most linguists would agree, on the basis of such similarities, that either one of the two documents was derived from the other or that both had been derived from a third. However, at the time of the original trial, no linguist was called to give evidence – in fact there were no forensic linguists practising in Britain at the time – so it was left to the lawyers to evaluate the linguistic significance of the similarities between the interview and the confession. As a result, the same phenomenon, massive identity in phrasing and lexical choice, was argued by the defence to be evidence of falsification, and by the prosecution to be evidence of the authenticity and reliability of both texts, on the grounds that here was an example of the accused recounting the same events, in essentially the same linguistic encoding, on two separate occasions.

The prosecution assertion, that identity of formulation in two separate texts is indicative of reliability, depends on two commonly held mistaken beliefs: first, that people can and do say the same thing in the same words on different occasions and second, that people can remember and reproduce verbatim what they and others have said on some earlier occasion. The former belief can be demonstrated to be false either by recording someone attempting to recount the same set of events on two separate occasions, or by simply asking a witness to repeat word for word what s/he has just said. The second belief used to have some empirical support, at least for short stretches of speech (see Keenan *et al.* 1977 and Bates *et al.* 1980), but was seriously questioned by Hjelmquist (1984) who demonstrated that, even after only a short delay, people could remember at best 25 per cent of the gist and 5 per cent of the actual wording of what had been said in a five minute two-party conversation in which they had themselves participated. Confirmatory evidence about the inability to remember even quite short single utterances verbatim was specially commissioned from Professor Brian Clifford and presented at the 2003 'Glasgow Ice Cream Wars' Appeal. This was used to challenge successfully the claim of police officers that they had independently remembered, some of them for over an hour, verbatim and identically, utterances made by the accused at the time of arrest. Clifford's experiment tested the ability to remember a short, 24-word utterance and found that most people were able to recall verbatim no more than 30 to 40 percent of what they had heard (BBC News 17 February 2004).

By the time of the Bridgewater Appeal in 1997 it was possible to provide extra evidence to support the claim that identity of expression was indeed evidence that one text was derived from the other. First, as a direct result of Johnson's work on plagiarism discussed above, which demonstrated the significance of vocabulary overlap, an analysis was done of the shared vocabulary in the two Molloy texts;

it became evident that the highlighting in the extracts presented above actually understates the similarities between the two texts – a closer examination revealed that there was in fact not one single token in Molloy's statement, neither lexical nor grammatical, which did not also occur in the interview record. We have only seen that degree of overlap on one other occasion, when two students submitted identical essays for assessment. Ironically, the computer analysis showed the degree of similarity to be only 97 per cent – the 3 per cent apparent difference was in fact made up of spelling mistakes.

In the Bridgewater case there also was secondary linguistic evidence, of a different kind, to support the claim that the interview record was both falsified and based on the statement. If we assume that the police officers had indeed, as Molloy claimed, set out to create a dialogue based on the monologue statement, they would have faced the major problem of what questions to invent in order to link forward and apparently elicit the actually pre-existing candidate answers, which they had derived from the statement. In this scenario one would expect there to be occasions when a question did not fit entirely successfully into the text into which it had been embedded – and indeed there are.

In a developing interview, a police question usually links backwards lexically, repeating word(s) from the previous answer. However, in designing a question to fit a pre-existing answer, there is always the danger that the question will only link forward. For example, the original statement has a two-sentence sequence

(21) 'They all looked shocked and were shouting at each other.'
(22) 'I heard Jimmy say 'it went off by accident''

which appears word for word in the interview record, except that the two sentences are separated by the question 'Who said what?'. However, in this context the word 'said', although it is cataphorically unremarkable – *said* links with *say* – it is anaphorically odd because the men have just been described as 'shouting'. One would therefore have expected an anaphorically cohesive follow-up question to be either 'What/Why were they *shouting?*' or 'Who was *shouting* (what/at whom)?'; one would certainly not predict 'who *said* what?'. The choice of 'said' is a most unexpected choice – except of course for someone who already knows that the next utterance will be 'I heard Jimmy *say*…'; then it has an evident logic.

There are also *grammatical* misfits. For example, the statement version 'on the settee I saw the **body** of the **boy**. **He** had …' is transformed into 'Q. Did you see **the boy's body**? Yes sir, **he** was on the settee'. The statement version correctly uses the pronoun 'He' because the referent is the 'boy' in 'the body of the boy', but the reformulated version in the police interview, 'the boy's body', would be more likely to have elicited '**it**' as a referent. There are also examples of *verbal process* misfit: in the exchange reproduced below, the question 'what happened' requires a report of an action or an event, but in fact the response is a description of two states:

P.   What **happened** then?
M.   I **was appalled** and **felt sick**.

Had the reply been 'I vomited', it would, of course, have been cohesive.

There was no opportunity to test the persuasiveness of this evidence in court as, a few weeks before the date of the appeal, an ESDA test was carried out on the first page of the handwritten record of Molloy's confession. The traces revealed the last few lines of the confession which Molloy had always insisted had been read out to him, while he was being persuaded to make his own, along with the forged signature of the supposed confessee. The credibility of the police evidence was destroyed, the three surviving 'murderers' were released immediately and their convictions quashed shortly afterwards, without the need of linguistic evidence.

The evidential value of single identical strings

As we have just seen, in the Bridgewater Four case there was a whole series of identical strings of words to support the claim that the interview record was derived from the statement and, for anyone unconvinced by the assertion that the identical phrasings were due to borrowing, rather than identical encoding on two separate occasions, the claim of fabrication was supported by other linguistic evidence of a different and independent kind. We now ask how much weight can be placed on a single identical string and how important is the length of a string when assessing its evidential significance? These questions go to the heart of current thinking about uniqueness in language production.

As Sinclair (1991) pointed out, there are two complementary assembly principles in the creation of utterances/sentences; one is the long-accepted principle that sequences are generated word by word on an 'open choice' basis. When strings are created in this way, there is, for each successive syntagmatic slot, a large number of possible, grammatically acceptable, paradigmatic fillers and thus one can easily, if not effortlessly, generate memorable grammatical but meaningless sequences like 'colorless green ideas sleep furiously'. The other assembly principle proposed much more recently, as a result of corpus work (Sinclair 1991), is the 'idiom principle', according to which pre-assembled (idiomatic) chunks, made up of frequent collocations and colligations, are linked together to create larger units. In practice, both principles work side by side, which means that any given short string might be produced by either principle and therefore might be either an idiosyncratic combination or a frequently occurring fixed phrase. However, the longer a sequence is, the more likely that some of its components, at least, have been created by the open choice principle and thus the more likely the whole sequence is to be a unique formulation. For this reason, the occurrence of long identical sequences in two texts supposedly independently created is less likely to be a result of two speaker/ writers coincidentally selecting the same chunk(s) by chance and more likely to be a product of borrowing.

The data we will use for exemplificatory purposes come from the appeal of Robert Brown in London in 2003. As in the Bridgewater Four case, here too there was a disputed statement and a disputed interview record; the difference was that Brown claimed that his statement was in reality a dialogue which had been represented as if it had been a monologue. He claimed that a police officer had asked questions to which he had simply replied 'Yes' (Judge's Summing-up, p. 95, section E), and that, although the interview did occur, the record of it was made up afterwards – 'no police officer took any notes' (Judge's Summing–up, p. 93, section E).

Below are two sentences from the statement matched with items occurring in the (disputed) interview record:

i)	Statement	I asked her if I could carry her bags she said 'Yes'
	Interview	I asked her if I could carry her bags and she said 'yes'
ii)	Statement	I picked something up like an ornament
	Interview	I picked something up like an ornament

The figures below were taken in 2002 from Google. Google was used, rather than a corpus such as the *Bank of English* or the *British National Corpus*, on the grounds that it was accessible to the layperson, for whom the argument was designed – they could go home and test the claims for themselves as indeed can you. While the paired utterances/sentences may not seem remarkable in themselves, neither occurred even once in the hundreds of millions of texts that Google searched and, as can be seen below, even the component sequences quickly became rare occurrences:

String	*Instances*
I picked	1,060,000
I picked something	780
I picked something up	362
I picked something up like	1
I picked something up like an	0
an ornament	73,700
like an ornament	896
something like an ornament	2
I asked	2,170,000
I asked her	284,000
I asked her if	86,000
I asked her if I	10,400
I asked her if I could	7,770
I asked her if I could carry	7
I asked her if I could carry her	4
I asked her if I could carry her bags	0
if I could	2,370,000
if I could carry	1,600

It is evident that 'if I could' and perhaps 'I asked her' have the characteristics of pre-assembled idioms in Sinclair's sense, but even then their co-selection in the same sequence is rare, at 7,770 occurrences. The moment one added a seventh word, 'carry', the odds against it occurring became enormous, with only seven instances.

From evidence like this we can assert that even a sequence as short as ten running words has a very high chance of being a unique occurrence. Indeed, rarity scores like these begin to look like the probability scores that DNA experts proudly present in court. The next few years will tell whether courts are willing to place the same reliance on linguistic evidence.

Coda

When we were revising this chapter in May 2007, we checked Google again and discovered to our horror that there are now four examples of 'I asked her if I could carry her bags'. But thankfully it was a case of the exception proving the rule. Since Brown's successful appeal there is a website devoted to his case, which reproduces the contested statement. Two other hits are from internet versions of Coulthard (2004), which discusses the case, and the fourth hit is a Dutch Powerpoint presentation, which quotes Coulthard (2004). So the claim about uniqueness still stands – what Google found was a set of four repetitions of the same unique uttering.

Further reading

Angélil-Carter (2000); Hanlein (1999); Johnson (1997); Pecorari (2003); Woolls (2003).

Research tasks

1   On plagiarism
    Examine the official definition of plagiarism in your own institution, discover what the penalties are and study the documents that give advice to students on how to avoid plagiarizing. Then devise a questionnaire to discover: (i) how well do your colleagues understand the rules and know the penalties; (ii) what are their views on the penalties; and (iii) what solutions do they propose for reducing the problem?

2   Patchwriting
    Here are two texts (a and b) taken from biographies of Andrew Carnegie – are the similarities sufficient to suggest *patchwriting*? If you think so, get copies of both books and check whether this is an isolated instance or a more general writing strategy.

    a.   With all of these problems it was little short of a miracle that the 'stichting' board was ready to lay the cornerstone for the building in the summer of 1907 at the opening of the Second Hague International Conference. It then took six more years before the Palace was completed during which time there continued to be squabbles over details, modifications of architectural plans and lengthy discussions about furnishings. For ten years the Temple of Peace was a storm of controversy, but at last, on 28 August 1913, the Grand Opening ceremonies were held.

(J.F. Wall, Andrew Carnegie, 1970)

b.   The foundation stone was not laid until the summer of 1907, in nice time for the opening of the Second Hague International Conference. Actual construction of the palace took a further six years, delayed and exacerbated by constant bickering over details, specifications and materials. For an entire decade the Peace Palace was bedevilled by controversy, but finally, on 28 August 1913, the opening ceremony was performed.

(J. Mackay, Little Boss: A Life of Andrew Carnegie 1997)

3   Web plagiarism
    Stage 1 *Textual 'Creation' and Detection*
    Work in pairs
    1   First create a 1,000 word essay on a topic of your choice by taking extracts from Internet texts and pasting them together – each extract must be at least 80 words long and at most 120.
    2   Make two versions of each 'essay' – the first with minimal sewing together. For the second spend 90 minutes making it into a readable text.
    3   Then exchange version 2 with your partner and see how many of the extracts they can find on the Internet. Then exchange version 1 and do the same.
    Stage 2 *Reflection on the process of plagiarizing*
    4   What have you learned about the detection of web plagiarism?

10 The linguist as expert witness

It is crucial for linguists to remain outside the advocacy that attorneys are ... required to have. Linguists must carry out their analyses in such a way that the same results would occur if they were working for the other side.

(Shuy 2002a: 4)

Prof Meadow wrongly stated in Mrs Clark's trial in 1999 that there was just a 'one in 73 million' chance that two babies from an affluent family like hers could suffer cot death. The actual odds were only one in 77.

(*The Guardian*, Friday July 15, 2005)

On being an expert witness

Some readers may aspire to become an expert witness, so we must emphasize at the outset that we know of only one forensic linguist and very few forensic phoneticians who work full time as expert witnesses – for the moment at least, it is essentially a part-time profession. It can also be a lonely profession, as the majority of experts work alone, on occasional cases and rarely go to court to give evidence; most of them average fewer than ten cases a year and one court appearance every two years. For this reason, giving evidence in person in court is, for the majority of forensic linguists, an uncommon and stressful event. As Shuy (2002a: 5–6)observes:

> For those who have never experienced cross-examination, there is no way to emphasize how emotionally draining it can be. ... Testifying is not for the weak at heart.

Nor indeed for the weak at stomach – one colleague eventually gave up, after some 25 years as an expert witness, saying he could no longer cope with vomiting before every appearance in the witness box.

There are frustrations as well. Maley (2000: 250) observes, in an excellent paper examining linguistic aspects of expert testimony, that

> expert witnesses, particularly if they are new and inexperienced, tend to be quite unaware of the extent to which shaping and construction of evidence

goes on. ... All too often they emerge frustrated from the courtroom, believing that they have not been able to give their evidence in the way they would like and that their evidence has been twisted or disbelieved

and this despite the fact that experts are allowed speaking turns on average two to three times longer than those of other witnesses (Heffer 2002).

Ever more frequently, intending experts are seeking professional training to enable them to cope more successfully with cross-examination, but even experienced experts can still struggle with two courtroom specific interactional conventions. The first is the suspension, for the lawyer, of the Gricean conversational maxim of *quality*, that is 'do not say what you believe to be false', in a situation in which the experts themselves have been required to commit themselves explicitly, by oath or affirmation, to telling the truth. Novice academic experts may be deceived into thinking that they are still in an academic environment and that, if they are sufficiently coherent and persuasive, they can convince the cross-examiner of the correctness of their opinion. The lawyer, of course, is paid not to be convinced, or at least not to admit that s/he has been convinced.

The second convention, which disorients all witnesses, expert and lay alike, is that, whilst the examining lawyer is in one sense both the speaker and the addressor, or, as Goffman (1981: 79) puts it, 'the author of the sentiments that are being expressed and the words in which they are encoded', the court convention is that s/he is actually acting as a spokesperson for the court and simply asking questions on its behalf. The physical consequence of this is that the witness is expected to treat the judge(s), and the jury if there is one, as addressee(s) and therefore to look at and direct answers to them and not to the lawyer. This can be particularly difficult in some courts, where the physical layout places the lawyer, judge and jury in such positions that the witness cannot face both at the same time. Thus, having turned to look at the speaker/lawyer who is asking the question, the witness may fail to turn back to direct the answer to the real addressee(s).

Expressing opinions

When acting as an expert the linguist will typically be asked first to write a report expressing an opinion (McMenamin 2002: 176–8 has a useful section on report writing), and then later s/he may be asked to go to court to present and defend that opinion.

In 2002 Stuart Campbell was tried and convicted for the murder of his niece Danielle. Part of the evidence against him was a couple of text messages sent to his phone from Danielle's shortly after she disappeared. The prosecution suspected that he had sent them to himself using her phone and Coulthard was asked to compare the style of the two suspect messages with a set of 70 which Danielle had sent over the previous three days; unfortunately there was no similar corpus of texts composed by the uncle to use for comparison purposes.

Below is the first of the suspect messages:

> HIYA STU WOT U UP 2.IM IN SO MUCH TRUBLE AT HOME AT
> MOMENT EVONE HATES ME EVEN U! WOT THE HELL AV I DONE
> NOW? Y WONT U JUST TELL ME TEXT BCK PLEASE LUV DAN XXX

The text displays a series of linguistic choices which were either absent from, or rare in, the Danielle corpus: the use of capitals rather than sentence case, the spelling of 'what' as 'wot', the spelling in full of the morpheme 'one' in 'EVONE', rather than its substitution by the numeral '1', the omission of the definite article in the abbreviation of the prepositional phrase 'AT MOMENT' and the use of the full form of the word 'text' rather than an abbreviation in the phrase TEXT BCK. The problem was how to reach and then express an opinion on the likelihood that Danielle did or did not produce the message.

Expressing opinions semantically

The majority of forensic linguists and phoneticians have traditionally felt that they were unable to express their findings statistically in terms of mathematical probability and so expressed them as a semantically encoded opinion. Indeed, some experts simply express their opinion without giving any indication to the court of how to evaluate its strength, or of how that opinion fits with the two legally significant categories of 'on the balance of probabilities' and 'beyond reasonable doubt'. However, a growing number of experts now use a fixed semantic scale and attach that scale as an Appendix to their report to enable the reader to assess the expert's confidence in the opinion s/he has reached. All members of the International Association of Forensic Phonetics also attach a note warning that their evidence should only be used corroboratively in criminal cases, because it is their collective opinion that it is not possible to establish the identity of a speaker with absolute certainty.

   At the time of the Danielle case Coulthard was using the scale of opinions below, which he had adapted from the scale being used by members of the International Association of Forensic Phoneticians:

Most Positive
   5   'I personally feel *quite satisfied* that X is the author'
   4   'It is in my view *very likely* that X is the author'
   3   'It is in my view *likely* that X is the author'
   2   'It is in my view *fairly likely* that X is the author'
   1   'It is in my view *rather more likely than not* that X is the author'
   0   'It is in my view *possible* that X is the author'
  −1   'It is in my view *rather more likely than not* that X is *not* the author'
  −2   'It is in my view *fairly likely* that X is *not* the author'
  −3   'It is in my view *likely* that X is *not* the author'
  −4'   'It is in my view *very likely* that X is *not* the author'
  −5   'I personally feel *quite satisfied* that X is the *not* author'
Most Negative

The opinion he gave was -2 on the above scale, that is that it was *fairly likely* that Danielle had *not* written the text message, but he agonized long and hard over which semantic label would best convey his assessment of the strength of the evidence as indeed he had with previous cases. Broeders (1999) suggested that what was happening in such cases was that:

> experts, in using degrees of probability, are actually making categorical judgements, i.e. are really saying yes or no. Even if they use a term like *probably (not)*, I think they are subjectively convinced that the suspect did or did not produce the sample material.
>
> (Broeders 1999: 237)

That was certainly true for Coulthard. Broeders went on to observe that the choice of a given degree of likelihood on a scale like this is irremediably subjective, which is why two experts might reach opinions of differing strengths based on exactly the same data. Even so, he stressed that a subjective judgement should not be condemned simply because it is subjective:

> The crucial question is not whether [it] is subjective or objective, but whether it can be relied on to be correct.
>
> (Broeders 1999: 238)

Nevertheless, a growing body of opinion is opposed to the use of such semantic scales, especially because, even when they *are* accepted by a court, an unsolvable problem remains – how can one be sure that judges and juries will attach the same meanings to the labels as did the experts who chose and applied them? This point was brought home in a court martial where Coulthard expressed his opinion as 'very likely' on the above 11-point scale and another expert expressed her opinion as 'very strong support' on a 9-point scale. Neither was allowed to tell the jury how many points there were on their respective scales, let alone show the full scale or even gloss the particular category chosen, even though the defence lawyer did his best to persuade the other expert to lower her opinion from 'very strong' to 'strong'.

An added complication is that, at the end of a trial, the triers of fact themselves are not allowed the luxury of degrees of confidence; they have to work with a binary choice of 'Guilty' or 'Not Guilty'. So, however hedged the individual expert's opinion is when s/he presents it, the judge and jury have ultimately to make a categorical judgement as to whether to interpret the evidence as supportive of the prosecution or the defence case or as simply inconclusive.

Expressing opinions statistically

Broeders (1999: 238) argued that one should be worried about opinions expressed semantically, not because they are subjective, but rather because far too often the experts who use them are expressing their opinions in the wrong way. Broeders

(1999: 229) and later Rose (2002) noted that an expert can offer an opinion on two things: first, on the probability of a hypothesis – so in linguistic cases, for example, on the hypothesis that the accused is the speaker/author – given the strength of the evidence which the expert has analysed; and second, on the probability that the evidence would occur in the form and quantity in which it does occur, given the *two* hypotheses that the accused is and, crucially, also is *not* the speaker/author.

Both authors recommend the second approach. Indeed, Rose quotes Aitken (1995: 4) in arguing that the former type of opinion, which, he says, is tantamount to deciding on the likelihood of the accused being guilty, is the exclusive role of the judges of fact and for this reason responsible scientists must confine themselves to talking about the likelihood of the evidence. Rose supports his argument by pointing out that no expert can make an estimate of the likelihood of guilt or innocence on the basis of the linguistic evidence alone; only those with access to all the available evidence can assess the value of each piece. So, for example, a forensic handwriting colleague concluded, after exhaustive comparisons, that it was very likely on the basis of the evidence he had analysed, that a disputed signature on an Irish will, which had been written with a ballpoint pen, was genuine. But then, fortunately before committing his opinion to paper, he realized that the signature was dated before the invention of ballpoint technology!

Broeders and Rose both argue that not only does their approach have logic on its side, but also that it has the added advantage that it enables probability to be expressed mathematically rather than semantically. Essentially the method involves first looking at the *likelihood* of the prosecution hypothesis given the raw data on each of the particular features being examined. For example, imagine an anonymous letter which includes the non-standard spelling 'ofcourse'. In support of the prosecution hypothesis that the accused wrote the letter we discover that 80 per cent of a sample of attested letters written by the suspect also display this feature. However, in support of the defence hypothesis that the accused was not the author, we discover that, in the general population, writers use the feature 10 per cent of the time. How do we now assess the evidential strength of this finding; that is, that we would expect the suspect to use it 10 per cent of the time anyway, but that in fact s/he is using it so much more?

To start with, we produce a *likelihood ratio* by dividing one percentage by the other, so 80/10 provides a likelihood ratio of 8. Interpretation of this ratio, however, is not quite so simple. It is certainly true that, as Broeders (1999: 230) expresses it, 'to the extent that the likelihood ratio exceeds 1 the evidence lends greater support to the [prosecution] hypothesis, [while] if it is smaller than 1 it supports the alternative hypothesis'. Unfortunately, that does not tell us exactly how much greater support a likelihood ratio of 8 gives – we will return to this question of interpretation below.

A major advantage of this method of expressing the weight of evidence statistically is that it allows the user to combine several pieces of evidence, or several likelihood ratios, by multiplication, in order to produce a composite likelihood ratio: when combined together, all ratios that are greater than 1 will increase the overall likelihood, while any ratio of less than 1 will reduce it. So, to continue our imaginary example, there might be a series of other distinctive features co-occurring in the anonymous and attested letters like 'their' spelled as 'there', 'you're' spelled as 'your' and possessive 'its' spelled as 'it's'. These features may be found in themselves to have low likelihood ratios of, respectively, 1.4, 1.5, 1.7, but when they are combined with the likelihood ratio of 8 already calculated for 'ofcourse', they produce, by multiplication, the much higher ratio of 25.86. In other words after examining the four features, we can now say on a principled basis that it is 25 times more likely that the suspect wrote the letter than that anyone else did.

One strong argument in favour of this mathematical approach is that it allows the easy incorporation of counter indications as well. Whereas experts using the 'evidence to evaluate the hypothesis approach', as Coulthard was in the Campbell case, have to decide what weight to give to any evidence which does not support the indication of the majority of the features analysed – should they, for example, allow such evidence to reduce their opinion by one or two degrees of certainty or by none at all. By contrast, with a likelihood ratio approach, any measurement which supports the defence hypothesis, and so by definition has a likelihood ratio of less than 1, will simply reduce the cumulative ratio. So let us now imagine we add in the feature 'whose' spelled as 'who's', which has a ratio for the letters under consideration of 0.85, the cumulative ratio will now fall to 21.98.

While such a mathematical approach has obvious attractions, it does present very real problems to both phoneticians and linguists when they try to calculate the defence likelihood ratio. First, how does one establish what is a relevant comparison population of speakers or texts and how does one get access to, and then analyse, the data from that population, particularly in a world where lawyers and courts are not willing to pay for what might be thought to be basic research. At least in the area of forensic phonetics there are already agreed reference tables for such things as pitch of voice as well as solid evidence about the effects of telephone transmission on the pitch of the first formants of vowels. In the area of linguistics there is even less reference data, although specialist corpora are being created: McMenamin, for instance (2002: 154), reports using a corpus of 742 letters for comparison purposes, while of course for some purposes (see Coulthard 1993, 1994b) evidence can be drawn from general corpora like the Australian National Corpus, the British National Corpus, the Collins Bank of English and the American National Corpus which, at the time of writing, is still being constructed.

But then, even if we are able to calculate the defence ratios, we are still not out of the trees, because we need to know how to evaluate the significance of the resulting composite likelihood ratios. And there is the added problem of whether a lay jury can cope with likelihood ratios, or whether they will simply introduce even greater confusion.

Rose (2002: 62) proposes solving this problem by grouping all numerical likelihood ratios, once they have been calculated, into five semantically labelled categories, which, he suggests, should be transparent to the jury:

Likelihood ratio	Semantic Gloss
10,000+	Very strong
1,000–10,000	Strong
100–1,000	Moderately strong
10–100	Moderate
1–10	Limited

However, such a translation is by no means universally accepted and Professor Meadow, who was referred to in the epigraph at the beginning of the chapter, had a much more persuasive translation – he created what came to be known as 'Meadow's Law': 'one sudden infant death is a *tragedy*, two is *suspicious* and three is *murder*, unless proven otherwise'.

Even if one accepts Rose's argument for the theoretical advantages of his mathematically calculated likelihood ratio, there remain two major doubts. First, after rejecting a scale of *opinions* expressed semantically, we have ended up with a scale of *likelihoods* expressed semantically, although admittedly, in this case, if two experts agree on the facts to be considered they will necessarily agree on the likelihood ratio too. Even so, the same problem remains of whether juries can and will interpret the semantic expressions of the ratios as the expert intended. Second, we do not yet know how appropriate the labels are as glosses for the ratios, even though the category cut-off points are numerically neat. On the one hand, courts work with the concept of 'beyond reasonable doubt' which does not have a defined likelihood ratio, although a lay juror, along with statistician A.P. Dawid (2001: 4), might be happy to equate the phrase with one chance in 100. On the other hand, one area of forensic investigation, DNA analysis, seems to be working with much higher likelihood ratios:

> His counsel, Rebecca Poulet QC, reminded him of DNA evidence which showed his profile matched that of the attacker, with the chances of it being anyone else being one in a billion.
>
> (BBC News 17 February 2004)

In principle though, the judicial system should be attracted by the fact that likelihood ratios derived from a variety of types of evidence can be combined to produce a composite likelihood ratio. In an ideal Rosean world, juries would have a statistician to help them weigh all the evidence, and, unlike the individual expert, the jury would be able to take account as well of such *prior odds* as how many possible suspects there are. For example, if there are five suspects, then before any evidence has been considered the odds that one of them is guilty are $1/4 = 0.25$, if there are only two suspects the odds are $1/1 = 1$.

Despite obvious academic support for the use of likelihood ratios, it may be a long time before they get general acceptance in courts. *The Times* (9 May 1996: 36) reported the opinion in an Appeal Court judgement (*R v. Adams*) where, in the original trial, a statistician had been allowed to instruct the jury about both the Bayes theorem and the underlying likelihood ratios and then how to create and sum the ratios in order to produce a composite ratio. The Appeal Court judges ordered a retrial and observed that, although the likelihood ratio 'might be an appropriate and useful tool for statisticians … it was not appropriate for use in jury trials, nor as a means to assist the jury in their tasks'. After a second trial in which the same expert was allowed to instruct a different jury in the same way, there was a second appeal, at the end of which the judges opined:

> Introducing Bayes' Theorem, or any similar method, into a criminal trial plunges the jury into inappropriate and unnecessary realms of complexity, deflecting them from their proper tasks. Reliance on evidence of this kind is a recipe for confusion, misunderstanding, and misjudgement.
> (Sanderson, S.M., 10 October 2006)

And that, for the moment, is the situation in the British courts: experts are still able to express opinions without relating them to probabilities or likelihood ratios.

Admissible evidence

We have seen in previous chapters examples of most of the areas in which forensic linguists and phoneticians feel they have something to offer as expert witnesses and in which they have been willing to write reports. We will now look at the reaction of the courts to such evidence.

Australia and Britain

Australia and Britain share essentially the same position on expert evidence, although there are minor differences between the rules in the individual Australian States and between the three British jurisdictions of Scotland, Northern Ireland and England and Wales. Here it is the expert rather than the method that is recognized, so courts can allow opinion evidence from anyone considered to have

> specialised knowledge based on … training, study or experience [provided that the opinion is] wholly or substantially based on that knowledge.
> (Evidence Act 1995 Sec. 79)

For the UK the current position on the duties and responsibilities of all experts, irrespective of which side has retained and is paying them, was articulated in the case of *National Justice Compania Naviera SA* v. *Prudential Assurance Co* and the rules are very similar for experts working in Australia. Legally, 'an expert witness is appointed by the court, even though they appear as a witness for one of the parties' (Bromby 2002: 21). The rules include the following:

1 Expert evidence presented to the court should be, and should be seen to be, the independent product of the expert, uninfluenced as to form or content by the exigencies of litigation;

2 An expert witness should provide independent assistance to the court by way of objective, unbiased opinion in relation to matters within his expertise and should never assume the role of an advocate;

3 An expert witness should state the facts or assumptions on which his opinion is based. He should not omit material facts which could detract from his concluded opinion.

There are, however, no explicit rules, as there are in the US following the Daubert ruling (see below), on the nature of the theoretical position or the methodology or the evidence on which the expert bases his/her opinion and so once an expert has been retained, the court will determine, '*ad hoc*, the sufficiency of expertise and the relevance of that expertise to each case in question' (Bromby 2002: 9). As part of this process both the competence of the expert and the reliability of the method(s) s/he has used can be subjected to detailed examination, which can last for many hours. Even after deciding to allow an expert to give evidence, the judge(s) and/or jury may decide it is not helpful, persuasive or relevant and ignore it and occasionally, at the end of a trial, experts are severely censured by the court and particular methodologies are deemed to be unacceptable.

What this means as far as linguistic evidence is concerned is that almost all of the techniques and resulting expert opinions discussed in the previous four chapters are acceptable in British and Australian courts, with the exception of auditory evidence in speaker identification cases. French (1994: 173) wrote:

> Despite a recent English Court of Criminal Appeal ruling (*R* v. *Robb* 1991) that forensic speaker identification evidence based upon auditory analysis alone is admissible in a criminal trial, its shortcomings are quite apparent.

And this observation was prophetic because, at the time of writing, a recent ruling in Northern Ireland has forbidden such unsupported evidence, although for the moment this is only 'persuasive' rather than 'binding' in the other two jurisdictions – England and Wales, and Scotland (French personal communication).

The United States

Unlike the Anglo-Australian system, the American legal system approves the technique(s) that a witness uses rather than the witness him/herself. Rule 702 of the Federal Rules of Evidence allows an expert to testify as a witness if:

> the testimony is based upon sufficient facts or data, [and]
> the testimony is the product of reliable principles and methods, and
> the witness has applied the principles and methods reliably to the facts of the case.

Rule 702 is designed to take account of the 1993 Daubert Ruling which dramatically changed the nature of allowable evidence and distanced the American system even further from the Anglo-Australian one. In what follows we draw substantially on Tiersma and Solan (2002) and Solan and Tiersma (2004), which readers are advised to study in their entirety.

There have been three stages in defining the admissibility of expert evidence in the United States. Until 1975, the main standard for evaluating expert testimony was the Frye test, named after a ruling in a 1923 case involving the admissibility of lie detector evidence, which required there to be general acceptability of the principles and/or methodology which the expert had used:

> while courts will go a long way in admitting expert testimony deduced from a well-recognized scientific principle or discovery, the thing from which the deduction is made must be sufficiently established to have gained general acceptance in the particular field in which it belongs.
>
> (293 F. at 1014, as quoted in Tiersma and Solan 2002: 223)

As time went by Frye came to be seen as too rigorous. It was argued that scientific knowledge advances by argument and dissent, so there was pressure to allow the judge and/or jury to hear opinions from both sides when there was serious academic disagreement and in 1975 the Federal Rules of Evidence were introduced with the following observation on the admissibility of expert evidence:

> if scientific, technical, or other specified knowledge will assist a trier of fact to understand the evidence or to determine a fact in issue, a witness qualified as an expert by knowledge, skill, experience, training, or education, may testify thereto in the form of an opinion or otherwise.
>
> (Rule 702 as quoted in Tiersma and Solan 2002: 223)

Even so, and confusingly, some federal courts continued to apply Frye until 1993, when the Supreme Court ruled in the case of *Daubert* v. *Merrell Dow Pharmaceuticals*. The main argument in that appeal was over whether expert evidence could be rejected on the grounds that the experts involved had not published their work and had thereby failed to meet the Frye test. In their ruling the Supreme Court observed that 'the adjective "scientific" implies a grounding in the methods and procedures of science' and then went on to propose four criteria with which to evaluate 'scientific-ness':

1 whether the theory ... has been tested;
2 whether it has been subjected to peer review and publication;
3 the known rate of error; and
4 whether the theory is generally accepted in the scientific community.
   (509 US at 593 as quoted in Tiersma and Solan 2002)

This ruling left open the question of whether it covered evidence which was descriptive rather than theoretical, but a ruling in 1999, in the case of *Kumho Tire Co.* v. *Carmichael*, confirmed that it did:

'the general principles of Daubert' apply not only to experts offering scientific evidence, but also to experts basing their testimony on experience.

(119 S.Ct. 1173 as quoted in Tiersma and Solan 2002: 224)

So, where does that leave the American forensic linguist? On the positive side Tiersma and Solan (2002: 221) note that:

> courts have allowed linguists to testify on issues such as the probable origin of a speaker, the comprehensibility of a text, whether a particular defendant understood the Miranda warning, and the phonetic similarity of two competing trademarks.

However, in other areas the situation is more problematic, partly, perhaps, because non-linguists have claimed ownership of the labels for linguistic concepts. The Van Wyk case in 2000 seemed to set a precedent for excluding *stylistic analysis*, as the court refused to allow the expert to give evidence about the authorship of disputed documents, but, as McMenamin (2002) points out, the expert in the case had no qualifications in linguistics. McMenamin (2004) argues a strong case for the scientific nature of his own brand of forensic stylistics and therefore for its acceptability under Daubert. Indeed he shows how to express opinions statistically in terms of mathematically calculated probabilities, in a case study of the significant documents in the JonBenét Ramsey case (McMenamin 2004: 193–205). It appears that the linguistic area of *discourse analysis* may have suffered similar loss of credibility through a non-linguist claiming expertise. Tiersma and Solan quote a judge's observation in a 1984 case, *State v. Conway*, following evidence from a psychologist, that discourse analysis is a 'discipline allowing [the expert] to determine the intent of the speaker in covertly recorded conversations', which shows just how much re-education needs to be done.

Nevertheless, it must be conceded that, in cases where conclusions depend on observations about the frequency or rarity of particular linguistic features in the texts under examination, many linguists would have considerable difficulty in stating a 'known rate of error' for their results, even if this phrase is interpreted as a likelihood ratio. It is for this reason that some linguists will be forced to change their way of reaching and presenting their opinions, while others may choose to see their role more as that of 'tour guides' than opinion givers (Solan 1998).

Consulting and testifying as tour guides

So what remains for the linguist whose findings cannot be appropriately presented in a mathematical way? Solan (1998) addresses a problem which is unique to experts in linguistics, the fact that the judges of fact, whether they be actual judges or jury members, are seen for most purposes to be their own experts in the area of language use and interpretation – the law is, much of the time, concerned with the meaning(s) that ordinary speakers attach to words and expressions. Even so, there is a role for the linguist, which is to explain and elucidate facts about language and usage as a result of which judge and jury will then be in the same position as the linguist and so can make linguistically informed decisions. In Solan's words:

> my linguistic training has made me more sensitive to possible interpretations that others might not notice and I can bring these to the attention of a judge or jury. But once I point these out and illustrate them clearly, we should start on an equal footing.
>
> (p. 92)

To expand Solan's observation, linguists are not only 'experts in the nature of meaning' but also experts in the nature of linguistic encoding at both lexico-grammatical and textual levels and so there is a guiding role for the linguist in these areas as well, both before and during a trial.

Shuy (2002a: 8) notes that some lawyers prefer to use the linguist as consultant and not as expert witness:

> Some use my analysis as part of their opening and closing statements ... but the most common use ... is for cross-examination.

Shuy (2002a: 11–12) reports several examples of such assistance, one of them where a tape-recorded conversation with an undercover agent was being used by the prosecution to show the accused, a Mr Richards, apparently incriminating himself by referring to drug related money. Richards counter-claimed that in the conversation he had in fact been referring to legal money, which he understood to be coming from Mexico. Shuy provided the attorney with a simple table showing how and by whom places were referred to in the conversation:

Place reference	By Agent	By Richards
Columbia(n)	7	0
Down south	5	0
Down there	1	4
Mexico	0	8

and the attorney was able to use this as a basis for aggressive cross-examination (Extract 10.1) to establish that his client had not in fact used any of the incriminating references; rather they had been fed into the conversation by the agent himself:

Extract 10.1

Q. In all of your conversations you use the reference 'Colombian' seven times. Is it your experience that everyone from Colombia is a drug dealer?
A. No, but these were.
Q. I notice that you referred to the source of the money as coming from 'down south'. Is everyone from down south a drug dealer?

A. No, but these guys were.
Q. And did Richards ever use the expressions, 'Colombians', or 'drug dealers?'
A. I think so.
Q. You may think so, but would it surprise you to know that he never used these expressions?
A. Yeah.
Q. The tape speaks for itself. I assure you, there are none. But did Richards ever refer to a possible source of the money?
A. I don't know.
Q. Look at page 17 and at page 24. What does he say there?
A. Mexico.

One British example of the expert sensitizing the lay audience comes from Coulthard's evidence in the appeal of *R v. Robert Brown*. In Brown's disputed statement there occurs the phrase *my jeans and a blue Parka coat and a shirt*. The accused claimed that a monologue confession attributed to him had in fact been elicited by question and answer and transformed by the interviewing officers into monologue form. As part of his evidence in support of Brown's claim, Coulthard focussed on the two clauses:

> I was covered in blood, my jeans and **a** blue Parka coat and **a** shirt were full of blood.

To a linguist it is clear that the phrasing of the subject of the second clause is most unnatural; no one would refer to their own clothes with the indefinite article once they had begun a list with the possessive determiner. The most likely use of 'a' in this context would be to distinguish between 'mine' and 'not-mine'. For example, 'I looked round the room and I saw my jeans and a blue Parka coat and a shirt; they were full of blood' would be perfectly natural, but that meaning, of course, did not make any sense in a narrative where all the clothes referred to belonged to the narrator. The phrase 'a blue Parka coat and a shirt' could occur quite naturally, of course, as a result of a careless conversion of a sequence of short questions and answers into monologue form and one could see how it might have happened by looking at the following sequence taken from the record of an immediately preceding interview with Brown:

> What were you wearing?
> I had **a** blue shirt and **a** blue parka.

In this context the use of the indefinite article is normal; as just noted above, when items are introduced for the first time, the indefinite article is the natural choice. Once the oddity of the phrase and the occurrence of a similar phrase in the interview had been pointed out to the appeal court judges they were as competent as any linguist to draw inferences from this oddity.

A *substitute prosecution witness*

One of the important points that Solan makes is that, although juries and judges may well be able to analyse words, phrases and even sentences as well as any professional linguist, they may have problems with long documents or a series of related documents, because they may not be able to make the necessary links:

> Of course a jury can read the document[s]. … But not all jurors, without help, can focus on a phrase in paragraph 24 of a contract that may have an impact on how another word should be interpreted in paragraph 55.
>
> (Solan 1998: 94)

In the Paul Blackburn case, discussed above on pp. 196–8, it was also important to draw the attention of the judges to two phrases occurring in two different documents, one a record of a dictated statement, the other a record of an interview:

i)	Statement	I asked her if I could carry her bags she said 'Yes'
	Interview	I asked her if I could carry her bags and she said 'yes'
ii)	Statement	I picked something up like an ornament
	Interview	I picked something up like an ornament

As we noted earlier, linguists of most persuasions are in agreement that the likelihood of two speakers independently producing exactly the same phrasing reduces dramatically with the length of the expression and the likelihood of them choosing two or more identical phrasings is even more unlikely. However, the linguist's 'knowledge' is the total opposite of lay belief. When faced with the problem of convincing the Appeal Court judges of the significance of the identical expressions, Coulthard chose the following procedure.

First, he demonstrated that even short sequences of words can be unique encodings, by looking at the occurrences of the individual words and component phrases of the utterance 'I asked her if I could carry her bags' and presenting the figures discussed on page 197.

Using this evidence Coulthard argued that, if there was not a single instance of anyone having ever produced this sequence, the chances of even longer sequences occurring twice in different documents was infinitesimal, unless, of course, one was derived from the other.

Then, to strengthen the argument, Coulthard used Google to find another case, this time one involving Lord Justice Rose, who was to preside at the trial. On typing in the words 'Lord', 'Justice', 'Rose' and 'Appeal' the first three citations he found were concerned with an appeal by a famous British politician – Lord Archer – against his conviction for perjury. The first hit of all was:

Guardian Unlimited – Special reports – Archer loses *appeal* bid
… was not present at today's hearing, had his application for permission to *appeal* against the conviction rejected within hours. *Lord Justice Rose*, sitting with …

(*Guardian Unlimited* 22 July 2002)

Coulthard accessed the full citation, which is reproduced in part as Extract 10.2, and from it selected the first phrase quoted from Lord Rose 'For reasons we will give later in the day', which is highlighted in *italics*.

Extract 10.2

Archer loses appeal bid
Lord Justice Rose, sitting with Mr Justice Colman and Mr Justice Stanley Burnton in London, told Archer's QC Nicholas Purnell: '*For reasons we will give later in the day* we are against you in relation to conviction'.

At the start of the hearing Nicholas Purnell QC, outlining the grounds of appeal, said: 'The submission that we make on behalf of Lord Archer is that *the first and fundamental ground* which interconnects with all the other grounds of appeal was that the learned trial judge wrongly exercised his discretion not to sever the trial of Edward Francis.'

Mr Purnell said the decision of the judge, Mr Justice Potts, not to sever the trial of Francis had an '*unbalancing effect on the equilibrium*' of the trial.

Counsel argued that Mr Francis was 'in a position effectively as *a substitute prosecution witness* and a substitute prosecutor'.

Given the nature of Appeal Court judgements this seems to be an unremarkable phrase for an appeal court judge to use, particularly as a lot of judgements are produced some time after the verdict is announced. Yet a search returned only seven occurrences. Every single one of them was about Lord Rose; indeed they were all reports of this same single utterance at the end of the Archer appeal.

Coulthard then took three other short phrases quoted in the article, this time from Nicholas Purnell, Lord Archer's lawyer, each of them apparently not unusual phrases for a lawyer to utter: 'the first and fundamental ground', an 'unbalancing effect on the equilibrium' of the trial and a 'substitute prosecution witness'. For these phrases Google found seven, ten and four instances respectively, but again all the instances were versions of the same single utterings.

This seemed to be a simple and efficient way of illustrating uniqueness of expression in court, but when Coulthard presented this illustration to the lawyers, they declined to submit it to the judges and one of them described it as 'whimsical'.

Conclusion

We started this book with a chapter entitled 'Approaching a forensic text', in which we asked you to consider what skills and knowledge you could bring to bear on a text which had significance in a legal context, and now we have just ended the book with a chapter for aspiring experts that provides a sketch of the work of the linguist as expert witness. In between our concern has been with all aspects of language use and description in a legal context. Our two-fold aim was: first, to give you a much deeper insight into the language of the legal process, from first contacts with the emergency services, through interactions with the police and legal professionals to the end of legal proceedings in court; second, we wanted to exemplify how language and the forensic linguist's analysis of it can be significant evidence used by both prosecution and defence in criminal and civil trials.

This book has been our examination of the case in two parts; but we do not know how persuasive our advocacy was. For the moment, the jury is out; we hope your verdict goes in our favour.

Further reading

Coulthard (2005); Rose (2002, chapters 4 and 11); Shuy (2006); Solan and Tiersma (2004, 2005); Tiersma and Solan (2002).

Research task

Work with a colleague.

Stage 1. Take the ten text messages you collected from your friend for Research Task 2 in Chapter 8 and add 20 more messages, ten produced by yourself and ten by another friend. Give the three sets of texts to your colleague and ask him/her to analyse the underlying rules. Then give your colleague your friend's version of the 'Hiya Stuart' text and ask him/her to identify the most likely author. At the same time you should undertake the same task using your colleague's set of texts.

Stage 2. Now choose one of the two cases and jointly write a formal expert's report, as if for a court, expressing and justifying your opinion and giving your degree of certainty using the 11-point scale presented on page 202. Attach all the texts as an appendix. Remember that, even if you know who produced the texts, the linguistic evidence alone may not be strong enough to enable you to demonstrate that in court.

Stage 3. Finally exchange your joint report for one produced by another pair of colleagues. You should now take on the role of expert for the defence and test the strength of the case made in the other report, while they do the same with yours.

Stage 4. Select two other colleagues to act as courtroom lawyers who will examine and cross-examine the expert for the prosecution and then the expert for the defence. Ask the rest of the class, acting as jury, to indicate what weight they would give to the evidence.

References

ABC News (20 February 2007) Online. Available HTTP: <http://www.abc.net.au/news/ newsitems/200207/s604549.htm> (accessed 9 May 2007).

Aitken, C.G.G. (1995) *Statistics and the Evaluation of Evidence for Forensic Scientists*, Chichester: John Wiley.

Aldridge, M. and Wood, J. (1998) *Interviewing Children: A Guide for Child Care and Forensic Practitioners*, London: Wiley.

Amsterdam, A.G. and Bruner, J. (2000) *Minding the Law*, Cambridge, MA: Harvard University Press.

Anderson, J. (1998) *Plagiarism, Copyright Violation and other Thefts of Intellectual Property*, Jefferson, NC: McFarland.

Angélil-Carter, S. (2000) *Stolen Language? Plagiarism in Writing*, Harlow: Longman.

Archer, D. (2005) *Questions and Answers in the English Courtroom (1640–1740): A sociopragmatic analysis*, Amsterdam: John Benjamins.

Atkinson, J.M. and Drew, P. (1979) *Order in Court*, London: Macmillan.

Atkinson, J.M., Heritage, J.C. and Watson, D.R. (1979) 'Suspects' rights and the standardization of interrogation procedures: a case for greater formality', *Written Evidence to the Royal Commission on Criminal Procedure*, Mimeo.

Atwood, W. and Hollien, H. (1986) 'Stress monitoring by polygraph for research purposes', *Polygraph*, 15, 47–56.

Auburn, T., Drake, S. and Williy, C. (1995) 'You punched him, didn't you?': versions of violence in accusatory interviews', *Discourse and Society*, 6, 3, 354–86.

Austin, J.L. (1962) *How to Do Things with Words*. J.O. Urmson (ed.). Oxford: Clarendon; reprinted in Jaworski and Coupland (2006) *The Discourse Reader*, 2nd edn, London: Routledge, 55–65.

Avon and Somerset Constabulary Interactive webchat (9 February 2007) Online. Available HTTP: <http://www.avonandsomerset.police.uk/Interactive/Webchat/ PreviousChatsView.aspx?scid=25> (accessed 27 March 2007).

Avon and Somerset Constabulary Interactive webchat (27 February 2007) Online. Available HTTP: <http://www.avonandsomerset.police.uk/Interactive/Webchat/ PreviousChatsView.aspx?scid=28> (accessed 27 March 2007).

Baigent v. *Random House* (7 April 2006) *Summary of Judgment* Online. Available HTTP: <http://www.judiciary.gov.uk/judgment_guidance/judgments/summary.htm> (accessed 27 May 2007).

Bakhtin, M. (1981) *The Dialogic Imagination: Four Essays*, M. Holquist (ed.), trans. C. Emerson and M. Holquist, Austin, TX and London: University of Texas Press.

—— (1986) *Speech Genres and Other Late Essays*, C. Emerson and M. Holquist (eds), trans. V.W. McGee, Austin, TX: University of Texas Press.

Baldwin, J. and French, J. (1990) *Forensic Phonetics*, London: Pinter.

Bamberg, M. (2004) 'Considering counter narratives' in M. Bamberg and. M. Andrews (eds), *Considering Counter Narratives: Narrating, resisting, making sense*, Amsterdam: John Benjamins, 351–71.

Bank of English (2007) Online. Available HTTP: <http://www.titania.bham.ac.uk/docs/svenguide.html> (accessed 12 May 2007).

Barry, A. (1991) 'Narrative style and witness testimony', *Journal of Narrative and Life History*, 1, 4, 281–93.

Bates, E., Kintsch, W., Fletcher, C.R. and Giulani, V. (1980) 'The role of pronominalisation and ellipsis in texts: some memorisation experiments', *Journal of Experimental Psychology: Human Learning and Memory*, 6, 676–91.

BBC (10 January 2007) 'Little Britain' Online. Available HTTP: <http://www.bbc.co.uk/bbc7/comedy/progpages/littlebritain.shtml> (accessed 20 January 2007).

BBC (20 January 2007) 'Little Britain: Interview with Matt Lucas and David Walliams' Online. Available HTTP: <http://www.bbc.co.uk/bbcthree/tv/littlebritain/interview.shtml> (accessed 20 January 2007).

BBC Crime (10 August 2006) Crime – Case Closed – Fred West (accessed 10 August 2006).

BBC News (31 January 2000) Online. Available HTTP: <http://news.bbc.co.uk/1/hi/uk/616692.stm> (accessed 10 August 2006).

BBC News (17 February 2004) Online. 'Doubt over murder trial evidence'. Available HTTP: <http://news.bbc.co.uk/1/hi/scotland/3494401.stm> (accessed 3 September 2006).

BBC News (17 February 2004) Online. 'Rape accused tells jury "hang me"'. Available HTTP: <http://news.bbc.co.uk/1/hi/england/3496207.stm> (accessed 3 September 2006).

BBC News (16 March 2004) Online. 'Kelly inquest will not be reopened'. Available HTTP: http://news.bbc.co.uk/1/hi/uk_politics/3513812.stm (accessed January 2007).

BBC News (20 October 2005) Online. Available HTTP: <http://news.bbc.co.uk/1/hi/england/4360026.stm> (accessed 10 August 2006).

BBC News (21 March 2006) 'Man jailed for Ripper deception'. Online. Available HTTP: < http://news.bbc.co.uk/1/hi/england/west_yorkshire/4828828.stm (accessed 10 August 2006).

BBC News (7 April 2006) Online. Available HTTP: <http://news.bbc.co.uk/1/hi/entertainment/4886234.stm> (accessed 10 August 2006).

BBC News (1 February 2007) Online. Available HTTP: <http://news.bbc.co.uk> (accessed 4 February 2007).

Berk-Seligson, S. (2002) *The Bilingual Courtroom: Court interpreters in the judicial process*, Chicago, IL: University of Chicago Press.

Bennett, W.L. and Feldman, M.S. (1981) *Reconstructing Reality in the Courtroom: Justice and judgment in American culture*, New Brunswick, NJ: Rutgers University Press.

Bhatia, V.K. (1993) *Analysing Genre: Language Use in Professional Settings*, London: Longman.

—— (1994) 'Cognitive structuring in legislative provisions', in J. Gibbons (ed.), *Language and the Law*, London: Longman, 136–55.

—— (2004) *Worlds of Written Discourse*, London: Continuum.

Biber, D. (1988) *Variation across Speech and Writing*, Cambridge: Cambridge University Press.

—— (1995) *Dimensions of Register Variation: A cross-linguistic comparison*, Cambridge: Cambridge University Press.

Bloch, B. (1948) 'A set of postulates for phonemic analysis', *Language*, 24, 3–46.

BNC (2000) British National Corpus, BNC World Edition, Oxford: Humanities Computing Unit, Oxford University.

Braun, A. (1994) 'The audio going with the video: some observations on the Rodney King case', *Forensic Linguistics*, 1, ii, 217–22.

Brazil, D.C. (1985) *The Communicative Value of Intonation*, Birmingham: English Language Research.

Brennan, M. (1994a) 'The discourse of denial: cross-examining child victim witnesses', *Journal of Pragmatics*, 23, 71–91.

—— (1994b) 'Cross-examining children in criminal courts: child welfare under attack', in J. Gibbons (ed.), *Language and the Law*, London: Longman, 199–216.

Brennan, M. and Brennan, R.E. (1988) *Strange Language*, Wagga Wagga, NSW: Riverina Literacy Centre.

Broeders, A.P.A. (1996) 'Earwitness identification: common ground, disputed territory and uncharted areas', *Forensic Linguistics*, 3, i, 1–13.

—— (1999) 'Some observations on the use of probability scales in forensic identification', *Forensic Linguistics*, 6, ii, 228–41.

—— ms 'Forensic speech and audio analysis in forensic linguistics 1998 to 2001: a review', quoted in Rose (2002) *Forensic Speaker Identification*, London: Taylor and Francis.

Broeders, A.P.A. and Rietveld, A.C.M. (1995) 'Speaker identification by earwitnesses', in A. Braun and J.-P. Köster (eds) *Studies in Forensic Phonetics*, Trier: Wissenschaftlicher Verlag, 24–40.

Bromby, M.C. (2002) *The Role and Responsibilities of the Expert Witness within the UK Judicial System*, dissertation presented for the Diploma in Forensic Medical Science, awarded by The Worshipful Company of Apothecaries, London. Online. Available HTTP: <http://cbs1.gcal.ac.uk/law/users/~mbro/documents/DipFMSDissertation.pdf> (accessed 12 September 2006).

Brown, P. and Levinson, S. (1978) 'Universals in language use: politeness phenomena', in E.N. Goody (ed.) *Questions and Politeness: Strategies in social interaction*, Cambridge: Cambridge University Press, 56–311; reprinted in A. Jaworski and N. Coupland (2006) *The Discourse Reader*, 2nd edn, London: Routledge, 311–24.

Bull, R. and Clifford, B. (1999) Special supplement on Expert Witnesses *New Law Journal*, 149, Feb., 216–20.

Buranen, L. and Roy, A.M. (eds) (1999) *Perspectives on Plagiarism and Intellectual Property in a Postmodern World*, Albany, NY: State University of New York Press.

Caldas-Coulthard, C.R. and Coulthard, M. (1996) *Texts and Practices: Readings in critical discourse analysis*, London: Routledge.

Canale, M., Mougeon., R. and Klokeid, T.J. (1982) 'Remarks: forensic linguistics', *Canadian Journal of Linguistics*, 27, 2, 150–5.

Canter, D.C. and Chester J. (1997) 'Investigation into the claim of weighted Cusum in authorship attribution studies', *Forensic Linguistics*, 4, ii, 252–61.

Chomsky, N. (1965) *Aspects of the Theory of Syntax*, Cambridge, MA: MIT Press.

Clemit, P. and Woolls, D. (2001) 'Two new pamphlets by William Godwin: a case of computer-assisted authorship attribution', *Studies in Bibliography*, 54, 265–84.

Clifford, B.R. (1983) 'Memory for voices: the feasibility and quality of earwitness evidence', in S.M.A. Lloyd-Bostock and B.R Clifford (eds) *Evaluating Witness Evidence*, New York: Wiley and Sons, 189–218.

Coke, Sir E. (1979) *The Third Part of the Institutes of the Laws of England*, vol.2, New York: Garland Publishing.

Conley, J.M. and O'Barr, W.M. (1998) *Just Words: Law, language and power*, Chicago: University Chicago Press.

Cooley, A., Bess, C. and Rubin-Jackson, M. (as told to Tom Byrnes with Mike Walker) (1995) *Madam Foreman: A rush to judgment?* Beverly Hills, CA: Dove Books.

Corder, S.P. (1973) *Introducing Applied Linguistics*, Harmondsworth: Penguin.

Cotterill, J. (ed.) (2002) *Language in the Legal Process*, London: Palgrave.

—— (2003) *Language and Power in Court: A linguistic analysis of the O.J. Simpson trial*, Basingstoke: Palgrave.

Coulthard, R.M. (1977) *An Introduction to Discourse Analysis*, London: Longman.

—— (1992) 'Forensic discourse analysis', in R.M. Coulthard (ed.) *Advances in Spoken Discourse Analysis*, London: Routledge, 242–57.

—— (1993) 'Beginning the study of forensic texts: corpus, concordance, collocation', in M.P. Hoey (ed.) *Data Description Discourse*, London: HarperCollins, 86–97.

—— (1994a) '*Powerful* evidence for the defence: an exercise in forensic discourse analysis', in J. Gibbons (ed.), *Language and the Law*, London: Longman, 414–42.

—— (1994b) 'On the use of corpora in the analysis of forensic texts', *Forensic Linguistics*, 1, i, 27–43.

—— (1997) 'A failed appeal', *Forensic Linguistics*, 4, ii, 287–302.

—— (2002) 'Whose voice is it? Invented and concealed dialogue in written records of verbal evidence produced by the police', in J. Cotterill (ed.) *Language in the Legal Process*, London: Palgrave, 19–34.

—— (2004) 'Author identification, idiolect and linguistic uniqueness', *Applied Linguistics*, 25, 4, 431–47.

—— (2005) 'The linguist as expert witness', *Linguistics and the Human Sciences*, 1, i, 39–58.

Crown Prosecution Service (2002) *Achieving Best Evidence in Criminal Proceedings: Guidance for Vulnerable or Intimidated Witnesses, including Children*. Online. Available HTTP: <http://www.cps.gov.uk/publications/prosecution/bestevidencevol1.html> (accessed 14 May 2007).

CRTC Decision 2006-45 (2006) Online. Available HTTP: <http://www.crtc.gc.ca/archive/ENG/Decisions/2006/dt2006-45.pdf> (accessed 12 August 2006).

Crystal, D. (2003) *Cambridge Encyclopedia of the English Language*, 2nd edn, Cambridge: Cambridge University Press.

Davies, E. (2004) 'Register distinctions and measures of complexity in the language of legal contracts', in J. Gibbons *et al.* (eds) *Language in the Law*, Hyderabad: Orient Longman, 82–99.

Davis, T. (1986) 'Forensic handwriting analysis', in R.M. Coulthard, (ed.) *Talking About Text*, Birmingham: ELR, 189–207.

—— (1994) 'ESDA and the analysis of contested contemporaneous notes of police interviews', *Forensic Linguistics*, 1, i, 71–89.

—— (1996) 'Clues and opinions: ways of looking at evidence', in H. Kniffka, R.M. Coulthard and S. Blackwell (eds) *Recent Developments in Forensic Linguistics*, Frankfurt: Peter Lang, 53–73.

Dawid, A.P. (2001) 'Bayes theorem and weighing evidence by juries', Online. Available HTTP: <http://www.ucl.ac.uk/~ucak06d/evidence/1day/ba.pdf> (accessed 12 September 2006).

de Morgan, S.E. (ed.) (1882) *Memoir of Augustus de Morgan by his wife Sophia Elizabeth de Morgan with selections from his letters*, London: Longman's Green and Co.

Drew, P. (1979) 'Comparative analysis of talk-in-interaction in different institutional settings: a sketch', in P. Glenn, C.D. LeBaron and J. Mandelbaum (eds) *Studies in Language and Social Interaction: in honor of Robert Hopper*, Mahweh, NJ: Lawrence Erlbaum, 293–308.

—— (1990) 'Strategies in the contest between lawyer and witness in cross-examination', in J. Levi and A. Graffam Walker (eds), *Language in the Judicial* Process, London: Plenum, 39–64.

—— (1992) 'Contested evidence in courtroom cross-examination: the case of a trial for rape', in P. Drew and J. Heritage (eds), *Talk at Work*, Cambridge and New York: Cambridge University Press, 470–520.

Drew P. and Heritage J. (eds) (1992) *Talk at Work*, Cambridge and New York: Cambridge University Press.

Dumas, K. (1992) 'Adequacy of cigarette package warnings: an analysis of the adequacy of federally mandated cigarette package warnings', *Tennessee Law Review*, 59, 261–304.

—— (2002) 'Reasonable doubt about reasonable doubt: assessing jury instruction adequacy in a capital case', in J Cotterill (ed.), *Language in the Legal* Process, London: Palgrave, 246–59.

Duranti, A. and Goodwin, C. (eds) (1992) *Rethinking Context: Language as an interactive phenomenon*, Cambridge: Cambridge University Press.

Eades, D. (1994) Forensic linguistics in Australia: an overview, *Forensic Linguistics*,1, ii, 113–32.

—— (2002) '"Evidence given in unequivocal terms": gaining consent of Aboriginal young people in court', in J. Cotterill (ed.), *Language in the Legal Process*, London: Palgrave, 162–79.

—— (2005) 'Applied linguistics and language analysis in asylum seeker cases', *Applied Linguistics*, 26, 4, 503–26.

Eades, D., Fraser, H., Seigel, J., McNamara, T. and Baker, B. (2003) 'Linguistic identification in the determination of nationality: a preliminary report', *Language Policy*, 2: 179–99.

Eagleson, R. (1994) 'Forensic analysis of personal written texts: a case study', J. Gibbons (ed.), *Language and the Law*, London: Longman, 362–73.

Edwards, D. (ed.) (2007) 'Calls for help', Special issue of *Research on Language and Social Interaction*, 40, 1, 1–144.

Ehrlich, S. (2001) *Representing Rape: Language and Sexual Consent*, London: Routledge.

—— (2002) '(Re)Contextualizing complainants' accounts of sexual assault', *Forensic Linguistics*, 9, 193–212.

Eisenberg, U. (1995) 'Visuelle und auditive Gegenüberstellung im Strafverfahren', *Kriminalistik*, 49, 458–65.

Ellen, D. (1989) *The Scientific Examination of Documents: Methods and Techniques*, Chichester: Ellis Horwood.

—— (1997) *Scientific Examination of Documents: methods and techniques*, 3rd edn, London: Taylor and Francis

Ellis, S. (1994) 'Case report: The Yorkshire Ripper enquiry, Part 1', *Forensic Linguistics* 1, ii, 197–206.

Fairclough, N. (1989) *Language and Power*, London: Longman.

—— (1995) *Critical Discourse Analysis: The Critical Study of Language*, London: Longman.

Farringdon, J.M. (1996) *Analysing for Authorship: A guide to the Cusum technique*, Cardiff: University of Wales Press.

Foster, D. (2001) *Author Unknown: on the trail of Anonymous*, London: Macmillan.

Fox, G. (1993) 'A comparison of "policespeak" and "normalspeak": a preliminary study', in J.M. Sinclair, M. Hoey and G. Fox (eds) *Techniques of Description: Spoken and Written Discourse*, Routledge: London, 183–95.

Frade, C. (2007) 'Power dynamics and legal English', *World Englishes*, 26, 1, 48–61.

French, J.P. (1994) 'An overview of forensic phonetics', *Forensic Linguistics*, 1, ii, 169–81.

—— (1998) 'Mr Akbar's nearest ear versus the Lombard reflex: a case study in forensic phonetics', *Forensic Linguistics*, 5, 1, 58–68.

French, P., Harrison, P. and Windsor Lewis, J. (2007) 'R v John Humble: The Yorkshire Ripper hoaxer trial', *International Journal of Speech, Language and the Law*, 13, ii, 255–73.

Garfinkel, H. and Sacks, H. (1970) 'On formal structures of practical actions', in J.C. McKinney and E.A. Tiryakian (eds) *Theoretical Sociology*, New York: Appleton-Century-Crofts, 187–238.

Garner, M. and Johnson, E. (2006) 'Operational Communication: a paradigm for applied research into police call-handling', *International Journal of Speech, Language and the Law*, 13, i, 55–75.

Gibbons, J. (ed.) (1994) *Language and the Law*, London: Longman.

—— (1996) 'Distortions of the police interview process revealed by video-tape', *Forensic Linguistics*, 3, ii, 289–98.

—— (2003) *Forensic Linguistics: an introduction to language in the justice system*, Oxford: Blackwell.

—— (2004) 'Taking legal language seriously', in J. Gibbons *et al.*, *Language in the Law*, Hyderabad: Orient Longman, 1–16.

Gibbons, J., Prakasam, V., Tirumalesh, K.V. and Nagarajan, H. (eds) (2004) *Language in the Law*, Hyderabad: Orient Longman.

Gimson, A.C. (1962) *An Introduction to the Pronunciation of English*, London: Arnold.

Goffman, E. (1964) 'The neglected situation', *American Anthropologist*, 66, 6, part II (Special Issue), 133–6.

—— (1967) 'On face-work' in E. Goffman *Interaction Ritual Essays on Face-to-Face Behaviour*, Garolen City, NY: Anchor/Doubleday, reprinted in A. Jaworski and N. Coupland, 2006, 299–310.

—— (1981) *Forms of Talk*, Oxford: Blackwell.

Grant, T.D. (2005) *Authorship Attribution in a Forensic Context*, unpublished PhD thesis, University of Birmingham.

Grice, H.P. (1975) 'Logic and conversation', in P. Cole and J. Morgan (eds) *Syntax and Semantics III: Speech acts*, New York: Academic Press, 41–58; reprinted in A. Jaworski and N. Coupland (eds) *The Discourse Reader*, 2nd edn, London: Routledge, 66–77.

Guardian Unlimited (22.7.02) Online. Available HTTP: <http://www.guardian.co.uk/archer/article/0,2763,759829,00.html> (accessed 12 September 2006).

Gudjonsson, G. (2003) *The Psychology of Interrogations and Confessions: A handbook*, Chichester: John Wiley and Sons.

Gumperz, J. (1982) *Discourse Strategies*, Cambridge: Cambridge University Press.

—— (2003) 'Interactional Sociolinguistics: A personal perspective', in D. Schiffrin, D. Tannen and H.E. Hamilton (eds) *The Handbook of Discourse Analysis*, Oxford: Blackwell, 215–28.

Gustafsson, M. (1984) 'The syntactic features of binomial expressions in legal English', *Text*, 4, 1-3, 123–41.

Haddon, M. (2003) *The Curious Incident of the Dog in the Night-time*, London: Jonathan Cape.

Halldorsdottir, I. (2006) 'Orientations to law, guidelines, and codes in lawyer–client interaction', *Research on Language and Social Interaction*, 39, 3, 263–301.

Halliday, M.A.K. (1975) *Learning How to Mean*, London: Edward Arnold.

—— (1989) *Spoken and Written Language*, 2nd edn, Oxford: Oxford University Press.

—— (1994) *An Introduction to Functional Grammar*, 2nd edn, London: Edward Arnold.

Halliday, M.A.K. and Hasan, R. (1989) *Language, Context and Text: Aspects of language in a social semiotic perspective*, Oxford: Oxford University Press.

Halliday, M.A.K., McIntosh, A. and Strevens, P. (1964) *The Linguistic Sciences and Language Teaching*, London: Longman.

Hanks, W.F. (2005) 'Explorations in the deictic field', *Current Anthropology*, 46, 2, 191–220.

Hanlein, H. (1999) *Studies in Authorship Recognition: a corpus-based approach*, New York: Peter Lang.

Hannam (1953) extract from the court transcript of the examination of Chief Inspector Hannam in the trial of Alfred Charles Whiteway.

Hans, V. and Vidmar, N. (1986) *Judging the Jury*, New York: Plenum.

Hardcastle, R.A. (1997) 'Cusum: a credible method for the determination of authorship?', *Science and Justice*, 37, 2, 129–38.

Harris, S. (1989) 'Defendant resistance to power and control in court', in H. Coleman (ed.) *Working with Language: a multidisciplinary consideration of language use in work contexts, Vol 52 in Contributions to the sociology of language*, Berlin: de Gruyter, 131–64.

—— (1991) 'Evasive action: how politicians respond to questions in political interviews', in P. Scannel (ed.) *Broadcast Talk*, London: Sage, 76–99.

—— (2001) 'Fragmented narratives and multiple tellers: witness and defendant accounts in trials', *Discourse Studies*, 3, 1, 53–74.

—— (2005) 'Telling stories and giving evidence: the hybridisation of narrative and non-narrative modes of discourse in a sexual assault trial' in J. Thornborrow and J. Coates (eds) *The Sociolinguistics of Narrative*, Amsterdam: John Benjamins Publishing Company, 215–37 and Online. Available HTTP: <http://www.courttv.com> (accessed 15 May 2007).

Hasan, R. (2000) 'The uses of talk', in S. Sarangi and M. Coulthard (eds) *Discourse and Social Life*, London:Longman, 30–81.

Heffer, C. (2002) *Making a Case: Narrative and paradigmatic modes in the legal-lay discourse of English jury trial*, unpublished PhD thesis, University of Birmingham.

—— (2005) *The Language of Jury Trial: A corpus-aided analysis of legal-lay discourse*, Basingstoke: Palgrave Macmillan.

Heritage, J.C. (1985) 'Analyzing news interviews: aspects of the production of talk for an overhearing audience', in T.A. van Dijk (ed.) *Handbook of Discourse Analysis Volume 3*, New York: Academic Press, 95–119.

Heritage, J.C. and Watson, D.R. (1979) 'Formulations as conversational objects', in G. Psathas (ed.) *Everyday Language: Studies in ethnomethodology*, New York: Boston University Irvington Press Inc., 123–62.

—— (1980) 'Aspects of the properties of formulations in natural conversations: some instances analysed', *Semiotica*, 30, 3/4, 245–62.

Heritage, J.C., and Sorjonen, M.L. (1994) 'Constituting and maintaining activities across sequences: and-prefacing as a feature of question design', *Language in Society*, 1, 1–29.

Heydon, G. (2005) *The Language of Police Interviewing: A critical analysis,* Basingstoke: Palgrave Macmillan.

Hiltunen, R. (1984) 'Some complex types of embedding in legal English', in H. Ringbom and M. Rissanen (eds) *Proceedings from the Nordic Conference for English Studies,* np.

Hjelmquist, E. (1984) 'Memory for conversations', *Discourse Processes*, 7, 321–36.

—— (1991) 'Recognition memory for utterances in conversations', *Scandinavian Journal of Psychology*, 29, 168–76.

Hoey, M. (1983) *On the Surface of Discourse,* London: George Allen & Unwin.

—— (2000) *Textual Interaction: An Introduction to Written Discourse Analysis,* London: Routledge.

Hollien, H. (1990a) 'The phonetician as expert witness', in R.W. Rieber and W.A. Stewart (eds) *The Language Scientist as Expert in the Legal Setting: Issues in forensic linguistics,* New York: The New York Academy of Sciences, 33–45.

—— (1990b) *The Acoustics of Crime,* London: Plenum.

—— (2001) *Forensic Voice Identification,* London: Academic Press.

Hollien, H., Huntley, H., Kunzel, H. and Hollien, P. (1995) 'Criteria for earwitness lineups', *Forensic Linguistics*, 2, ii, 143–53.

Holmes, J. (1992) 'Women's talk in public contexts', *Discourse and Society*, 3, 2, 131–50.

Holt, E.J. and Johnson, A.J. (2006) 'Formulating the facts: questions and repeats in police/ suspect interviews', Paper presented at the International Conference on Conversation Analysis, Helsinki (May 2006).

Honoré, A. (1979) 'Some simple measures of richness of vocabulary', *Association for Literary and Linguistic Computing Bulletin*, 7, 2, 172–7.

Howard, R.M. (1999a) 'The new abolitionism comes to plagiarism', in L. Buranen and A.M. Roy (eds) *Perspectives on Plagiarism and Intellectual Property in a Postmodern World,* Albany, NY: State University of New York Press, 87–95.

—— (1999b) *Perspectives on Writing: Theory, research, practice, vol. 2: Standing in the shadows of giants,* Stamford, CT: Ablex Publishing.

Hymes, D.H. (1972) 'On communicative competence', in J. Pride and J. Holmes (eds) *Sociolinguistics*, Penguin, 269–93, reprinted under the title 'Modes of the interaction of language and social life' in C. Bratt Paulston and G.R. Tucker (2003) *Sociolinguistics: the essential readings,* Oxford: Blackwell, 30–47.

—— (1974) 'Ways of speaking', in R. Bauman and J. Sherzer (eds) *Explorations in the Ethnography of Speaking,* Cambridge: Cambridge University Press, 425–32.

—— (1986) 'The interaction of language and social life', in J.J. Gumperz and D. Hymes (eds) *Directions in Sociolinguistics: The ethnography of communication,* Oxford: Blackwell, 35–71.

Imbens-Bailey, A. and McCabe, A. (2000) 'The discourse of distress: a narrative analysis of emergency calls to 911', *Language and Communication*, 20, 3, 275–96.

Jackson, B.S. (1988) *Law, Fact and Narrative Coherence,* Roby: Deborah Charles.

—— (1995) *Making Sense in Law: Linguistic, psychological and semiotic perspectives,* Liverpool: Deborah Charles.

Jacquemet, M. (1996) *Credibility in Court: Communicative practices in the Comorra Trials,* Cambridge: Cambridge University Press.

Jaworski, A. and Coupland, N. (eds) (2006) *The Discourse Reader,* 2nd edn, London: Routledge.

Jessen, M., Gfroerer, S. and Köster, O. (2003) 'Forensic study of a case involving SMS text-to-speech conversion', *The International Journal of Speech, Language and the Law*, 10, i, 113–37.

Johns, T.F. (1994) 'The text and its message', in R.M. Coulthard (ed.) *Advances in Written Text Analysis*, London: Routledge, 102–16.

Johnson, A.J. (1997) 'Textual kidnapping: a case of plagiarism among three student texts', *Forensic Linguistics*, 4, ii, 210–25.

—— (2002) 'So...? Pragmatic implications of *So*-prefaced questions in formal police interviews', in J. Cotterill (ed.) *Language in the Legal Process*, London: Palgrave, 91–110.

—— (2006) 'Police questioning', in Brown, K (ed.) *The Encyclopedia of Language and Linguistics*, 2nd edn, vol. 9, Oxford: Elsevier, 661–72.

Jönsson, L. and Linell, P. (1991) 'Story generations: from dialogical interviews to written reports in police interrogations', *Text*, 11, 419–40.

Kaplan, J.P. (1998) 'Pragmatic contributions to the interpretation of a will', *Forensic Linguistics*, 5, ii, 107–26.

Kaplan, J.P., Green G.M., Cunningham, C.D. and Levi J.N. (1995) 'Bringing linguistics into judicial decision making: semantic analysis submitted to the US Supreme Court', *Forensic Linguistics*, 2, i, 81–98.

Keenan, J.M., MacWhinney, B. and Mayhew, D. (1977) 'Pragmatics in memory: a study of natural conversation', *Journal of Verbal Learning and Verbal Behavior*, 16, 549–60.

Kelly, L., Lovett, J. and Regan, L. (2005) 'A gap or a chasm? Attrition in reported rape cases', Home Office Research Study Online. Available HTTP: <http://www.homeoffice.gov.uk/rds/pdfs05/hors293.pdf> (accessed 12 March 2007).

Kersta, L.A. (1962) 'Voiceprint identification', *Nature*, 196, 1253–7.

Kilgariff, A. (24 May 2007) 'BNC database and word frequency lists', Online. Available HTTP: <http://www.kilgarriff.co.uk/bnc-readme.html> (accessed 24 May 2007).

Klarreich, E. (2003) 'Bookish math: statistical tests are unraveling knotty literary mysteries', *Science News Online*, 164, 392, Online. Available HTTP: <http://www.sciencenews.org/articles/(2003)1220/bob8.asp> (accessed 14 September 2006).

Kniffka, H. (1990) (ed.) *Texte zu Theorie und Praxis forensischer Linguistik*, Tübingen: Max Niemeyer Verlag (Linguistische Arbeiten Nr. 249).

Koenig, B.J. (1986) 'Spectrographic voice identification: a forensic survey', letter to the editor of *J. Acoustic Soc. Am.*, 79, 6, 2088–90.

Knox, M. (with M. Walker) (1995) *The Private Diary of an O.J. Juror: Behind the scenes of the trial of the century*, Beverly Hills, CA: Dove Books.

Komter, M.L. (1994) 'Accusations and defences in courtroom interaction', *Discourse and Society*, 5, 3, 165–188.

—— (1998) *Dilemmas in the Courtroom: A study of trials of violent crime in the Netherlands*, Mahwah, NJ: Lawrence Erlbaum Associates.

—— (2003) 'The interactional dynamics of eliciting a confession in a Dutch police interrogation', *Research on Language and Social Interaction*, 36, 4, 433–70.

—— (2006) 'From talk to text: the interactional construction of a police record', *Research on Language and Social Interaction*, 39, 3, 201–28.

Kredens, K. (2000) *Forensic Linguistics and the Status of Linguistic Evidence in the Legal Setting*, unpublished PhD dissertation, University of Lodz.

Kremer-Sadlik, T. (2004) 'How children with autism and Asperger's Syndrome respond to questions: a "naturalistic" theory of mind task', *Discourse Studies*, 6, 2, 185–206.

Künzel, H.J. (1987) *Sprechererkennung*, Heidelberg: Kriminalistik Verlag.

—— (1994) 'On the problem of speaker identification by victims and witnesses', *Forensic Linguistics*, 1, i, 45–58.

Kurzon, D. (1997) '"Legal Language": Varieties, genres, registers, discourses', *International Journal of Applied Linguistics*, 7, 2, 110–39.

—— (2000) 'The right to understand the right of silence: a few comments', *Forensic Linguistics*, 7, ii, 244–8.

—— (2001) 'The politeness of judges: American and English judicial behaviour', *Journal of Pragmatics*, 33, 1, Jan, 61–85.

Labov, W. (1972) *Language in the Inner City: Studies in the Black English vernacular*, Philadelphia, PA: University of Pennsylvania Press.

—— (1988) 'The judicial testing of linguistic theory', in D. Tannen (ed.) *Linguistics in Context*, Norwood, NJ: Ablex, 159–82.

Labov, W. and Fanshel, D. (1977) *Therapeutic Discourse: Psychotherapy as conversation*, New York: Academic Press.

Ladefoged, P. and Ladefoged, J. (1980) 'The ability of listeners to identify voices', *UCLA Working Papers in Phonetics*, 49, 43–51.

Lafone-Walshe, K. (2004) *An Examination of the Characteristics of Freehand Simulated Signatures*, unpublished MPhil. thesis, University of Birmingham.

Laver, J. (1980) *The Phonetic Description of Voice Quality*, Cambridge: Cambridge University Press.

Legge, G.E., Grosmann, C. and Pieper, C.M. (1984) 'Learning unfamiliar voices', *Journal of Experimental Psychology*, 10, 298–303.

Leo, R.A. (1996) 'Inside the interrogation room', *Criminal Law and Criminology*, 86, 266–303.

Levi, J.N. (1993) 'Evaluating jury comprehension of the Illinois capital sentencing instructions', *American Speech*, 68, i, 20–49.

—— (1994a) *Language and the Law: A bibliographical guide to social science research in the USA*, Chicago, IL: American Bar Association.

—— (1994b) 'Language as evidence: the linguist as expert witness in North American Courts', *Forensic Linguistics*, 1, i, 1–26.

Levi, J.N. and Graffam Walker, A. (eds) (1990) *Language in the Judicial Process*, London: Plenum.

Levinson, S. (1979) 'Activity types and language', *Linguistics*, 17, 5/6, 356–99; reprinted in P. Drew and J.C. Heritage (1992), *Talk and Work*, Cambridge and New York: Cambridge University Press, 66–100.

Liberman, K. (1985) *Understanding Interaction in Central Australia: an ethnomethodological study of Australian Aboriginal people*, Boston, MA: Routledge.

Linell, P. and Jönsson, L. (1991) 'Suspect stories: perspective setting in an asymmetrical situation', in I. Markovà and K. Foppa (eds) *Asymmetries in Dialogue*, Hemel Hempstead: Harvester Wheatsheaf, 75–100.

Linfoot-Ham, K. (2006) 'Conversational maxims in encounters with law enforcement officers', *International Journal of Speech, Language and the Law*, 13, i, 23–54.

de Lotbinière, M. (21.07.06) *The Guardian Weekly*, Learning English. Online. Available HTTP: <http://education.guardian.co.uk/tefl/story/0,,1825851,00.html> (accessed 12 September 2006).

Love, H. (2002) *Attributing Authorship: An introduction*, Cambridge: Cambridge University Press.

Louw, B. (1993) 'Irony in the text or insincerity in the writer?', in M. Baker, G. Francis and E. Tognini-Bonelli (eds) *Text and Technology: In honour of John Sinclair*, Philadelphia, PA and Amsterdam: John Benjamins, 157–76.

Lucas, M. and Walliams, D. (2004) *'Little Britain': The complete scripts and all that*, series 1: vol. 1., London: HarperCollins.

McClelland, E. (1994) 'Regina versus Neil Scobie', *Forensic Linguistics*, 1, ii, 223–7.

McGehee, F. (1937) 'The reliability of the identification of the human voice', *Journal of General Psychology*, 17, 249–71.

McMenamin, G. (1993) *Forensic Stylistics*, Amsterdam: Elsevier.

—— (2002) *Forensic Linguistics: Advances in forensic stylistics*, London: CRC Press.

—— (2004) 'Disputed authorship in US law', *International Journal of Speech, Language and the Law*, 11, i, 73–82.

Maddox, J. (1991) 'Another mountain from a molehill', *Nature*, 351, 13.

Maley, Y. (1994) 'The language of the law', in J. Gibbons (ed.), *Language and the Law*, London: Longman, 11–50.

—— (2000) 'The case of the long-nosed potoroo: the framing and construction of expert witness testimony', in S. Sarangi and M. Coulthard (eds) *Discourse and Social Life*, London: Longman, 246–69.

Maley, Y., Candlin, C.N., Crichton, J. and Koster, P. (1995) 'Orientations to lawyer–client interviews', *Forensic Linguistics*, 2, i, 42–55.

Malinowski, B. (1923) 'The problem of meaning in primitive languages', in C.K. Ogden and I.A. Richards (eds) *The Meaning of Meaning*, London: Routledge and Kegan Paul, 296–336; extract reprinted as 'On phatic communion' in A. Jaworski and N. Coupland (eds) (2006), *The Discourse Reader*, 2nd edn, London: Routledge, 296–8.

Marlow, K., Cherryman, J. and Lewis-Williams, S. (2006) 'Improving the ability of vulnerable adults with learning disabilities through effective use of rapport to establish a free narrative', paper presented at Second International Investigative Interviewing Conference 5–7 July 2006, University of Portsmouth, UK.

Martin, J.R. (1992) *English Text*, Amsterdam: John Benjamins.

Maryns, K. (2004) 'Identifying the asylum speaker: reflections on the pitfalls of language analysis in the determination of national origin', *International Journal of Speech, Language and the Law*, 11, ii, 240–60.

Matoesian, G. (2001) *Law and the Language of Identity: Discourse in the William Kennedy Smith rape trial*, Oxford: Oxford University Press.

—— (2003) *Reproducing Rape: Domination through talk in the courtroom*, Chicago, IL: University of Chicago Press.

Matthews, R. and Merriam, T. (1993) 'Neural computation in stylometry. I. An application to the works of Shakespeare and Fletcher', *Literary and Linguistic Computing*, 8, 203–9.

Mendenhall, T.C. (1887) 'The characteristic curves of composition', *Science*, 11, 237–49.

—— (1901) 'A mechanical solution to a literary problem', *Popular Science Monthly*, 60, 97–105.

Merriam, T. (2002) *Marlowe in Henry V: a crisis of Shakespearian identity?*, Oxford : Oxquarry Books.

Merriam, T. and Matthews, R. (1994) 'Neural computation in stylometry. II. An application to the works of Shakespeare and Marlowe', *Literary and Linguistic Computing*, 9, 1–6.

Morton, A.Q. (1991) 'Proper words on proper places', Department of Computing Science Research Report, R18, University of Glasgow.

—— (1995) 'Response' [to Sanford *et al.* (1994)], *Forensic Linguistics*, 2, ii, 230–3.

Morton, A.Q. and McLeman, J. (1964) *Christianity and the Computer*, London: Hodder and Stoughton.

—— (1980) *The Genesis of John*, Edinburgh: St Andrew Press.

Morton, A.Q. and Michaelson, S. (1990) *The Q-Sum Plot*, internal report CSR-3-90, Department of Computer Science, University of Edinburgh.

Mosteller, F. and Wallace, D.L. (1964) *Inference and Disputed Authorship: The federalist*, New York: Springer-Verlag.

Muir, H. (24 September 1996) 'Big Mac puts the bite on McMunchies', Online. Available HTTP: http://www.telegraph.co.uk/htmlContent.jhtml?html=/archive/1996/09/24/nmac24.html (accessed 22 August 2006).

Munro, A. (2007) '"Reform in Law" Awarded for First Plain-Language Rewrite of Federal Civil Court Rules in 70 Years', Online. Available HTTP: <http://enewschannels.com/2007/05/12/enc1282_012728> (accessed 27 May 2007).

Nakasone, H. and Beck, S.D. (2001) 'Forensic automatic speaker recognition', *Proc. (2001) Speaker Odyssey Speaker Recognition Workshop*, 1–6.

Newbury, P. and Johnson, A.J. (2006) 'Suspects' resistance to constraining and coercive questioning strategies in the police interview', *International Journal of Speech, Language and the Law*, 13, ii, 213–40.

Nolan, F. (1994) 'Auditory and acoustic analysis in speaker recognition', in J. Gibbons (ed.), *Language and the Law*, London: Longman, 326–45.

—— (2003) 'A recent voice parade', *International Journal of Speech, Language and the Law*, 10, ii, 277–91.

Nolan, F. and Grabe, E. (1996) 'Preparing a voice lineup', *Forensic Linguistics*, 3 i, 74–94.

Nolan, F. and Oh, T. (1996) 'Identical twins, different voices', *Forensic Linguistics*, 3, i, 39–49.

O'Barr, W.M. (1982) *Linguistic Evidence: Language, power, and strategy in the courtroom*, New York: Academic Press.

Ochs, E. and Capps, L. (2001) *Living Narrative: Creating lives in everyday storytelling*, Cambridge, MA: Harvard University Press.

Olsson, J. (2004) *Forensic Linguistics: An introduction to language, crime and the law*, London: Continuum.

Oxford English Dictionary 2nd edn (1989) J.A. Simpson and E.S.C. Weiner (eds), Additions 1993–7, J. Simpson, E. Weiner and M. Proffitt (eds) and 3rd edn (in progress) J. Simpson (ed.) OED Online, Oxford University Press (Online. Available HTTP: <http://oed.com> Accessed 27 March 2007).

Pagano, A. (1994) 'Negatives in written text', in R.M. Coulthard (ed.) *Advances in Written Text Analysis*, London: Routledge, 250–75.

Pecorari, D.E. (2002) *Original Reproductions: An investigation of the source use of postgraduate second language writers*, unpublished PhD thesis, University of Birmingham.

—— (2003) 'Good and original: plagiarism and patchwriting in academic second-language writing', *Journal of Second Language Writing*, 12, 317–45.

Pennycook, A. (1996) 'Borrowing others' words: text, ownership, memory and plagiarism', *TESOL Quarterly*, 30, 201–30.

Philbrick, F.A. (1949) *Language and the Law: The semantics of forensic English*, New York: Macmillan.

Plain English Campaign (1996a) *Language on Trial*, London: Robson Books.

—— (1996b) *A–Z of Legal Words and Phrases*, High Peak: Plain English Campaign.

Pomerantz, A. (1984) 'Agreeing and disagreeing with assessments: some features of preferred/dispreferred turn shapes', in J.M. Atkinson and J. Heritage (eds) *Structures of*

Social Action, Cambridge: Cambridge University press, 57–101; reprinted as 'Preference in conversation: agreeing and disagreeing with assessments' in A. Jaworski and N. Coupland (eds) (2006) *The Discourse Reader*, 2nd edn, London: Routledge, 246–61.

Prakasam, V. (2004) 'The Indian Evidence Act 1872: a lexicogrammatical study', in J. Gibbons *et al*. (eds) *Language in the Law*, Hyderabad: Orient Longman, 17–23.

Prince, E. (1981) 'Language and the law: a case for linguistic pragmatics', *Working Papers in Sociolinguistics*, Austin: Southwest Educational Development Laboratory, 112–60.

Projeto COMET (2007) *Projeto COrpus Multilíngüe Ensino e Tradução*, Online. Available HTTP: <http://www.fflch.usp.br/dlm/comet/> (accessed 15 January 2007).

Quirk, R. (1982) *Style and Communication in the English Language*, London: Edward Arnold.

Raymond, G. (2000) 'The voice of authority: the local accomplishment of authoritative discourse in live news broadcasts', *Discourse Studies*, 2, 3, 354–79.

Ricks, C. (1998) 'Plagiarism', British Academy lecture, 10 February 1998.

Robertson, G. (06.08.06) 'Comma quirk irks Rogers' *Globe and Mail*, Online. Available HTTP: <http://www.theglobeandmail.com/> (accessed 24 August 2006).

Robertson, B., Vignaux, G.A. and Egerton, I. (1994) 'Stylometric evidence', *Criminal Law Review*, 645–9.

Rock, F. (2001) 'The genesis of a witness statement', *Forensic Linguistics*, 8, ii, 44–72.

—— (in press) *Communicating Rights: The language of arrest and detention*, London: Palgrave.

Rose, P. (2002) *Forensic Speaker Identification*, London: Taylor and Francis.

Royce, T. (2005) 'Case Analysis. The negotiator and the bomber: analysing the critical role of active listening in crisis negotiations', *Negotiation Journal*, 21, 1, 5–27.

Sacks, H., Schegloff, E. and Jefferson, G. (1974) 'A simplest systematics for the organization of turntaking for conversation', *Language*, 50, iv, 696–735.

Sanderson, S.M. 'Bayes' theorem … a simple example', Online. Available HTTP: <http://www.herkimershideaway.org/writings/bayes.htm> (accessed 10 October 2006).

Sandhya, G.K. (2004) 'Teaching the language of the law: patterns, problems and challenges', jn J. Gibbons *et al*. (eds) *Language in the Law*, Hyderabad: Orient Longman, 133–9.

Sanford, A.J., Aked, J.P., Moey, L.M. and Mullin, J. (1994) 'A critical examination of assumptions underlying the cusum technique of forensic linguistics', *Journal of Forensic Linguistics*, 1, ii, 151–67.

Sarangi, S. (2000) 'Activity types, discourse types and interactional hybridity: the case of genetic counselling', in S. Sarangi and M. Coulthard (eds) *Discourse and Social Life*, London: Longman, 1–27.

Sarangi, S. and Coulthard, M. (eds) (2000) *Discourse and Social Life*, London: Longman.

Schank, R.C. and Abelson, R. (1977) *Scripts, Plans, Goals and Understanding*, Hillsdale, NJ: Lawrence Erlbaum Associates.

Schank, R. and Nash-Webber, B. (eds) (1975) *Theoretical Issues in Natural Language Processing*, Menlo Park, CA: Association for Computational Linguistics.

Scheffer, T. (2006) 'The microformation of criminal defense: on the lawyer's notes, speech production, and a field of presence', *Research on Language and Social Interaction*, 39, 3, 303–42.

Schlichting, F. and Sullivan, K.P.H. (1997) 'The imitated voice: a problem for voice line-ups?', *Forensic Linguistics*, 4, i, 148–65.

Scott, M. (2006) *Wordsmith Tools*, version 4, Oxford: Oxford University Press.

Searle, J. (1969) *Speech Acts: An essay in the philosophy of language*, Cambridge: Cambridge University Press.

Shuy, (1993) *Language Crimes: the use and abuse of language evidence in the courtroom*, Cambridge, MA: Blackwell.

—— (1994) 'Deceit, distress and false imprisonment: the anatomy of a car sales event', *Forensic Linguistics*, 1, 2, 133–49.

—— (1998) *The Language of Confession, Interrogation and Deception*, London: Sage.

—— (2002a) 'To testify or not to testify', in J. Cotterill (ed.) *Language in the Legal Process*, London: Palgrave, 3–18.

—— (2002b) *Linguistic Battles in Trademark Disputes*, New York: Palgrave.

—— (2005) *Creating Language Crimes: How law enforcement uses and abuses language*, Oxford: Oxford University Press.

—— (2006) *Linguistics in the Courtroom: A practical guide*, Oxford: Oxford University Press.

Sinclair, J.McH. (1991) *Corpus, Concordance, Collocation*, Oxford: Oxford University Press.

—— ms Unpublished expert opinion on the ordinary man's understanding of the word 'visa'.

Singler, J.V. (2004) 'The "linguistic" asylum interview and the linguist's evaluation of it, with special reference to applicants for Liberian political asylum in Switzerland', *International Journal of Speech, Language and the Law*, 11, ii, 222–39.

Slembrouck S. (1992) 'The parliamentary Hansard "verbatim" report: the written construction of spoken discourse', *Language and Literature*, 1, 2, 101–19.

Snell, J. (2006) 'Schema theory and the humour of Little Britain', *English Today*, 22, 59–64.

Solan, L. (1993) *The Language of Judges*, Chicago, IL: University of Chicago Press.

—— (1998) 'Linguistic experts as semantic tour guides', *Forensic Linguistics*, 5 ii, 87–106.

—— (2002) 'Ordinary meaning in legal interpretation', in *Pohjois-Suomen Tuomarikoulu*; reprinted in B. Pozzo (ed.) (2005) *Ordinary Language and Legal Language*, Milan: Giuffrè, 125–52.

Solan, L.M. and Tiersma, P.M. (2004) 'Author identification in American courts', *Applied Linguistics*, 25, 4, 448–65.

—— (2005) *Speaking of Crime: The language of criminal justice*, Chicago, IL: University of Chicago Press.

Stern, S. and Wiggins, J. (19 March 2007) ft.com, 'McDonald's seeks to redefine "McJob"' Online. Available HTTP: <http://www.ft.com/cms/s/2065c45e-d65d-11db-99b7-000b5df10621.html> (accessed 9 April 2007).

Stubbs, M. (1996) *Text and Corpus Analysis*, Oxford: Blackwell.

—— (2004) 'Conrad, concordance, collocation: heart of darkness or light at the end of the tunnel?', The Third Sinclair Open Lecture, University of Birmingham.

Stygall, G. (1994) *Trial Language: Discourse processing and discursive formation*, Amsterdam: Benjamins.

Svartvik, J. (1968) *The Evans Statements: A case for forensic linguistics*, Gothenburg: University of Gothenburg Press.

Swales, J.M. (1990) *Genre Analysis: English in academic and research settings*, New York: Cambridge University Press.

Syal, R. (29 September 2006) The Times Online 'Blair aide questioned in cash for peerages investigation', Online. Available HTTP: <http://www.timesonline.co.uk/tol/news/politics/article654507.ece> (accessed 14 February 2007).

Tannen, D. and Wallat, C. (1987) 'Interactive frames and knowledge schemas in interaction: examples from a medical examination/interview', *Social Psychology Quarterly*, 50, 2,

205–16; reprinted in A. Jaworski and N. Coupland (eds) (2006), *The Discourse Reader*, 2nd edn, London: Routledge, 332–48.

The Hutton Inquiry (2003a) Online. Available HTTP: <http://www.the-hutton-inquiry.org.uk> (accessed 10 January 2007).

——— (2003b) Online. Available HTTP: <http://www.the-hutton-inquiry.org.uk/content/rulings/ruling01.htm>, section 12 (accessed 10 January 2007).

——— (2003c) Online. Available HTTP: http://www.the-hutton-inquiry.org.uk/content/transcripts/hearing-trans22.htm (accessed 10 January 2007).

——— (2004a) Online. Available HTTP: <http://www.the-hutton-inquiry.org.uk/content/report/chapter01.htm#a1> section 1 (accessed 10 January 2007).

——— (2004b) Online. Available HTTP: <http://www.the-hutton-inquiry.org.uk/content/report/ chapter09.htm#a58> section 292 (accessed 10 January 2007).

The Shipman Inquiry (2001) *The Shipman Inquiry*, Online. Available HTTP: http://www.the-shipman-inquiry.org.uk/> (accessed 14 February 2007).

The Shipman Trial Transcript (2001) *The Shipman Inquiry*, Online. Available HTTP: <http://www.the-shipman-inquiry.org.uk/trialtrans.asp/> (accessed 12 August 2006).

The Test of Legal English website. Online. Available HTTP: <http://www.toles.co.uk/> (accessed 11 June 2006).

Tiersma, P. (1999) *Legal Language*, Chicago, IL: University of Chicago Press.

——— (2001) 'Textualising the law', *Forensic Linguistics*, 8, ii, 73–92.

——— (2002) 'The language and law of product warnings', in J. Cotterill (ed.) *Language in the Legal Process*, London: Palgrave, 54–71.

Tiersma, P. and Solan, L. (2002) 'The linguist on the witness stand: forensic linguistics in American courts', *Language*, 78, 221–39.

Toolan, M. (2001) *Narrative: a critical linguistic introduction*, 2nd edn, London: Routledge.

Trow, M.J. (1929) *"Let him have it Chris"*, London: HarperCollins.

Trudgill, P. (1992) *Introducing Language and Society*, London: Penguin.

Turchie Affidavit. Online. Available HTTP: <http://www.unabombertrial.com/documents/turchie_affidavit.html> (accessed 10 October 2006).

Turrell, T. (2004) 'Textual kidnapping revisited: the case of plagiarism in literary translation', *International Journal of Speech, Language and the Law*, 11, i, 1–26.

Watson, R. (1976) 'Some conceptual issues in the social identifications of victims and offenders', in E.C. Viano (ed.) *Victims and Society*, Washington, DC: Visage, 60–71.

——— (1983) 'The presentation of victim and motive in discourse: the case of police interrogations and interviews', *Victimology: An International Journal*, 8, 1-2, 31–52.

——— (1990) 'Some features of the elicitation of confessions in murder interrogations', in G. Psathas (ed.) *Interactional Competence, Studies in Ethnomethodology and Conversation Analysis 1*, Washington, DC: University Press of America, 263–95.

Wells, G.L. (1993) 'What do we know about eyewitness identification?', *American Psychologist*, 48, 553–71.

West Yorkshire Police (1 March 2007) 'Call Handling/Incidents', Online. Available HTTP: <http://www.westyorkshire.police.uk/section-item.asp?sid=66&iid=753> (accessed 15 May 2007).

Whalen, J., Zimmerman, D.H. and Whalen, M.R. (1988) 'When words fail: a single case analysis', *Social Problems*, 35, 4, Special Issue: Language Interaction and Social Problems, 335–62.

Whalen, M.R. and Zimmerman, D.H. (1987) 'Sequential and institutional contexts in calls for help', *Social Psychology Quarterly*, 50, 2, Special Issue: Language and Social Interaction, 172–85.

Windsor Lewis, J. (1994) 'Case report: The Yorkshire Ripper enquiry: Part II', *Forensic Linguistics*, 1, ii, 207–16.

Winter, E.O. and Woolls, D. (1996), 'Identifying authorship in a co-written novel', Internal report for University of Birmingham.

Woolls, D. (2002) *Copycatch Gold*, a computerised plagiarism detection program. Online. Available HTTP: <http://www.copycatchgold.com> (accessed 20 May 2007).

—— (2003) 'Better tools for the trade and how to use them', *International Journal of Speech, Language and the Law*, 10, i, 102–12.

Woolls, D. and Coulthard, R.M. (1998) 'Tools for the trade', *Forensic Linguistics*, 5, i, 33–57.

Yule, G.U. (1938) 'On sentence length as a statistical characteristic of style in prose, with application to two cases of disputed authorship', *Biometrica*, 30, 363–90.

—— (1944) *The Statistical Study of Literary Vocabulary*, Cambridge: Cambridge University Press.

Zander, M. (1999) *Cases and Materials on the English Legal System*, 8th edn, Cambridge: Cambridge University Press.

Zimmerman, D.H. (1992) 'The interactional organization of calls for emergency assistance', in P. Drew and J. Heritage (eds) *Talk and Work*, Cambridge and New York: Cambridge University Press, 418–69.

Acts of Parliament

Offences Against the Person Act (1861).

Police and Criminal Evidence Act 1984 and its Codes of Practice, Online. Available HTTP:<http://police.homeoffice.gov.uk/operational-policing/powers-pace-codes/> (accessed 1 May 2007).

Theft Act (1968).

Theft (Amendment) Act 1996, Online. Available HTTP: <http://www.opsi.gov.uk/acts/acts1996/1996062.htm> London: HMSO (accessed 27 March 2007).

Index

Related titles from Routledge

Corpus-Based Language Studies: An advanced resource book

Routledge Applied Linguistics series
Anthony McEnery, Richard Xiao and Yukio Tono

Corpus-Based Language Studies, like all books in the *Routledge Applied Linguistics* series, is a comprehensive resource book that guides readers through three main sections: Section A establishes the key terms and concepts, Section B brings together influential articles, sets them in context, and discusses their contribution to the field and Section C builds on knowledge gained in the first two sections, setting thoughtful tasks around further illustrative material. Throughout the book, topics are revisited, extended, interwoven and deconstructed, with the reader's understanding strengthened by tasks and follow-up questions.

Corpus-Based Language Studies:

- covers the major theoretical approaches to the use of corpus data
- adopts a 'how to' approach with exercises and cases, providing students with the knowledge and tools to undertake their own corpus-based research
- gathers together influential readings from key names in the discipline, including: Biber, Widdowson, Stubbs, Carter and McCarthy
- supported by a website featuring long extracts for analysis by students with commentary by the authors

Written by experienced teachers and researchers in the field, *Corpus-Based Language Studies* is an essential resource for students and researchers of Applied Linguistics.

ISBN13: 978-0-415-28622-0 (hbk)
ISBN13: 978-0-415-28623-7 (pbk)

Available at all good bookshops
For ordering and further information please visit:
http://www.routledge.com/rcenters/linguistics/series/ral.htm

Related titles from Routledge

English for Academic Purposes: An advanced resource book

Routledge Applied Linguistics series
Ken Hyland

English for Academic Purposes, like all books in the *Routledge Applied Linguistics* series, is a comprehensive resource book that guides readers through three main sections: Section A establishes the key terms and concepts, Section B brings together influential articles, sets them in context, and discusses their contribution to the field and Section C builds on knowledge gained in the first two sections, setting thoughtful tasks around further illustrative material. Throughout the book, topics are revisited, extended, interwoven and deconstructed, with the reader's understanding strengthened by tasks and follow-up questions.

English for Academic Purposes:

- introduces the major theories, approaches and controversies in the field
- gathers together influential readings from key names in the discipline, including: John Swales, Alastair Pennycook, Greg Myers, Brian Street and Ann Johns
- provides numerous exercises as practical study tools that encourage in students a critical approach to the subject.

Written by an experienced teacher and researcher in the field, *English for Academic Purposes* is an essential resource for students and researchers of Applied Linguistics.

ISBN13: 978-0-415-35869-9 (hbk)
ISBN13: 978-0-415-35870-5 (pbk)

Available at all good bookshops
For ordering and further information please visit:
http://www.routledge.com/rcenters/linguistics/series/ral.htm